HOW TO KEEP OUR LIBERTY

A Program for Political Action

HOW TO

KEEP OUR LIBERTY

A Program for Political Action

BY

RAYMOND MOLEY

NEW YORK

ALFRED·A·KNOPF

1952

L. C. CATALOG CARD NUMBER: 51-11984

THIS IS A BORZOI BOOK,
PUBLISHED BY ALFRED A. KNOPF, INC.

FIRST EDITION

To those Americans

who share the middle interests

and who can save themselves,

if they will.

The Purpose of This Book

The people of this nation are today presented with a choice between two forms of political and economic life. One form is that of our traditions, in which individual liberty prevails and is guarded by "the long, still grasp of law." The other is the dominance of the state in human affairs. With us the intrusion of the state is not a frightening threat but a seemingly benign alternative to the perplexities, the anxieties, and the labors that must attend the possession of true liberty. My purpose is to describe this alternative and, for those who prefer liberty, to offer the means for its preservation. Merely to bewail a trend is not to correct it. The American wants to know what to do about it.

"Abstract liberty," said Edmund Burke, "like other mere abstractions is not to be found. Liberty inheres in some sensible object; and every nation has formed to itself some favorite point, which by way of eminence becomes the criterion of their happiness." Our concept of liberty has enveloped and permeated our complex structure of associated living. Like oxygen in a physical organism, it is the means for burning away waste and decay and for the liberation of living forces. Its presence explains our material and spiritual achievements.

In those very achievements, however, there lurks a threat

to the liberty that made them possible. For we have a material abundance that seems to have no limit. And we have forms of government so excellent that our trust in them is ardent and complete. It is the very excellence of the fruit which may induce us to neglect the tree.

We are not and never have been threatened by authority in any of its more obvious or repellent forms—no armed master, no tyrannous mob, no foreign conqueror. We know nothing of what the peoples of Asia and Europe have seen and felt. The danger we may encounter is quite unlike theirs.

In a sense, our enemy is ourselves. It is clothed in the benign habiliments of men of good will. It phrases its appeal in terms that we have learned to love and trust— welfare, security, democracy, justice, and humanitarianism. More than a century ago, Alexis de Tocqueville warned us that we need fear not "tyrants" but "guardians."

"I have always thought," said that unrivaled commentator on our institutions, "that servitude of the regular, quiet and gentle kind . . . might be combined more easily with some of the outward forms of freedom, and that it might even establish itself under the wing of the sovereignty of the people."

Since gentleness is not always equipped with superlative capacity of mind, those who would thus lead us are generally unable to comprehend the inexorable facts of life. Nor are they able to comprehend what may come of their ministrations. The warm-hearted, God bless them, are sometimes the soft-minded, God keep them. Their charity may and generally does cover a multitude of errors and delusions. These errors and delusions may through seductive appeals be transmitted to most of us. And most of us will ultimately have to make the fatal decisions.

Not all who use these appeals are guileless. There are many among our leaders who have no illusions about what they are promoting. There are many who have no faith in the permanence of liberty and who would gain by its decline.

We have seen the meek armed with visionary purpose possess other lands. And we have seen them fail. Such disillusioned British socialists as Ivor Thomas are already publishing their confessions. We may well consider those failures abroad. "Whenever our neighbor's house is on fire," said Burke, "it cannot be amiss for the engines to play a little on our own."

The philosophy of statism already has sharp emphasis in the acts, plans, and policies of those who exercise predominant influence in our Federal Administration, in the presently dominant national political party, in several of our state governments, in an influential part of our press, in unofficial organizations, and in immense organized special interests.

The impairment of constitutional protections and our party system, the immense growth of Federal power, the increasing dependence of millions of people upon government bounties, and the insidious attack of alien philosophies—all these are evidences of a threat to those republican institutions which collectively have been the shield of our liberty.

The intervention of government in our economic and social life proceeds in what we may roughly call geometric progression. With each new encroachment upon the area of liberty, government grows more potent and liberty weaker. Ultimately, an unseen line is crossed, and resistance becomes impossible. The individual cannot regain his liberty, because his capacity for self-determination is exhausted. As a nation, we reach a point of no return.

This book is not an essay in pessimism. The means and the vitality remain in the United States to check this powerful trend, to save our liberty, and to enjoy through that liberty a luminous destiny. I believe that, as the problem is better understood by those who have the most to lose, and as those people create the organized force to resist, the reality of liberty can be assured for generations to come. I hope I can make a small contribution to that end.

The plan of this book can be stated simply. There are presented first, as essential background, the traditional principles of liberty and the institutions in which they are embodied in our republic.

I next consider what I call the "middle interests" of America. The immense stakes, material concerns, and potential power of those who share these interests are described in some detail.

Next there are presented in detail the theories, manifestations, and policies that are impairing our capacity to preserve our essential liberty. The consequences of this impairment, both in the present and the future, are then considered.

The challenge of statism—that there be given a "better way" to achieve the goal of a progressively better life—is then met by a series of alternative policies, which I have called "a road away from socialism."

The second half of the book is a consideration of how political means can be used for the preservation of liberty. Traditionally, such responsibility rests in the two-party system. But that system has fallen into decay. It is now an inadequate means of registering national decisions by the people. Finally, I suggest how political action by people most concerned with liberty can preserve not only their own interests but the essential integrity of the republic.

The pages that follow are addressed to all Americans who share my sense of the danger of government ascendancy and who want to do something to minimize that threat. The mail that comes to me as a journalist, my contacts with people in my travels through the states, my professional experience in measuring the nature and effects of government policies, and a feeling for public sentiment acquired in forty years of political observation, teaching, writing, and practice all give me positive evidence that the public is aware of the danger of statism.

While many of my conclusions and suggestions are the product of years of experience and reflection, this book embodies a number of conclusions reached in the three years since the great Republican debacle in 1948. During that period I have also had an opportunity to study directly the British political scene, during the 1950 Parliamentary campaign.

Millions of Americans are willing to meet the danger of statism with positive political action, but they lack organization, information, and direction. Of course, many would delegate the task to a political party or to some heaven-sent leader. That is a vain course. The parties will act only as citizens compel them to act. There is no savior but the citizen himself. He must first in his community, his Congressional district, his state, and finally at the national level, create the sinews of political organization to oppose the forces that would lead us down the road to socialism.

At this moment our parties are not truly national. In many states there is no real Republican Party. And the national machinery of the Democratic Party has been captured by virulent minorities. Those citizens who would preserve American institutions by political action must use the state and local machinery of whatever party is best able to elect candidates who think and believe as they do.

My insistence upon citizen action is not meant to minimize the value of political parties. Two strong parties are indispensable to republican government. But a party is only a vehicle for citizen action. The party, with its legal machinery, should be used to further the purposes of politically conscious citizens.

Above all, this book considers what I have called the "middle interests" of America. These interests are vital to a free society. Those who share them have both an immense stake and a massive potential power. Their action can be decisive. In England it was the middle class that decisively checked socialism in the elections of 1950 and 1951.

They should realize that it is a firm dogma of Marxism that "the middle class" must and will be destroyed. The people in America who correspond to that class are divided between the parties or are without party ties. They are paying the costs of statism, with little to say about the policies of their government.

Some will call this book a conservative manifesto. It does propose to conserve a faith and tradition through which America has emerged as the hope of a free world. It insists that the assurance of the future rests upon the experience of the past. If that be conservatism, let my critics make the most of it.

The reactionary is the person who tells us that progress is possible only through more and more government. That is a real retreat to the past. Anglo-Americans once lived under an omnipotent government, and paid with blood to escape from it. Before the rights of Anglo-Americans were established, the state was supreme; it failed to satisfy the material needs, the aspirations, and the dreams of men. Individual freedom finally seized the torch of progress. Individual freedom is still the authentic means of a better life.

While this book only incidentally touches foreign affairs, I am well aware that war vitally influences domestic policies. A war, of course, enlarges the power of government over private life and property. A withdrawal of liberty in the face of foreign peril must never be more than temporary. If, beyond the bare necessity of national survival, there is any reason for fighting, that reason must be the preservation of the domestic institutions under which we have lived. We must not, in opposing the ultimate in Marxism, surrender our cause at home.

The present emergency, occasioned by the cold war and vast rearmament, provides greater rather than less significance for the lesson that I am seeking to present in this book. And since the emergency may be of many years' duration, the need is still more important to stress the dangers of narrowing our sphere of liberty. For such vast military preparations bring into increasing prominence a military psychology among our people. Since that attitude of mind has to do with an emergent crisis, it is concerned with the expenditure and protection, rather than the production, of national wealth. It stresses discipline, authority, and uniformity.

Moreover, tremendous expenditures for military purposes sharpen problems of taxation and inflation. The production of immense quantities of military materiel also has a debilitating effect on business enterprise. Controls, cost-plus contracts, and other wartime factors in production weaken the business psychology that makes for vital competition. Wholesome control by Congress over expenditures is impaired by constant limitations, because of military secrets, on discussion. There is also the fear on the part of members of Congress to question military expenditures because of the danger that they will be charged with impairing essential national security. In short, a considerable part of the economy is enclosed in a sort of military sanctuary. All this is due to neither the ambitions of military men nor a deliberate acceptance of government dominance. It is inherent in the world situation. But it is a factor in the current growth of state power which must be appraised.

I have inflicted upon many patient and able friends the task of looking over sections of this book. Their suggestions have been of inestimable help. But since the sin and the sentence of any shortcomings must rest with me and me alone, I shall not evade my responsibility by naming these friends. My gratitude, however, is here acknowledged.

In this task I have had the competent advice and editorial help of my assistant, Marjorie Wilson.

A very important debt is due Frances Moley for patience, encouragement, and counsel.

—RAYMOND MOLEY

December, 1951

A Note on Terminology

One of the most difficult problems I have faced in writing this book was that of choosing a specific name to describe the trend of state intervention by which our personal liberties are progressively usurped. The problem of terminology is especially difficult in writing of politics, especially contemporary politics. Politicians habitually follow the unscrupulous practice of seizing words of positive and pleasant connotation to describe what they advocate, and of using unpleasant words to describe what they oppose. The result is a steady deterioration in the value of words that once had specific meaning. A "liberal," for example, was once a person who opposed the intervention of the state in the life and affairs of the individual. Now the word is used as self-description by those who favor such intervention. A similar fate has overcome such words as "welfare," democracy," and "planning."

Without attempting to explore the wilderness of semantics, I shall attempt to define three of the terms that I shall be using frequently.

An accurate word to describe the trend toward a socialist state is "interventionism." This word has the blessing of lexicographers and is widely used in British economic and political writing. In American political discussion it has two disadvantages. It is a long word with a somewhat technical overtone. And it has been commonly used to describe a form of foreign policy. I shall, however, feel free to use it in its proper sense from time to time.

A better, shorter word to describe state intervention is "statism." Recent use of the term, mainly by opponents of the trend, has anticipated the lexicographers. The most recent edition of the *New College Standard Dictionary* has caught up with this meaning. It has, in fact, somewhat overstated it. Statism, it says, is "A theory of government which holds that the returns from group or individual enterprise are vested in the state, as in communism." The same dictionary lists as obsolete an older definition, "statecraft."

The most recent *Webster's New Collegiate Dictionary* provides a more workable definition. Statism is defined as the "Concentration of all economic controls and economic planning in the hands of a highly centralized state government."

I shall use the word in a sense somewhat short of that definition to describe a policy or philosophy that advocates a progressive trend of intervention by government in economic, social, and personal life. Those who favor such intervention will deny that state socialism is the ultimate goal of such a trend. I cannot agree with that denial.

I shall use the word "socialism" to describe a form of society in which the main instruments of production, credit, and distribution are owned or fully controlled by the state. It is unnecessary to include in this definition the customary statement, largely a product of socialistic dialectic, that such instruments of production and distribution shall be "democratically" controlled. The use of the word "democratic" has been so mauled and distorted by socialists and Communists alike that such a qualification has no relevance to the main point, which is government ownership and control.

There are, of course, many varieties of socialism, some of which are now embedded in governmental and economic systems. There is the Communistic socialism of Soviet Russia, which is an adaptation of Marxian theory to fit conditions in Russia and the ever-changing caprice of Russia's masters. There is the mild socialism of Scandinavia, in which state intervention lives side by side with nongovernmental co-operatives and a fairly large residue of capitalism. British Labor socialism, also an adaptation of Marxism, when defined by its exponents, may be taken to mean a partial nationalization of the private economy, coupled with vast tax-supported welfare activities and much state planning of elements hitherto free in the economy. Stripped of all sophistry and frills, however, British socialism seeks complete state ownership and control of economic life to a degree limited only by compromise within the party itself and by the dictates of political expediency.

Contents

PART ONE: PRINCIPLES AND PEOPLE

xix

Contents

PART THREE: A ROAD AWAY FROM SOCIALISM

xxiii

Contents

Contents

PART ONE

PRINCIPLES AND PEOPLE

CHAPTER I

Principles We Live By

Principles Live in Institutions

"Individualities may form communities, but it is institutions alone that can create a nation." This was a comment by Benjamin Disraeli a century ago when he was beginning the task of building the Conservative Party, a party that still lives a lusty, constructive life. The institutions to which Disraeli referred were the Crown, the House of Commons, the Lords Temporal and Spiritual, and the Empire. Behind each of these institutions were ageless principles. These institutions cemented the loyalty of the people—loyalty to the principles of unity symbolized by the Crown, popular rule in the Commons, distinction in the Lords Temporal, morality and religion in the Church, and world influence in the Empire.

We Americans have no Crown, no Lords Temporal or Spiritual, and no Empire. Our institutions were created in a vastly shorter period than were England's. But they are nevertheless rooted in the verities of human nature and of human nature in America. They are derived from and are the embodiments of principles long tested and cherished by human beings. We have projected living principles into massive institutions.

These principles which we live by are in part inherited and in part the product of our experience here as a nation.

They assure our unity, our national security, and our common happiness. They should guarantee the permanence of our republic. Unless our immediate objectives are sought in terms of the principles behind our institutions, we will lose not only our objectives but our institutions as well.

Principles by Inheritance

CONSTITUTIONAL GOVERNMENT

The creation of constitutional government is a most significant mark of the distrust of human beings in human nature. It signalizes a profound conviction, born of experience, that human beings vested with authority must be restrained by something more potent than their own discretion. When exacted from a ruler, a constitution is a guarantee of rights which may not be denied, even by the sovereign who granted it. When adopted by a majority, it is a manifestation of self-denial. It is law and the source of law. With us, the Constitution is the repository of sovereignty. And since it is the creator of our Federal government, its terms govern the institutions of that government.

For the most part the Constitution of the United States is an inheritance from a body of principle, built up over many generations by Englishmen here and in their native land. That body of principle became in America a guide to associated living. Those who created the Constitution in 1787, and subsequently adopted the Bill of Rights, extracted from the inheritance known as the English Constitution a number of provisions and made written record of them with some important adaptations of their own, based upon colonial experience. Hence, our constitution is not an expression of all the liberties and rights of those Englishmen who became Americans. They, like those who remained behind, were still bound by the broader principles that dis-

4

tinguish Anglo-American civilization. In that inheritance of constitutional principle, as well as in the common law, lie the precepts under which we live together as a nation.

The purpose of constitutional government is described very well by Cornelia LeBoutellier in her *American Democracy and Natural Law:* "Gregarious and social and political, loving to be free, man builds a state, the cornerstone of which is his inherent liking for his fellowman. Along with this inherent liking goes inherent faith, and a shrewd appraisal of his fellowman as a good sort, but a sort who 'wants watching.' So he sets up machinery for watching his fellowman through the ministrations of constitutional democracy and charges the state with the solemn duty both to keep him free and to hold him safe, insofar as this is possible." [1]

THE REIGN OF LAW

The concept of constitutional government was born of a venerable principle—the supremacy of law. Bracton said in 1250: "Right is derived from what is unwritten and that which usage has approved." This was fixed in the medieval conscience, despite the ascendancies of various forms of religious and political authority. Law is not the offspring of the state, but the reason for the state. The instruments of government should merely give effective application to law.

As we search through antiquity for the origin of law, we lose a sense of the state in the interminable succession of authorities that have vainly conceived themselves masters of men's conduct. But we do find patterns of action, guided by some vague but positive rules. And because their roots are hidden in mystery, it seems sometimes that these rules were shaped by an unconscious process.

Law, says Edward Jenks in his *Law and Politics of the Middle Ages,* is "an authority which for some reason or an-

[1] Cornelia LeBoutellier: *American Democracy and Natural Law* (New York: Columbia University Press; 1950), p. 55.

5

other, great masses of men feel themselves bound to follow, not because they choose, but because they must. And yet certainly it is not a command of the State, direct or indirect. Upon critical examination, it may turn out to be the work of a mere private composer. Why do men obey it? Further back again, we find a purely impersonal document, compiled, no one exactly knows how, or by whom; and yet it is the controlling force which shapes the daily conduct of men. . . . It is not the work of the State, it may not be recognized by the State, there may be no State to recognize it. Yet the essential ideas of Law, the evident ancestors of our modern juristic notions, are clearly there." [2]

Thus, law in its essence is neither the act of a legislature, the proclaimed will of a sovereign, nor "judge-made." It is the creation of individuals, countless individuals, making patterns of action and relationships that rest one upon another likes the mites that make up a coral reef. The power that guides such individuals may be—indeed is believed by a great proportion of men to be—divine. But whatever the guiding power—the "right reason" of men or supernatural inspiration—it has manifested itself in the will and obedience of men. This power grows as men give it obedience. [3]

Perhaps that is why law is so often called the product of public opinion and why that law which violates public opinion is soon broken and liquidated.

[2] Edward Jenks: *Law and Politics in the Middle Ages* (London: John Murray; 1898), pp. 2, 3.

[3] The following is an excellent definition of the natural law as understood by those who hold to the doctrine of its divine origin. It was written by Edward F. Barrett of the School of Law, Notre Dame University: "The Natural Law is as old as Man himself. In ancient days Chinese sage and Hebrew Prophet, Greek philosopher and Roman jurist, alike caught the vision of a Supreme Law transcending and therefore necessarily informing the laws men make for men. From that Law resulted certain basic human rights. These rights the State was morally competent to implement and protect but not to impair or destroy. Nor could the State's commands be the sole criteria of right and wrong, for, independent of the State there existed an objective Standard, rationally ascertainable, by which the final value of all human laws can and must be tested."

6

The goal of law is justice. The need for definition brings into being courts of justice and so-called "lawmakers." Lord Coke spoke of reason as the life of law.

The earlier enemies of the concept of a right above the written law were the "positivists." They held that there was only positive or man-made law and that the laws made by the state or government were the only directions of conduct binding upon men living in society.

Various applications of pragmatism and other denials of natural law have all but captured American thinking. Pragmatism, instrumentalism, behaviorism, economic determinism, and rationalization have been the more recent spearheads of the attack on the verities of the past.

Because law is essentially the expression of what individuals deem best for their guidance, it has been and is a jealous guard against encroachment by those in political authority. "If justice be thy shield and it be broken, whence cometh thy succour?" Liberty under law is an old and useful maxim. But it implies a separation that does not exist. Law is the individual's expression of liberty in his relations with his fellow men.

This comment on the nature of law has a special application for the United States. For in no other country has the influence of men trained in the law been greater in creating and developing political institutions. The dominant influence in making the Constitution was that of the lawyer. Our legislative assemblies have proverbially been dominated by lawyers. Most of the presidential successors of Washington have been lawyers.

THE CONSENT OF THE GOVERNED

The great customary constitutional principle of the con- X sent of the governed means something quite different from, and more important than, majority rule. Majority "rule" is not in fact a principle of our constitution, for a majority does X

7

not rule but governs. It performs certain functions under the terms of fundamental law.

What, then, is consent? Is it mere resignation to the inevitable? Is it impotent acquiescence? Is it agreement secured under duress? Is it agreement obtained as the result of promises that, under proof, can be shown to be deceitful and fraudulent?

In the long history of the common law, which is in large measure the application of common sense and the fruits of experience to human situations, these questions are answered largely in the negative. Consent is not valid when it is given under duress, physical or even political. It is not valid if obtained by false representations. Nor do I believe it to be valid when it is obtained by political bribery. And I cannot believe it to be valid consent when a people submit because they can find no way to refuse.

Consent is real when those involved freely, knowingly, willingly, and with a part in creating the situation, enter into the benefits and responsibilities of the decision.

Consent is not present when a decision is made in the face of a virile and sizable opposition. We often see such decisions and we learn how futile they are. Sumptuary laws whose dictates are neither respected nor believed in by a large part of the population become either dead letters or sources of corruption and blackmail.

The consent of the governed is not only a basic principle of a free society but a corrective for injustice and oppression. It is essentially a principle demanding that government proceed in pace with the slow evolution of public opinion. It is the assurance of stability and public order.

PERSONAL RIGHTS

Like the recurrent theme in a great symphony, the concern for personal liberty runs through and through the language of the Constitution. The very climax of the Preamble is "to secure the Blessings of Liberty to ourselves and our Posterity." There are numerous protections in the body of the document. Subsequently, the Bill of Rights specified the traditional liberties. And, as if the authors were prone to linger on the theme and sum up everything in a sentence, the final, Tenth Amendment embodies an all inclusive stricture: "The powers not delegated to the United States by the Constitution, nor prohibited by it to the States, are reserved to the States respectively, or to the people."

The specified rights in the Bill of Rights of the Constitution are life, liberty, and property. This trilogy was carried over from the English tradition, well expressed by the philosophy of John Locke, who was Jefferson's major inspiration.

These rights were affirmed and in fact established in the second half of the eighteenth century. That was the half-century of Rousseau, of Chatham, of Burke, of Paine, of Jefferson the philosopher, of Hume, of Diderot, of Voltaire, of Adam Smith, of the American Constitution-makers, and of two great revolutions. It was a half-century when, under the prodigious assault of intellectual giants and of popular revolt, absolutism crumbled in the Western world and the state was mastered, tamed, and reduced to the status of a domestic servant.

It was an era in which the individual was delivered from captivity and proclaimed to have inalienable political rights. These rights were based in part upon the concept of his possession of an immortal soul and in part upon the rational concept that, unless a state is built with the powerful and resilient fiber of human personality, it cannot endure and grow. The state had been stolen by selfish men and, under the guise of unproved right, in the darkness of human ignorance, and under the cover of armed might, it was an engine of exploitation, superstition, and oppression.

The unity and integrity of the concept of individual rights

9

are shown by the singular parallelism in all the great expressions of human rights which marked victories over state power.

In the specification of rights—those imprescriptible personal rights which no state could either give or take away but could only protect—property was invariably linked with all the rest. The American Constitution linked life, liberty, and property. The French Declaration of Rights of 1793 specified equality, liberty, security, and property. These rights were equal, indivisible, and interdependent. Equality meant that men were born equal and were equal before the law.

The eighteenth-century revolution in political rights and practices was accompanied by a parallel and related revolution in economic principle. Adam Smith and his successors conceived of economic liberty as the freeing of individual enterprise from the restraints and compulsions of government. To them, the pursuit of personal good in a free market was the ideal means of attaining the general good of all. This was the concept of political democracy, couched in economic terms. That is, the sum total of individual well-being is not only best for the individual, but best for the nation.

According to John Locke, "the preservation of property" is "the end of government." Property that the individual "removes out of the state that nature hath provided and left it in, he hath mixed his labor with, and joined it to something that is his own." This property therefore becomes indivisible from his other liberties and rights.

There can be no hierarchy of values among human rights. They stand or fall together.

CONTROLLED AND BALANCED POWER

The most vivid proof that the American Constitution was created in the light of a profound knowledge of human na-

10

ture is in its meticulous distribution, division, and balance of the power of government. It drew its wisdom from centuries of experience of man's way with man. Its creators resolved that once and for all they would guard essential liberties from destruction at the hands of those vested with the powers of government.

It has been aptly said that the principle of balanced power is a "Gothic principle." The architects of the Constitution contemplated that with the three branches of government and with the Federal establishment and the states nicely balanced, one against the other, there would remain broad scope for free action by those who lived under the system.

To govern must mean to exercise power. Ultimately, a government must have physical power. But the sources of power appear in many forms, corresponding to the characteristics of human nature—ambition, appetite, gratitude, fear, pride, hatred, and revenge. In politics the manifestation of power is in the capacity of those who exercise it to persuade people to give them support. In government it manifests itself in the use of law and administrative action to compel people to act or not act in accordance with the purposes of those who have authority.

That governmental power is a dangerous thing to entrust to frail human beings is proverbial. Power is a toxic draught. It may activate dormant but dangerous traits in human character. It impairs judgment, closes the windows of the mind, creates illusions, and deadens sensibilities. Long possession of power may completely transform character. Anyone who has been near the high seats of government and who has himself escaped the infection deeply realizes these effects.

The literature of statecraft is full of warnings. There has been no better delineation of the need for checks upon power than by the experienced wisdom of Hamilton and Madison in *The Federalist:*

11

The great security against a gradual concentration of the several powers in the same department, consists in giving to those who administer each department the necessary constitutional means and personal motives to resist the encroachments of the others. . . . Ambition must be made to counteract ambition. . . . It may be a reflection on human nature, that such devices should be necessary to control the abuses of government. But what is government itself, but the greatest of all reflections on human nature? If men were angels, no government would be necessary. . . . In framing a government which is to be administered by men over men, the great difficulty lies in this: you must first enable the government to control the governed; and in the next place oblige it to control itself. A dependence on the people is, no doubt, the primary control on the government; but experience has taught mankind the necessity of auxiliary precautions. This policy of supplying, by opposite and rival interests, the defect of better motives, might be traced through the whole system of human affairs, private as well as public. We see it particularly displayed in all the subordinate distributions of power, where the constant aim is to divide and arrange the several offices in such a manner as that each may be a check on the other that the private interest of every individual may be a sentinel over the public rights.

INDESTRUCTIBLE STATES

The principle that ours is a union of indestructible states has been galvanized by experience. The Constitution and all of its judicial interpretations hold that the Federal government is vested with limited and specified powers and with only such unspecified powers as are implied or necessary to specified powers. By the same authority, states reserve all other powers not given to the Federal establishment or denied to the states. Jefferson expressed it as a means "to make us several as to ourselves but one as to all others."

The vast size of the nation, the diversity of its characteristics and interests, the vital need that the people have their government within reach, the great value of experimentation in government in many states, all add the logic of facts to this constitutional guarantee. Add to this the clear value to individual liberty when government power is cut into so many units. The states are in truth our best security against revolutionary change.

Jefferson, echoing the prevailing sentiment of his time, wrote: "Were not this country already divided into States, that division must be made that each might do for itself what concerns itself directly." He wrote also: "A single consolidated government would become the most corrupt government on earth."

Nothing in present conditions invalidates the truth of these judgments. Experience has in fact strengthened them.

Principles by Custom and Experience

THE ENDLESS GROWTH OF PRINCIPLE

It would be absurd to claim that the quest for perfect institutions ended with the adoption of the Constitution. History went its way, and out of the slow growth of custom there came adaptations shaped partly by special conditions in America and partly by the growth of human enlightenment. These were not abrupt breaks with the past. They were, in fact, in keeping with the past.

New principles of government spring from all sorts of sources. They perish, or they enter the structure of a free society. Only rarely do they come from the heights of formal authority. They are born humbly and move outward into an area of general acceptance. Ultimately they become the expression and the tools of statesmen. For political leaders do not create; they discover and exploit.

In this respect our system contrasts most violently with

the Communist world. There the Marxian ideology came as the tool and the weapon of a revolutionary elite that came to power amid chaos. The people themselves knew little of the alien principles that governed them. And so the ideological pattern has had to be kept by the iron discipline of police power.

The modifications of our system, to a degree, have been associated with the names of such statesmen as Washington, Jefferson, Marshall, Lincoln, Theodore Roosevelt, and Wilson, not because those men originated the innovations but because they gave them the sponsorship of high office. Embodied in these innovations, new principles came to be impressed upon the mind and conscience of the nation.

THE PRESIDENCY AS THE EMBLEM AND AGENT OF NATIONAL UNITY

If George Washington had fallen in the Revolution, it is possible that there would have been no new constitution for many years after independence. Certainly, if he had not been before the eyes of those who made the Constitution, they would have created a quite different Presidency. The office was given vast power and prestige only because it was self-evident that Washington would be the first President and as such would create the pattern and customs of the office. For the men who had revolted against the British Crown were fearful of executive power. They felt that in Washington power would be associated with restraint.

They were right, for Washington not only lent incomparable prestige and dignity to his office, but by almost regal detachment from faction established himself as an embodiment of national unity. His Farewell Address, in which he solemnly warned his country against factionalism, heightened the impression thus created. And his refusal to accept more than two terms was an emphatic reminder that a re-

14

public was best served through the principle of limited tenure. His example was frozen into a custom that lasted for a century and a half and has now been legally established by constitutional amendment.

There have been Presidents who lent themselves to the lesser level of partisanship. Some have descended to the arena of class conflict and have joined some Americans in contending with others. But despite these perversions, the office has kept the essential attributes of a chief magistracy, a final recourse for the mediation of great domestic conflicts and a potential source of unity when all else fails.

THE PARTY SYSTEM

The liberties so carefully guarded in the Constitution gave to individuals and interests full rights to organize movements to secure governmental policies and actions favorable to them. The field for party action was thus left open under the Constitution, although specific provision for parties was wisely omitted. The statesmen of that day were of course quite aware of the inevitability of party action, and in fact in their several experiences they had no little part in creating it. But since the creation of party alignments inevitably follows changing conditions and situations, it was left for the free action of citizens to determine what those alignments should be.

But there were sharp warnings, by Washington and Madison and others, of the dangers inherent in factions. It is clear that by this term was meant not national parties but smaller minority-interest groups. For when two parties made their appearance, they were vastly more than factional groups. They were, and for the most part continued to be, so broad in their base that they came to be unifying rather than divisive forces in our society.

It is not without reason that history has attributed to

15

Jefferson and Hamilton the major contribution in the creation of the first parties. These were class-dominated only to a degree, for the country was already too big for any single class or faction to capture the national government. And because the Constitution was so contrived and the division of the nation into states so effective, a mere majority was unable to exercise absolute power. This has been of inestimable value in the preservation of our free life.

The parties can be valuable agencies for popular government. They should be vehicles for the use of like-minded people in attaining their objectives. They should provide cohesion in activating a government that is based upon a sharp division of powers. And they should serve over the generations to awaken the consciousness of people to common interests and ideals.

THE INDEPENDENCE OF THE JUDICIARY

When John Marshall boldly asserted the power of the Supreme Court to invalidate an act of Congress, his authority to do so was sharply challenged. It was claimed then, and has repeatedly been claimed since, that this is a clear usurpation of power by one branch of government over two others. Marshall based his case on the proposition that when he had to choose between a constitutional provision and a law made by Congress, a creature of the Constitution, he was compelled to respect and uphold only the higher law. The progeny, he inferred, must step down for the progenitor.

This was disputed on two notable grounds, one based upon tradition and the other upon logic. Considerable authority said that Anglo-American custom had never allowed a court to invalidate a legislative act. Also, it was claimed that the determination of whether the act of Congress was incompatible with the Constitution was just as logically within the power of Congress as within the power of the Supreme Court.

16

Marshall, however, won his case with posterity. Slowly the massive force of public opinion accepted the principle of the independence, not to say the supremacy, of the Supreme Court and made it a national conviction. The Court rose to be a monumental institution. The strength of this conviction revealed itself generations later, when Franklin D. Roosevelt, an immensely popular President, sought in 1937 to bend the Court to his will. Public opinion through Congress sustained the Court as an institution.

But only a superficial view of history can regard the decision of Marshall as pure innovation. Throughout Anglo-American history since the Magna Charta, and in the struggles of Lord Coke and others with the Crown, individuals had relied upon the concept of justice embodied in the authority of the courts. In the choice among executive authority, legislative bodies, and the courts, the instinct of free men turned to the courts. We cannot completely fathom the basis of this choice. But it may be ventured that since in the executive—notably, the Crown—people saw personal selfishness, and in legislative assemblies the play of faction, ignorance, and chicane, they turned to judges who, although not always pure or wise, pursued in the main a quest for a fair balance of conflicting interests, for peace among men, for the restraint of the strong, for the protection of the weak, for the righting of wrong, and for a decent respect for precedent and tradition.

THE INDISSOLUBLE UNION

Woodrow Wilson, writing as a historian twenty years before his Presidency, has this to say about the growth of the principle of an indissoluble union:

The legal theory upon which secession proceeded was one which would hardly have been questioned in the early years of the government, whatever resistance might then have been offered to its practical execution. It was for long found difficult to deny that a State could withdraw from the federal arrangement, as she might have declined to enter it. But constitutions are not mere legal documents; they are the skeleton frame of a living organism; and in this case the course of events had nationalized the government once deemed confederate.[4]

Since the principle asserted by Abraham Lincoln and acted upon by him as President was finally and tragically sealed in blood, it is hardly necessary to summarize the long debate over the primacy of Union or states. The common sense of it is that the makers of the Constitution favored the permanence of the Union, made it the first objective of the Preamble, and no doubt prayed for its success. Nevertheless, there was over the years strong opinion North and South that the sovereignty retained by the states entitled them to leave the Union. Opinion against it was equal, perhaps preponderant. The pity is that extremists on both sides finally precipitated the ordeal by arms.

But military force, however overwhelming, is a poor, indecisive method of resolving an issue of principle. It has been, rather, the force of common and supervening interests and ideals, the increase in economic interdependence, the habit of peaceful solution of differences in Congress and among the states, and the widening of national culture that have cemented the Union beyond any chance of division.

It is well, however, to remember that union among equals, not consolidation, is our national ideal.

WORLD RESPONSIBILITY

Woodrow Wilson is widely believed to be the major architect of the principle of America's world responsibility. It is true that the military and legislative conflict in which he

[4] Woodrow Wilson: *Division and Reunion* (New York: Longmans, Green & Co.; 1909), p. 211.

18

figured gave a new meaning to the principle. But any conception of American isolation before the first World War must be drastically revised in the light of the facts. The United States has been a factor in world politics and world politics has been a factor in our public policy for a long, long time. It was more than an urge to assure our security that pushed the national boundaries to the Pacific, that waged wars of conquest against Mexico and Spain, that purchased Alaska and annexed Hawaii. A destiny, however "manifest," has constantly attracted America to the far reaches of the world.

Occasionally we have been diverted from world interests by internal strife or internal development, but generally our foreign policy has not been isolationist. A long succession of Secretaries of State and Presidents maintained a far-reaching concern beyond national boundaries. Seward, Hamilton Fish, Blaine, Hay, Theodore Roosevelt, Root, Hughes, and Hoover stand with Wilson and Franklin D. Roosevelt in the history of our foreign policy.

But these statesmen were discoverers, not creators, of the principle of world responsibility. The diverse origins of our people, our maritime importance, our immense economic resources, have made us a world power. Neither thrust upon us nor sought for, this destiny lies in what we are and where we are.

A CLASSLESS SOCIETY

The principle of a classless society dominates the mind and spirit of the American nation. It asserts the ideal if not the fact that one man is as good as another, that given the appropriate and due opportunity one person can achieve as much as another, and that self-reliance is the major key to success.

Whatever the origins of this ideal may have been, our

nation's conditions and resources have provided rich nourishment for the growth of a classless society. The stratification of a people in fixed classes is impossible in a society constantly in process of expansion, of internal flux, and of alluring personal opportunities. No society can stratify in the face of a constantly enlarging geographic and economic frontier. And that frontier is fortunately still far from the immobility that characterizes those of many older nations. A nation in which a Walter Chrysler can build a mighty industry from a beginning in the work-clothes of a mechanic is still enjoying lusty youth.

The signs of national youth are innumerable. There is personal independence, guiding vigorous minds to unconventional and imaginative purposes. There is plenty of wholesome and sometimes unfortunate disrespect for authority. There is always belief in another chance, another opportunity. And there is optimism, high thinking, daring, and aggressiveness.

In such an atmosphere, the principle of a classless society has found a firm home in America. This defies the philosophy of Marx and his school, for the concept of a systematic remaking of classes can find few converts in a society where groups have no fixed boundaries.

Principles and Institutions as Safeguards

These conservative safeguards were, in part, designed to protect democracy against itself. Farsighted men realized that a broad franchise and popular political institutions might allow a popular tyranny even more sinister than that of royal absolutism or aristocratic privilege. For the real enemies of liberty were recognized as the perversions and selfishness of human nature, whether attired in royal raiment or in the

rags and tatters of the masses. There had been many reminders of this danger, from Plato and Aristotle to Jefferson and
Burke.

There lived in the mind of Jefferson, along with a passion-
ate faith in the noble instincts of free men, a deep apprehension concerning their original sins of selfishness and affinity
with power. In his early *Notes on Virginia,* he wrote of the
dangers of masses in cities swayed by passion and infected by
demagogues. He noted that men in the mass might ruthlessly
invade the liberties of minorities and ultimately lend their
great power to a tyrant. The evolution of government from
democracy to tyranny was well known. Jefferson thus appreciated the fearful danger of what later came to be known as
"the tyranny of the majority." He feared a majority that
might create first a tyrannical legislature and then a tyranny
of an executive. He said in a letter to Madison:

> The tyranny of the legislative power is really the danger most
> to be feared and will continue to be so for years to come. The
> tyranny of the executive power will come in its turn, but at a
> more distant period.

The penetrating and prophetic Tocqueville in the 1830's
gave us further and more detailed warnings. "The very essence of democracy," he wrote, "consists in the absolute
sovereignty of the majority." Legislatures become the tools
of this majority. The executive can lose all stability and independence under the impact of a majority. And law made
under its influence can violate all the fine theories of parliamentary deliberation.

"This," Tocqueville continues, "comes to the same thing
as if the majority of the populace held its deliberations in the
market place."

This tyranny—and it is tyranny—of the majority exercises
"a prodigious actual authority and a moral force which is

21

scarcely less predominant." Of what value is legalized free expression of opinion if majority rule can crush complaints to earth?

In a complex society, various institutions serve by internal oppositions to counterbalance each other and provide stability. Many of these institutions are mentioned by Tocqueville. With the malign Paris Commune in mind, he noted that the strength of America did not lie in a single great capital city. He laid great stress on education. He pointed to religion and the great organized churches as conservative forces. The profession of law was another. Private associations of various sorts were on his list.

Most important among Tocqueville's safeguards was local and state self-government as a balance against a national establishment. Next were the courts, in the exercise of their power to interpret legislation.

Jefferson also looked to these great fortresses of liberty, and he added another, the great national political parties.

Today these safeguards in the United States are confronted with formidable and dangerous threats.

Principles Are an Entailed Inheritance

Edmund Burke, in one of his memorable passages, observes that "From Magna Charta to the Declaration of Rights, it has been the uniform policy of our Constitution to claim and assert our liberties as an entailed inheritance derived to us from our forefathers, and to be transmitted to our posterity." This moral stricture never had more immediate meaning than it has to Americans today.

In our haste to achieve objectives, however worthy, we have strained our constitutional principles to the breaking point. We have set up new and strange interpretations of democracy which have seriously impaired the structure of the republic. We have greeted what some of our leaders have called "the great majority" (of those who have chosen to vote) as a divinely ordained authority, despite the fact that constitutional government restrains all, including majorities. We have, to borrow a phrase from Burke, considered human progress as a "problem in arithmetic."

If our folly prompts us to create new principles for succeeding generations, and if by some miracle we succeed, we should be robbing those generations of their own freedom of choice. Our wisdom should suggest that something be left to the hands and hearts and ingenuity of those yet to come. To name ourselves arbiters of history is to invite the pitiless judgment of the future.

Common sense, as well as a consideration of our puny importance in the stream of history, should bring us to realize that the past and the future constitute an indivisible whole. A backward glance can instill in an American a sense of belonging to a distinguished tradition. Those who prepared our way were illustrious men who conserved what they had and multiplied it for our use. In a world shaken by folly and violence, they held firm the best of their past. We, their heirs, have a responsibility to guard the future. Our inheritance is entailed. It is morally inalienable.

We are not creators, we are trustees. We serve in an endless succession of watches at the citadel of liberty.

CHAPTER II

Economic Liberty, Limited by Law

An Undetermined Principle

The ultimate in socialism is a condition in economic life in which the concerns of the individual are rigidly determined for him by authority over which he has only vague and indirect control.[1] The ultimate in liberty, superficially considered, is the antithesis of such restraint, in which every individual pursues his interests in utter freedom. Such a concept of individual freedom, however, implies a chaos in which very few individuals have any freedom at all. The development of restraint and regulation in economic life has been a major problem of authority from the beginning of civilization and is a major purpose of government. True economic liberty, therefore, must always be limited and defined by law. The determination of the proper sphere of law in the economic field involves the creation of a principle that has never been accurately defined or firmly fixed in public policy.

---

[1] In using the word "ultimate" I realize that theoretical socialists will reply that their "ultimate" is the stage when the state withers away. However, that is a consummation that has never been attained. The complete domination of the state is the ultimate, so far as experience has provided any evidence.

What a true believer in liberty is seeking in economic life is that minimum of government restraint, aid, and control which will leave the largest possible scope for the exercise of individual initiative and effort, and for reward.

It is not easy to define a boundary between individual economic freedom and government intervention, and it is still harder to secure a general recognition of such a boundary in the making of public policy. In the past three quarters of a century we have witnessed a conflict over this issue. The intensity of this conflict arises from several factors.

Economic interests grow more confused, complex, and interwoven. An individual may be the owner of real estate in a home, the employee of a great corporation from which he receives a stated wage, a dues-paying member of a labor union that has not only economic but political objectives, a member of a local school board sitting beside a banker and the physician who cares for his children, and the owner of an insurance policy in a company that owns bonds in a public utility corporation from which he purchases electric power. The individual's interest in what government does to protect these diversified interests is mixed, confused, and almost undefinable.

The claims of two or more economic interests may conflict and overlap. The determination of what is a fair value of capital invested, of services performed—whether in manual labor or judgment or skill—depends, in the mind of the individual concerned, upon personal predilections. And such judgments are almost impossible to reconcile.

There is also the superimposed interest of government itself. The ideal is a government holding the scales as an arbiter in economic affairs. The reality is a government operating as a positive, independent force. It has the incentive of seeking power. It is not a selfless agent but something that has claims for itself. It talks of a "public interest," but tends to identify its own ambitions and concerns with the "public interest." It becomes another interest against whose selfishness there must be protection for the individual.

The nature of this conflict and the decay of the true liberal ideal of the early nineteenth century can be well described in terms of British experience. Our course in this movement has lagged many years behind that of Britain, but it has followed the same general pattern.

The Decline and Fall of British Liberalism

The great enlightenment of the second half of the eighteenth century in Europe and America asserted the rights of the individual. His liberty was to be bounded only by the liberty of others. Government and law were to be devices for the protection of liberty.

In England this concept was later to be subjected to more than a century of revision, until the liberal faith of, say, 1910 was so compromised that it bore little resemblance to the great doctrine of the eighteenth-century revolution. It was a frail, anemic prospect for the virus of socialism.

Jeremy Bentham, James Mill, and his son, John Stuart Mill, were the leaders of the earlier stages of this revision. They were eagerly abetted by others of a more practical political strain. In their enthusiasm over the discovery of a state based upon political democracy, they conceived it wise to vest that state with an ever growing authority. They felt that such a people's government could work no wrong. In pursuing the greatest happiness for the greatest number, the Utilitarians, operating by a rule of thumb, would hasten the progress of the state by a mass of law and an army of bureaucrats. No man with intelligence and conscience, as he looks back, can blame those reformers for their objectives, for there was plenty of need for reform, much stark injustice to correct, in a new, raw industrial civilization. They little real-

26

ized, however, the need for protections against protection and for the reform of reform.

In 1846 the repeal of the Corn Laws marked the summit and the point of decline of the free market. From that point, government rode in the saddle.

The Liberal Party of Gladstone, Asquith, and Lloyd George, like every party, was on the trail of votes. Holding fast to the good name "liberal," it compromised the liberal faith with each passing year. Ultimately, socialism, embodied in the Labor Party, engulfed the Liberal Party, its desiccated faith, its followers, and its mission.

In the latter years of the nineteenth century, a final vain cry was raised by a great liberal, Herbert Spencer. Viewed in the light of today, his criticism of all social legislation is black and hopeless. But his prophecy can be read after seventy-five years with profit for all of us. He said:

The laws made by Liberals are so greatly increasing the compulsions and restraints over citizens that . . . it may by-and-by happen that the Tories will be the defenders of liberties which the Liberals, in pursuit of what they think popular welfare, trample under foot.

That prophecy has come true. The Tories of whom he spoke, despite their mistakes, held to a body of principle. They yielded the necessity of some intervention in economic life and, since they had no sacred vow not to use government to right wrongs, they were able to enact reform without revolution. Now they are the defenders of the liberty deserted by the Liberals. They have temporarily at least, checkmated socialism with the aid of the middle class—once the very bone and marrow of Liberalism.

The Origins of Government Intervention

It is ironic that government intervention in the United States should have been introduced by one of the revered architects of our constitutional system, Alexander Hamilton. In the second year of the Republic, 1791, the first Secretary of the Treasury presented his famous "Report on Manufactures" to the House of Representatives. It was a bold assertion of the desirability of government intervention in the free market, at the very moment when *laissez faire* was gaining ascendancy over the old practices and theories. Adam Smith had published his *Inquiry into the Nature and Causes of the Wealth of Nations* only fifteen years before and had himself died only the year before. The impact of that classic statement of economic freedom was very great, mingled as it was with all the other great revolutionary forces of the time. Against this tide moved Hamilton's appeal, an earnest argument for government intervention against the prevailing growing belief in full economic liberty.

Like most of those who urge more intervention now, Hamilton based his case, in part at least, on precedent. He granted the reasonableness of those who stood for a free market and who asserted that government help distorted the natural course of the economy and produced the evils of monopoly. But he claimed that, since the policies of nations had never been based on the ideal of a free economy, it would be inadvisable to follow theory in this instance, which he claimed to be exceptional. Foreign nations were offering aid to their own manufactures. Manufacturing in the United States, which he wanted government to encourage and subsidize, was essential to a growing nation, he said. And he claimed that his plan for subsidizing domestic manufactures out of special tariffs could be authorized under the welfare clause of the Constitution. He made clear, however, unlike many who now invoke the welfare clause in the Constitution, that his proposed bounties had general and not local purposes, and fully fitted the intent of that constitutional provision.

Since tariffs, bounties, and subsidies thus found a foothold in national policy, and continued through the generations, the concessions made for the manufacturing interests of Hamilton's time became the basis of arguments for miscellaneous aid of all sorts. From that day to this, every suppliant for government aid had claimed that "business has always had it." It is perhaps idle to note that once the free market was violated by a tariff for protection of favored parts of the economy, the way was opened far down the years for the threat of socialism that we now face.

Accepted Types of Government Action

By tradition and general acceptance, government activities can be classified roughly in two groups: first, services; and second, restraints and regulations.

Typical of government services are lawmaking, enforcing, and judging; coinage and regulation of currency; defense and police; postal service; care of the helpless and unfortunate; provisions for recreation; building of streets, roads, and highways; preservation of public health; and conservation of essential natural resources. There are also many purely informational services essential to the general public and specified interests, such as the census, health information, data for business, labor, agriculture, commerce, and scientific research.

Essential, sound, and safe government regulations limit and protect our freedom on every side, from the traffic light on the corner to the registration of security issues.

It would be false and futile to deny that it is right and necessary to maintain these economic services and economic restraints and regulations. The evolution of more complex relationships between buyer and seller, employer and em-

29

ployee, investor and investment, and generally between the individual and the economy as a whole, demands some intervention of government.

Practically everyone recognizes this. Even those whose property interests are most affected acknowledge the fact of more government. The 1950 statements of the National Association of Manufacturers and the United States Chamber of Commerce would in 1900 have been regarded as radical.

Limits and Conditions of Government Intervention

In approaching a general principle of what our future course should be in determining economic liberty limited by law, the following propositions should be useful:

1. The guiding ideal should be a free market.

2. Individual responsibility and voluntary co-operation, freely arrived at, are the characteristics of true economic liberty. They should be recognized as the ideal in the fields of agriculture, labor relations, and in business generally. Government can and should promote this ideal by suggestion and encouragement.

3. To promote this ideal to the fullest extent, those entrusted with government should always be detached and judicial in their attitude. Political alliances with specific groups destroy this role of impartiality, and by impairing the integrity of the executive and the Congress as courts of last resort invite class struggle and chaos.

4. When individual and co-operative efforts fail and government assumes regulatory power, its function should be the making of rules generally prohibiting, not compelling. It is valid for government to tell a man not to do something against another man; it is not only impracticable but a denial of liberty to tell him exactly what he should do for another. The lurking danger in all government regulation is like that

30

in press censorship. The censor will never be content to tell people what not to print. He will ultimately tell them what to print.

5. Government should not inject its will into matters that are within the realm of business judgment. It is not qualified to do that. The role of government as a judge, a mediator, and a regulator has been established over the centuries. Methods of operating in that capacity have been perfected. They are governed by principles, tested by experience, and fixed in common and statute law. It has been proved over the years that the proper exercise of this function is not only consistent with liberty but is an indispensable means of preserving liberty.

On the other hand, government administration of the activities generally known as business—manufacturing, buying, selling, lending, and the like—has not only in modern times been regarded as an improper function of a free government but has been casual and incidental as well. No body of skill or experience has been established.

6. In all government regulation, the essential structure of our constitutional system should be respected. Federal regulation is appropriate only in matters that are truly interstate in character or are genuinely related to other Federal powers. Regulation, like other government processes, is at its best when those responsible are close to and familiar with the problem they seek to solve.

7. Since economic life is in a state of constant change, regulatory laws should frequently be reconsidered and revised. In fact, they may well be regarded as temporary invasions of economic liberty, subject to withdrawal when normal, free relations are restored.

8. All groups and interests should be held equally accountable to the public interest. Corporations, trade associations, and labor unions should be subject to the same or similar regulations.

31

9. Regulation should have as its objective the preservation of fair and measurably free economic relations and, above all, free competition. Free competition was the keystone of classical liberal doctrine. Beyond that, the regulator should not use his power to further his personal notions of what the nature of economic institutions should be. For example, business regulation should have as its objective fair practices and healthy competition among units of all sizes. Bigness *per se* should not be regarded as monopoly.

10. The measure of the value of an economic system is its capacity to produce wealth; i.e., the goods that make for higher living standards, and the material means for human happiness. Government regulation should have this objective constantly before it. Thus, it should avoid unreasonably limiting by law the span of the individual's working hours and life. It should also restrict to a minimum the number of persons in nonproductive government employment. It should not curb efficiency or check the flow of capital.

11. Government regulations, moreover, should not contradict each other. At the moment, dozens of cross-purposes prevail.

12. In the bestowal of government benefits, aid, and relief, there should generally be required a demonstration of actual need. This principle is bitterly contested. It is demanded that aid be given as a matter of right. This is dangerous for two reasons. Generalized aid results in expenditures far beyond the resources of any nation. And promiscuous benefits destroy the moral fiber of those who receive them. The demand that aid be given as a matter of right is the adoption of the principal tenet of socialism—equal shares, equal everything. There are special forms of aid, such as compensation for industrial accidents, in which a means test is not necessary or appropriate and in which experience has shown no danger to economic liberty.

Government aid and relief are for genuine emergencies.

32

They are for the prevention of disaster, economic or personal. There is grave doubt whether the Federal government should directly exercise those powers at all. Generally, they should be exercised by states or local government, with perhaps some Federal help.

13. In the conservation of natural resources, there are alluring temptations for the undue exploitation of government power. It is self-evident that some natural resources, especially those in the public domain, are limited in amount and are essential to the economy as a whole. Government intervention, even acquisition, under fair terms is generally recognized as legitimate. This should apply to national parks and other time-tested government institutions and services. Government, however, should generally act as a trustee of property belonging to the people, ultimately to be used by them under conditions of private ownership and development and not to be exploited for the enlargement of government power as such.

14. The imposition of taxes should always be for the exclusive purpose of raising necessary revenue. The use of the taxing power for regulation or reform is self-defeating, unjust, and destructive.

15. Since the Federal government must have the power of issuing and regulating the value of money, its concern should be stability. As in the case of the taxing power, it should not use its control over currency to achieve regulation and reform.

16. Those who administer a public trust should believe in a free economy. A disparity between the nature of an economy and the beliefs of its administrators is dangerous. Former socialist Prime Minister Attlee has said: "A socialist party cannot hope to make a success of administering the capitalist system because it does not believe in it."

17. The operation of a business by government is the deadly enemy of economic liberty. In competition with pri-

vate business, government has overwhelmingly decisive advantages that lead to private ruin and state socialism.

David E. Lilienthal, for many years an advocate of a more "dynamic" government and an administrator first of government electric power and then of atomic energy, apparently has grown to recognize the deadly danger of government monopoly in such fields. He calls for the removal of the heavy hand of government monopoly from this form of energy and for putting it "back on the American track," on which the motive power is composed of "the great prizes of satisfaction, prestige and profit that have always spurred men on in every other new chapter of American industrial history." We need, he continues, "development know-how . . . based on wideopen competition of ideas, providing an open and free field for any man's idea of a better way to do something." [2] He expresses a principle of progress which can be applied to every aspect of economic life.

18. The test of all government intervention should be whether it truly contributes to the freedom, development, and security of the individual. What the lover of liberty must seek in the face of growing government and complex economic relationships is more and more voluntary co-operation among all the interests of the country, based on personal responsibility.

The foregoing propositions should be the guiding ideals in holding the line between a necessary measure of government authority and the freedom of the individual.[3]

Liberties are indivisible. If economic liberty is not attained and held, the entire structure of principles, inherited and developed by experience, must fall.

[2] David E. Lilienthal: "Free the Atom," *Collier's,* June 17, 1950, p. 13.

[3] Elaborations and illustrations of these propositions will be found in many of the sections of Chapter VII.

CHAPTER III

Our Middle Interests and Their Stakes in Liberty

We Have Interests without Classes

It is an elementary rule of politics that people group themselves according to their "interests." When we speak of economic interests, we mean common concern within a group about a matter of economic value. There are, of course, manifold interests—religious, sectional, or other forms of shared cultural, emotional, or idealistic concerns. These interests provide the incentive for group formation, consciousness, and action in politics.

The diversity of American society, its extreme fluidity, in which individuals constantly shift about within the scale of fortune, the absence of real barriers to ambition and competence, and our fundamental equalitarian philosophy have always prevented groups with common interests from hardening into what other countries know as classes.

When in the United States a group or class has become the subservient inferior of another class, such a distinction has later disappeared, not only because it was in conflict with the temper and moral sentiments of our people but because it proved to be highly inefficient and impractical. The tragedy of the South before the Civil War was its progressive economic decline, which has been attributed to the institution of slavery. The major plea in Helper's celebrated book, *The Impending Crisis,* published in 1860, was the economic blight of slavery.

From time to time, however, some interest has succeeded in achieving, under law or otherwise, a favored position over other interests. In political oratory we hear this called a "vested" interest. While, as is habitual in political debate, there has been reckless exaggeration of the "privileges" under attack, it goes without saying that in any human society and under any man-made law, unfair advantages are likely to be seized by some groups at the expense of other groups.

In the course of our history, groups engaged in manufacturing, banking, or possessed of other forms of property interest have acquired for a limited period such privileged positions. In our own time, also, we have seen new vested interests appear. Pensioners with a statutory or constitutional first claim on specific tax receipts, labor leaders with legal exemptions not accorded to management, political bosses operating under election laws of their own fashioning, groups of individuals who find employment, preference, or undue profit from government connections, and many other "special" or "vested" interests, old and new, might be cited.

It is the task of statesmanship, however, to eradicate special privileges, since they threaten the internal integrity and safety of the state. In undertaking that task, caution must always be exercised to avoid creating new privileges to offset old ones. The great defect in the Wagner Labor Relations Act lay in its assumption that because employers had enjoyed an unfair advantage in the past, there should be inequitable advantages for organized employees. Much of that lack of balance was ultimately corrected by the Taft-Hartley Act. A constant examination of the operation of laws, by vigilant political parties and legislators and fair-minded administrators, can eradicate special privilege.

Statists, however, following the line of Marx, regard interest groups as classes and seek to inculcate class consciousness in such groups. This is the very essence of demagoguery. It is a major threat to our institutions.

The Marxian Middle Class

Karl Marx and his school based their predictions and directives on the assumption that classes have always prevailed in society. Since Marx was intent upon creating a formula that would be readily understood by the masses, he made his classification of society exceedingly simple, disregarding its infinitely complex nature. Hence, he defined three classes—the capitalists, or owners of the means of production; the unpropertied "slaves" or the "proletariat"; and between these, the middle class. Even Marx was very vague in assigning specific interests to this middle class, and his followers were even more vague in defining it. However, Marxian dogma disposed of the middle class by assigning it to oblivion; it would be broken up and absorbed, chiefly by the proletarians on the D-Day of the class struggle.

Socialists have held the middle class to be inimical to their purposes because, as John Spargo, an American socialist, put it, "the members of the middle class would prefer to have all class conflicts cease." Spargo went on to accuse the middle class of talking too much about the "essential unity of the interests of the workers and their employers."

Thus, even the socialists recognized, in their way, the fundamental concern of the middle class with stability and internal peace, and for that reason they hated this *petite bourgeoisie* and resolved to destroy it. For, as long as it stood firmly, it proved a most certain barrier to the consummation of the class struggle and the dictatorship of the proletariat. The Irishman Seán O'Faoláin thus expressed the frustration of the radical: "Between England and the revolution there will always stand an army of bowler hats."

The American Middle Interests

The Marxists' hatred for and fear of what they call the middle class can easily be understood when we consider the nature and distribution of wealth among Americans, as well as the interests, economic and otherwise, and the ideals of those who are neither rich nor poor. For not only does the preponderant part of the nation's wealth lie with this middle group, but the preservation of national well-being utterly depends on the maintenance of individual liberty and the limitation of the power of government. Moreover, the nature and size of the interests of this group make it the appropriate trustee and defender of the interests and ideals of the nation itself.

In defining the group that shares the middle interests I would be adopting the basic fallacy of the socialists if I were to attempt a hard and fast definition based upon economic status. We are a nation of interdependent groups, not a fragmented collection of independent, mutually antagonistic units.

The most common bases for defining distinctions are either income or property ownership. If we adopt those criteria we find a gradation from very small to very large individual or family income or ownership. The broad picture of our society is a small fringe at either end, with the vast mass in the middle. The superficial impression is that of great, almost monolithic stability.

But the real situation is not so simple. Many hired workers have high incomes and many own property. Many employers and property owners have low incomes. The earnings of

38

many small businessmen come in part from their own personal labor and in part as a return from capital invested, with no clear distinction between these two sources. The bulk of American families have annual incomes between two and five thousand dollars. They form a fluid mass, constantly fed from above and below, and constantly losing members in both directions. Nearly every working American passes into or through this income group some time in his life: young men starting from scratch work up; old men reaching the age of retirement come down; men in the prime of life enter or leave the middle group according to their business fortunes.

Members of this middle group do not depend exclusively on income from property or from business or from their own labor, and their earnings from labor are not exclusively wages. They combine the characteristics of the theoretical proletariat and the theoretical *bourgeoisie* and have interests in common with the lower income levels and the higher ones. Some of the contrasts and resemblances between the middle-income group and the extremes at both ends are illustrated in Table A.[1] It will be observed there that all of the various types of income are received by persons in both the lowest and highest groups, although in different proportions, and that creditors and debtors, savers and dissavers, are found in all income groups.

It is this great diversity of interests which precludes any arbitrary, exact definition of the great middle group in the United States or a description of that group in terms of precise dollar-incomes or property values. It suffices for my purpose to describe the middle group in economic terms as people of what are commonly known as average means. The interests of this group, economic and otherwise, I call middle interests. The property of this group, measured either in terms of income or of capital values, comprises the great bulk

[1] See pp. 43-4.

of the nation's wealth. The property interests involved are diverse, but almost without exception they are dependent upon the conditions of a free economy.

Perhaps after the foregoing discussion it is unnecessary to deny any inconsistency in arguing on the one hand against political appeals to so-called class interests, while at the same time attempting to convince those who share the middle interests to become politically active in protecting free institutions and private property. What I deplore are appeals to specific elements within our society—farmers, workers, or what not. These appeals are divisive. They create hatred and strife. On the other hand, an appeal to the interests of the middle group is to remind people of the concerns that really unite them. For the middle interests are truly national. They cut through all so-called class lines. They traverse occupational, sectional, religious, and racial boundaries. They are neither vested, nor special, nor privileged in the ordinary connotations of those terms.

The significance of the middle interests and of those who share them will clearly stand out in the following review of the nature and distribution of the income and property of the nation.[2]

Income Groups

The Federal Reserve Board Survey of Consumer Finances estimated the following percentages of "spending units," [3] which roughly means families, according to annual incomes before taxes:

[2] It is important to consider, in reading the figures presented in this chapter as well as elsewhere in this book, that the distribution of property and income is constantly and rapidly changing. The changes since the dates of my figures, however, could not materially alter the nature of my conclusions.

[3] *Federal Reserve Bulletin,* June–December, 1950.

Under $1,000	14%
$1,000–$1,999	19%
$2,000–$2,999	21%
$3,000–$3,999	19%
$4,000–$4,999	11%
$5,000–$7,499	11%
$7,500 and over	5%

The bulk of our voting population and the center of political power is therefore probably in the range of incomes between $2,000 and $5,000.

However, we must not assume, as has been the practice, that there are essential economic antagonisms among such groups as wage earners, farmers, and independent proprietors. Farm proprietors have average incomes between $2,000 and $3,000. White-collar workers in such occupations as banking earn, on the average, less than automobile workers. The average annual wages of workers in the pipeline transportation industry—aristocrats of the "working class"—amounted to $4,296 in 1950. Insurance agents and related office employees earned about 14 per cent less than that. Workers in water transportation—also "aristocrats"—earned $4,413 in 1950. Employees of religious organizations fell far short of most industrial workers; they got $2,276. Employees in public education, which means for the most part teachers, earned $2,420.

Moreover, the increases in wages since the prewar year 1939 have been far greater among industrial workers than among the white-collar group. In 1939 workers in the automobile and automobile-equipment manufacturing industry received average annual wages of $1,762. In 1950 the figure was $4,007. Adjusted to the 1939 value of the dollar, the latter would be, at the end of 1950, approximately $2,120. That is a gain in purchasing power of 20 per cent. The pipeline worker mentioned above is 18 per cent better off, and

41

the worker in water transportation is 50 per cent richer in real income.

On the other hand, the employee of a religious organization is 7 per cent behind 1939 in real income, and employees in public education are only 9 per cent better off.

The real incomes of retired people living on fixed incomes are, of course, deplorably reduced.

There has been a tremendous process of readjustment which has pushed wage earners into the middle groups, a process that is creating fundamental changes in their political sympathies and outlook.

Who Owns What?

The facts about the income and property ownership of the people of the United States deny not only the dialectical assumptions of socialist theoreticians, but most of the calculations of politicians. The complexity and the fluid conditions revealed in property ownership are difficult to portray, although they clearly provide the basis for a number of simple conclusions. The best brief summary that I have seen on incomes and property ownership arranged by income groups is by the able economist, Rufus S. Tucker.[4]

The Federal Reserve survey was based on "spending units," and includes a sampling of cases. There are approximately fifty-two million such "units" in the United States. The following conclusions in the survey help to show the relatively great material stakes of those who share the middle interests.

Four out of ten American families have assets worth $5,000 or more. One out of ten has assets worth $25,000 or more.

[4] This appears as Table A on pp. 43–4. In the interest of simplicity, in the pages that follow the table I have used for illustration only one of Mr. Tucker's sources, the 1950 Survey of Consumer Finances, published by the Federal Reserve Board in the *Federal Reserve Bulletin,* June–December, 1950.

TABLE A, BY RUFUS S. TUCKER

Showing Comparisons between Certain Income Groups, 1949

Relative Importance of Groups

Income Range	Under $1,000	$3,000–$4,000	Over $10,000
Per cent of total population	14.0 to 19.0	19.0 to 20.0	2.6 to 3.0
Per cent of money income	2.0 to 2.7	19.0 to 20.0	15.6 to 16.4
Per cent of total income	2.7 to 3.7	18.9 to 19.9	15.5 to 16.2

Percentage of Units in Each Group with Specified Characteristics

Occupations of Head of Unit	Under $1,000	$3,000–$4,000	Over $10,000
Professional and semiprofessional	1 to 2	4 to 8	19 to 22
Managerial and self-employed (except farm)	4 to 6	10 to 12	44 to 51
Clerical and sales	1 to 3	12 to 15	5 to 8
Skilled and semiskilled	7 to 9	43 to 44	5 to 12
Unskilled and service	12 to 15	9 to 14	1 to 2
Farm operators	24 to 31	4 to 5	7 to 14
In armed forces, students, housewives or not employed	32 to 40	8 to 12	5 to 10

Composition of Unit			
Single person	44 to 48	7 to 12	2 to 4
Two persons	27 to 29	25 to 26	19 to 35
Three persons	10	24 to 26	25 to 26
Four persons	5 to 6	19 to 22	20 to 23
Five or more	9 to 11	17 to 21	16 to 31
No earners	3 to 41	0 to 1	0 to 1
Single earner	49 to 84	65 to 78	53 to 71
Two or more	9 to 13	22 to 35	29 to 47

Units with Children under 18			
None	76.2	40.6	51.6
One	9.5	23.3	21.5
Two	6.0	20.6	16.1
Three	3.3	9.0	7.4
Four or More	5.0	6.5	2.4

Buying Habits:	Under $1,000	$3,000–$4,000	Over $10,000
Percentage of units buying in 1949			
House (nonfarm)	1	5	6 †
Automobile	5	24	37 †
New	1	7	25 †
Used	4	18	11 †
Other durable goods *	17	46	54 †
Television sets	1	8	14 †

COMPARISONS BETWEEN CERTAIN INCOME GROUPS *(cont.)*

Source of Income	Under $1,000	$3,000–$4,000	Over $10,000
Wages or salaries	46 to 47	78 to 92	60 to 65
Self-employment	24 to 48	9 to 17	28 to 52
Pensions, annuities, alimony, gambling, relief, gifts, etc.	26 to 38	10 to 23	6 to 9
Interest, dividends, trust funds, and royalties	4 to 9	7 to 11	43 to 54
Rent, other than roomers and boarders	4 to 7	6 to 9	20 to 23

Age of Head			
Under 25	6 to 11	4 to 6	0
25–64	40 to 54	88 to 90	88 to 92
65 and over	35 to 53	5 to 6	8 to 12

Ownership			
Home or farm	50	46	66 ‡
(Per cent of nonfarm homes owned)	(43)	(50)	(71) ‡
Other real estate	9	16	44 ‡
Business interest	3 to 13	6 to 9	29 to 36
Corporation stock	2 to 3	5 to 7	30 to 54
Liquid assets	44 to 48	74 to 78	96 to 99 ‡
Automobiles	19 to 24	62 to 63	89 ‡

Financial Condition			
Had liquid assets	44	74	99 ‡
Liquid assets exceeded liabilities	92	92	100 ‡
Had some debt	34	58	48 ‡
Net savers during year	29 to 31	70 to 73	85 ‡
Net dissavers	45 to 52	12 to 29	7 to 15 ‡
Decreased debts	5	11	6 ‡
Increased debts	20	33	19 ‡
Increased liquid assets	9	28	47 ‡
Decreased liquid assets	28	35	26 ‡
Per cent of nonfarm owned homes mortgaged	16	53	46 to 47 ‡

* Including television sets, radios, furniture, refrigerators, washing machines, stoves, other electrical appliances.
† Over $5,000; more detailed breakdown not available.
‡ Over $7,500; more detailed breakdown not available.

Sources: 1950 Survey of Consumer Finances (Fed. Reserve Bull., June–Dec. 1950).
Report on Consumer Income, U.S. Census, Series P-60, No. 7 (Feb. 15, 1951).
Statistics of Income for 1947, Preliminary Report, U.S. Bureau of Internal Revenue.
Statistics of Income for 1948, U.S. Treasury Dept. Press Release No. S-2497 (Nov. 10, 1950).

Only one in ten has debts greater than assets. And strange though it may seem, red ink is relatively more common among people in higher-income groups.

The ownership of automobiles is very general. It ranges from 24 per cent in the lowest group to 89 per cent in the highest. The relatively low percentage in the lower groups must be partly accounted for by the presence in those groups of many elderly retired people. But in the groups with incomes from $1,000 to $3,999, automobile ownership from 1949 to 1950 made a spectacular increase.

One half of all nonfarm families, or approximately twenty-one million, owned their own homes. Among the various income groups, the percentages of home owners were as follows:

Income	Percentage of Home Ownership
Under $1,000	50
$1,000–$1,999	32
$2,000–$2,999	40
$3,000–$3,999	46
$4,000–$4,999	55
$5,000–$7,499	62
$7,500 and over	66

Members of all groups had considerable holdings of real estate other than their own homes. Nine per cent of the lowest income group, and 15 per cent in the group between $2,000 and $5,000, owned "other real estate."

The tabulation of ownership of "other real estate" follows:

Income	Other Real Estate
Under $1,000	9
$1,000–$1,999	12
$2,000–$2,999	11
$3,000–$3,999	16
$4,000–$4,999	18
$5,000–$7,499	26
$7,500 and over	44

45

Since the most serious threat of statism is to that kind of savings known as "liquid assets," it is most important to comprehend the distribution of that form of property.

First, let us see the percentage of each group that owns liquid assets, which include U.S. bonds, checking and savings accounts in banks, postal savings, shares in savings-and-loan associations, and credit unions. Currency is not included.

Income	Percentage Owning "Liquid Assets"
Under $1,000	44
$1,000–$1,999	54
$2,000–$2,999	68
$3,000–$3,999	74
$4,000–$4,999	86
$5,000–$7,499	94
$7,500 and over	99

The tabulation of ownership in some "business interest," which includes "whole or part ownership in a nonfarm unincorporated business or privately held corporation" is also significant:

Income	Business Interest
Under $1,000	3
$1,000–$1,999	5
$2,000–$2,999	5
$3,000–$3,999	6
$4,000–$4,999	10
$5,000–$7,499	15
$7,500 and over	36

The ownership of the industrial plant of the United States by various groups is shown in the figures of ownership of corporate stock. This includes all common and preferred stock open to investment by the general public. It excludes stock of privately held corporations, U.S. government securities, and bonds of all kinds. The following figures show the percentage of each group reporting such ownership for early 1949 and early 1950:

Income	Percentage Owning Corporate Stock	
	1950	1949
Under $1,000	2 '	3 '
$1,000–$1,999	2	3
$2,000–$2,999	5	5
$3,000–$3,999	7	6
$4,000–$4,999	10	9
$5,000–$7,499	10	15
$7,500 and over	30	36

The decline in stock ownership in the higher-income groups suggests that over the years there has been a shifting of stock ownership from high to lower incomes. A comparison of 1949 and 1950 can hardly be relied on to prove that point, because in an inflationary rising stock market, there is likely to be a lively, speculative interest in stock by people of lower incomes. Moreover, in the Federal Reserve survey, as well as in income tax returns, people owning only a few shares are not likely to report them. Stock owners, however, have greatly increased in number over the years. Mr. Tucker estimates that in 1916 not more than 2,500,000 people owned stock and possibly not more than 1,000,000 did so. His rough estimate for 1950 is 11,500,000.[5]

---

[5] On this point Mr. Tucker makes these observations: "I have studied this matter of the number of stockholders very carefully for a number of years, and the nearest I can come to a statement is that in 1916 not over 2,500,000 owned stock; perhaps not more than 1,000,000 did so. In 1949 at least 4,500,000 spending units or at least 6,000,000 individuals owned stock according to the Federal Reserve Board's survey. The income tax statistics combined with certain reasonable assumptions might make the number of individuals as high as 11,500,-000. The number of spending units might be in the neighborhood of 8,000,000, and the number of voters in the neighborhood of 10,000,000. In any sample

Along with this increase in the number of people who own the American industrial plant, there has been a shift in ownership from individuals with high incomes to those with lower incomes. The statistics of income issued by the United States Treasury provide proof of this.

This relative decline in the ownership of corporate stock among individuals with large incomes is mainly due to the fact that they have had less to invest after taxes.[6] It is also due to the fact that under present tax laws they can get only a small percentage of the earnings of companies in which they own stock. An individual with an income of $50,000 could realize only 1.325 per cent on his investment in the company. If his bracket was $200,000, he would get 0.461 per cent on his investment. This is on the assumption that the company earned not over 12 per cent on its capital. If it earned more, the return would be affected by the excess profits tax. This suggests why risk capital is so hard to find.

Some of the Material Stakes in Our Society

The foregoing section has shown the wide distribution of property among the various income groups, including those in the very low brackets.

Since there is this diffusion of property, it is unnecessary

survey it is the universal experience that people in the upper-middle and high-income brackets are less willing to co-operate and that people in the lower-income brackets are inclined to understate their incomes and to omit small items unless very carefully questioned. Since it is easy and quite common for persons receiving less than $100 in dividends to refrain from mentioning them on their income-tax returns, they would be inclined not to mention them to a survey field worker. At least $1,000,000,000 of dividends escapes income taxation every year; and if they were all received in amounts less than $100 there would be 10,000,000 stockholders in addition to the 3,449,000 who reported dividends in 1947. A few large evaders would reduce this number, but on the other hand the average dividend received by those who received less than $100 would probably be around $50. Therefore you can choose any number between 6,000,000 and 26,000,000 without exceeding the bounds of possibility. My own choice is 11,500,000."

[6] See pp. 56–60.

[7] These calculations are based on the Revenue Act of 1951.

and irrelevant to identify the specific property interests of the middle groups, even if such data were available and reliable.

An effort, however, to list the specific property holdings of the middle interests would be a long and tedious process. It will suffice to present a few important examples:

The ownership of life insurance policies is most characteristic of people of moderate means. The impact of statist policies of heavy spending, government debt, and inflation fall with crushing force on this form of property. Recent figures show 83,000,000 life-policy holders. These people own 203,-890,000 policies, of which the face value is $230,000,000,000. There are 3,355,000 annuity contracts in effect with insurance companies alone. The face value of all these policies I shall later consider as savings.

There are 20,000,000 prospective and present beneficiaries under pension and insurance plans whose "security" depends on private and government agencies and employers. (This is exclusive of government social security.) Under the present trend toward industrial pension plans, this number is rapidly increasing.

There are now 95,000,000 persons on the social security rolls, and more than 12,000,000 will be added under the 1950 act. A total of 3,600,000 are now receiving benefits; 20,-000,000 would not have to work any more to receive benefits; and an additional 40,000,000 are classified as fully insured but would have to work longer to receive full benefits.

The liquid savings of individuals on January 1, 1951, were approximately $226,481,000,000. This figure included $59,-255,000,000 in time deposits, $14,038,000,000 in savings and loan institutions, $58,019,000,000 in U.S. Savings Bonds, and $41,169,000,000 in government trust funds. The "present value" of life insurance policies (which constitute savings) was $54,000,000,000 in 1951.[8]

[8] The source of these figures is the National Industrial Conference Board.

49

It will be pointed out by politicians now in power that there has been a spectacular increase in savings since 1945. Individual savings represented by the surrender value of life insurance policies, time deposits, U.S. Savings Bonds, savings and loan association assets, and pension and trust funds rose from $168,578,000,000 in 1945 to $226,481,000,000 in 1951. This is an increase of 34.3 per cent in dollars. Several factors, however, need to be considered before we assume that Americans are actually better off. On that subject, Table B has been prepared for me by L. Robert Driver, who was formerly of the U.S. Bureau of Internal Revenue and the Securities Exchange Commission, and is now a tax consultant.

TABLE B

Individual Savings Represented by Surrender Value of Life Insurance, Time Deposits, U.S. Savings Bonds, Savings and Loan Association Assets, and Government Pensions and Trust Funds.

All Amounts Are Cumulative and at End of Each Year

Year	Amounts in Millions Savings	Consumer Credit *	Balance	Population in Thousands	Per Capita in Dollars Current Dollars	1945 Dollars
1945	$168,578	$ 5,627	$162,951	139,586	$1,168	$1,168
Index	100			100	100	100
1946	183,566	8,677	174,889	141,235	1,238	1,141
Index	108.9		107.3		106.0	97.7
1947	196,006	11,862	184,144	144,024	1,279	1,032
Index	116.3		113.0		109.5	88.4
1948	208,079	14,366	193,713	146,571	1,322	992
Index	123.4		118.9		113.2	84.9
1949	217.076	16,809	200,267	149,215	1,342	1,017
Index	128.8		122.9		114.9	87.1
1950	226,481 †	20,102	206,379	151,400	1,363	964
Index	134.3 ‡		126.7		116.7	82.5 ‡

* The Consumer Credit balances are from the Federal Reserve Bank's Statistics and cover installment credit, charge accounts, and personal bank-loans. They do not include personal business-debt. These items are proper deductions from gross amount of savings to arrive at the net savings.
† Preliminary as to amount of savings.
‡ *General Note:* It will be noted that the published amount of savings, which was calculated before deducting the debts, had at the end of 1950 increased 34.3%, but on a per capita basis had decreased 17.5% after being adjusted for the decrease in the purchasing power of the dollar since 1945.

50

Unlike most calculations of savings, Table B takes account not only of the total dollars in savings, but of individual indebtedness in the form of consumer credit. It reduces these savings to a per capita basis. Finally, it calculates the savings in terms of purchasing power. The conclusion is that the per capita savings of the American people have been whittled down 17.5 per cent in five years. That is at the rate of 3.5 per cent a year.[9]

To describe in any detail the range of large and small businesses would take volumes. Here again, I merely offer specimen figures. There were about 700,000 corporate businesses in the United States in 1950, and 10,599,000 active proprietors of unincorporated enterprises, including farms. The 1950 Census reports that in nonfarming enterprises—which, it may be assumed, means corporate and unincorporated businesses—5,010,000 persons were employed as managers, officials, and proprietors. There were 10,516,000 employed in clerical, sales, and kindred work. There were 4,944,000 professional technical and kindred workers.

Finally, there were employed in the various units of government, 7,900,000 men and women.

All these people are vitally and adversely concerned with government policies that produce inflation and high taxes. All except the government workers have a direct stake in private enterprise.

The Farmers and the Middle Interests

In 1950 there were 4,381,000 farm owners. In addition to the owners, there were working on these farms 1,427,000 members of the owners' families. There were 2,154,000 hired hands.

The farmers traditionally have had a vital stake in the

[9] The purchasing power of such dollars has declined since 1939 from 100 cents to 54.8 cents. Since 1945, the decline has been from 100 cents to 70.7 cents (January 1951).

middle interests of the nation. According to the following figures of the Department of Agriculture, they have done pretty well over the past decade and a half. Farm income in 1950 was about $13,687,000,000. This includes the estimated rental value of their owner-occupied homes, the estimated value of the food grown and consumed on the farm, and other items. It also includes return on capital, the value of the services of the unpaid proprietors and unpaid full-time family workers. The total return was $2,357 per unpaid worker.

Farm owners and workers have certain distinct concerns that provide a ready invitation for statism to single them out and thus seek to create a serious fissure in the structure of our society. Government has probably extended more control and paternalism there than elsewhere, particularly during the past seventeen years. Here the line between the interest of individual farmers in government benefits and their interest in a free economy is hard to draw. In Jeffersonian political philosophy the farmer was the very embodiment of individualism. He was a man of property. He was and still is a man who deals in business terms of profit and loss and in the conservation of land. He demanded and received protection from government, but he remained free and self-reliant. Agriculture is still a vital part of the middle interests.

But farmers are a minority within the middle groups, as well as within the total voting population. Thus, they are in real danger, despite their government benefits, unless they appreciate their common interest with all other middle groups.

Wage Earners and the Middle Interests

In 1950 there were 40,930,000 full-time employees in private industries.[1] An estimated 15,000,000 of these workers were members of labor unions of various kinds.

[1] U.S. Department of Commerce, Survey of Current Business, National Income Supplement, 1951.

When we measure the economic and social status of the people who used to be identified as the middle "classes" and compare it with the present status of wage earners in the more fortunate ranges of their groups, striking similarities appear. Millions of workers, both union and nonunion, are now receiving incomes that compare favorably with those received by small independent business, professional, and so-called white-collar workers. Their status as property owners is also favorable by comparison.

That being true, their sympathies, their associations, their standards of intelligence and culture and those of their children are merging with those who in earlier days were regarded as much more fortunate.[2] Their political outlook is rapidly approaching that of the other middle groups. They can no longer confidently be expected to vote as a "labor" group. This changed status should be thoroughly grasped by conservative political leaders. In fact, by tradition a large proportion of union members have never voted as their leaders and others have expected and hoped they would. In a day when their status was much less fortunate than it is now, Theodore Roosevelt said the Republican Party could normally expect to receive about a third of the vote of union members. John L. Lewis before one election rather bitterly remarked that, while he could tell his people how to vote, there was no assurance that they would do so.

The political shift of labor was clearly shown in the results of the 1950 Senatorial election in Ohio. In the face of stupendous efforts by the United Labor League of Ohio, which was composed of the political arms of the A.F.L., the C.I.O., the railway brotherhoods, and other labor organizations, Senator Taft carried his appeal to the workers themselves. He carefully avoided the implication that there was any issue at all between him and wage earners. He avoided identifying "labor" with the leaders who opposed him. In

[2] See p. 41.

53

fact, he clearly made a differentiation between the workers, including union members, and the official heads of the unions. He carried every industrial county.

Excellent evidence of what happened is in the results in Cuyahoga County, a great part of which is occupied by the city of Cleveland. I am familiar with that county, since I was born and lived many years in what was then its rural section. Our Congressional district comprised part of the county outside Cleveland, together with a section of Cleveland that was regarded as "silk stocking." It was heavily Republican. In sixty years only two Democrats had been elected to Congress, for only one term each.

In recent years, notably since 1940, thousands of industrial workers have moved out into the nonurban parts of Cuyahoga County. Many large industrial plants have been established there. The economic and cultural status of all those new residents is indistinguishable from the status of those who have been there for a generation. They all share in the life of the various communities, own property, and send their children to high school and college. In the election campaign of 1950, however, the political arms of labor unions, believing that these suburban wage earners were still excellent ground for vote-hunting, made a vigorous attempt to carry a majority in this old Republican district, not only against Taft, but for a Congressional candidate who himself was a labor union official. The result was a large majority for the Republicans. Labor union members simply did not vote as their leaders told them to vote.

There is irony in this. Most of the leaders of organized labor have worked for many years to get better wages for their members, to shorten their hours, and to increase their benefits. Only in the past decade and a half have they disregarded Samuel Gompers's judgment that labor should remain politically independent and have organized political auxiliaries. In doing so and in pressing a purely political drive to

54

elect only those who do their bidding, they have lost the confidence of their dues-paying members. To a degree, the economic objectives that they helped to gain have destroyed their capacity to attain their newly formed political objectives. The "exploited, downtrodden" working people have acquired a vital concern in the middle interests and are, to a degree, capitalists.

Well-paid workers are quite conscious of this change, far more so than are their leaders. They have a new outlook and new political sympathies. They do not vote as a working class.

For two reasons it will little avail political leaders to attempt to hold the loyalty of these workers by reminding them of how hard union officials worked to raise their economic standards. First, it is not a human habit to vote in payment for past favors. Votes are cast for what is ahead. And second, it can be demonstrated—and it is known by most workers—that union leaders have been only partially responsible for the rise in the standard of living of workers. Resources out of which higher wages and benefits could be paid had to be created before union leaders could gain by bargaining. The basic reason why living standards can be higher lies in the industrial process itself—in efficiency of production, in skillful management, and in scientific progress.

Another vital weakness in the effort of labor leaders to influence the voting of dues-paying members lies in the outdated nature of their appeals. The jargon in their oratory and printed propaganda dates back to another generation. The "vast profits" of "a few capitalists" are still standard phrases. The "empty" or "wrinkled" bellies of workers are prominent in the speeches of Walter Reuther and John L. Lewis. The "grinding heel" of industry is still mentioned. Cartoons in labor papers still portray fat capitalists in the best Hearst tradition of the 1900's. The intelligence of the modern, well paid industrial employee cannot seriously accept these political chestnuts.

The Vanishing Rich

The economic position of the so-called rich, the perennial whipping-boys of radicals, has vastly changed in the past three or four decades. The emergence of a managerial group has materially lessened control over economic life by owner-employers and capitalists. The proportion of the national income that goes to individuals in the higher brackets has precipitously declined. And as I have indicated earlier, the ownership of the industrial plant has been moving downward in the scale of incomes.

The process of expropriation that is now invading the middle interests first affected the rich and fully justifies my use of the adjective "vanishing." Three sets of figures prove this.

The first of these include the incomes of people in two of the high brackets in 1927 and 1947.[3]

The total income of those reporting $100,000 or over in 1927 was $2,833,000,000. In 1947, it was $2,311,000,000. This was a drop of 18.4 per cent.

The total income of those reporting $500,000 or over in 1927 was $979,000,000. In 1947, it was $438,000,000. This was a decline of 55.2 per cent.

These totals, however, are before taxes are deducted. After tax, the decline is much greater.

After tax in 1927, the total income of those reporting $100,000 or over was $2,386,000,000. In 1947 it was $1,037,-000,000. The drop was 56.6 per cent.

For those in the brackets of $500,000 or more in 1927,

---

[3] It should be noted that in these figures there has been no correction for the decline in the real value of dollars. If that were done, the decline would be much greater.

there remained after taxes $816,000,000. In 1947 there remained $166,000,000. The decline was 80 per cent.

The proportion of all personal incomes received by those with more than $100,000 was 3.8 per cent in 1927 and 1.2 per cent in 1947. The corresponding percentages for those above $500,000 were 1.3 and 0.2. That was before tax.

After tax, the percentages for those above $100,000 in 1927 and 1947 were 3.2 and 1.1. For those above $500,000, the percentages were 0.7 and 0.15.[4]

Another set of figures showing the same trend is in the income tax returns of 1916 and 1948.[5] A comparison of those years shows the following percentages of increases and decreases in the number of returns:

Incomes over $	50,000	plus	303%
" "	100,000	plus	146%
" "	150,000	plus	79%
" "	300,000	plus	17%
" "	500,000	minus	3%
" "	1,000,000	minus	23%

The best way to indicate the relative real income of the individuals in these groups for the years 1916 and 1948 is to show the value of the combined income of those reporting in 1948 after taxes (and with the purchasing power of the dollar corrected for 1948) compared with the value of their incomes in 1916.[6]

The combined incomes in 1948 of all persons receiving over $50,000 were worth, in the purchasing power of the dol-

---

[4] It is important to note that these statistics for 1927 were classified as "net income." Those for 1947 were "adjusted gross income." If "net income" had been used for 1947, the decline in these high brackets would have been much greater.

[5] These figures for 1916 and 1948 were assembled and tabulated for me by L. Robert Driver.

[6] To simplify the somewhat complicated character of this comparison, I present it in a series of sentences, rather than in tabular form. In all cases, the figures are after tax, and the relative purchasing power of the dollar is taken into consideration.

lar of 1948, 76 per cent of the combined incomes of all persons in the same brackets in 1916.

For the brackets above $100,000, the proportion in real value was 45 per cent.

For those above $150,000, the proportion in real value was 34 per cent.

Above $300,000, it was 24 per cent.

Above $500,000, it was 20 per cent.

Above $1,000,000, it was 15 per cent.

A third set of figures, already alluded to, shows the trend. These are stated in a summary, by Dr. Arthur F. Burns of the National Bureau of Economic Research, of a study of income by Dr. Simon Kuznets of the same institution: [7]

In 1929 the highest 5 per cent of the income recipients obtained 34 per cent of the total disposable income of individuals—that is, the total of personal incomes, inclusive of any capital gains but after deducting Federal income tax payments. By 1939 their share had dropped to 27 per cent of total income, and by 1946 to 18 per cent. . . . If we now compare 1929 and 1946, we find that the share going to the top 5 per cent group declined 16 points. Had perfect equality of incomes been attained in 1946 the share would have dropped from 34 to 5 per cent, that is, by 29 points. In other words, the income share of the top 5 per cent stratum dropped 16 points out of a maximum possible drop of 29 points; so that, on the basis of this yardstick, we may be said to have traveled in a bare two decades over half the distance separating the 1929 distribution from a perfectly egalitarian distribution. If we turn to the top 1 instead of the top 5 per cent group, the results are still more striking. The share of the top 1 per cent group in total income was 19.1 per cent in 1929 and 7.7 per cent in 1946. Since the share of this group dropped 11.4 points out of a total possible drop of 18.1 points, we have traveled since 1929 on the basis of this yardstick almost two-thirds of the distance towards absolute income equality.

[7] National Bureau of Economic Research, 31st Annual Report, May, 1951, p. 4.

This tremendous shift in the ownership of wealth is, as Dr. Burns puts it, "one of the great social revolutions in history." His further observations are most important:

These conclusions of Kuznets' investigation have great significance for the American people. If we are to look forward constructively to a material reduction of income inequalities in the future, we must seek to attain it principally by raising the productivity of those at the bottom of the income scale rather than by transferring income from the rich to the poor. . . . Thus the upper income stratum suffered a substantial decline in money income and a still larger decline in real income. The social experimentation of our own and other countries suggests that private incentives to embark on new and venturesome investments are more firmly rooted than was generally believed to be the case a quarter of a century or even a decade ago; but there can be no doubt that as high incomes are cut, a point must come when private investors have neither the will nor the power to launch major innovations. Substantial further redistribution of incomes may therefore affect adversely the size of the national income, while it cannot improve appreciably the living conditions of the great masses. The paramount source of the rising living standards of our workers and farmers has always been an increasing volume of production, and in the years ahead it bids fair to become the only source.

Perhaps the foregoing figures will show why the expensive luxuries enjoyed by people with high incomes in past years have been less obvious, why those people have so much less to invest in new industries and, what is very important, why they can contribute only a small fraction of what they did to various cultural and scientific causes. For the burden of such responsibilities must now fall upon those with smaller incomes. And since the process of expropriation moves relentlessly into the middle groups, they, in turn, will be unable to sustain these responsibilities.

The interests of the so-called "rich" therefore become

more and more at one with those of the middle interests. A very large majority of all income groups are facing the same problem. The remaining "rich" and the middle groups are at one in seeking to preserve the economic and political system under which they were born.

Some Material Conclusions

After the foregoing detailed and perhaps confusing delineation of the economic affairs of the people of the United States, it may be helpful to draw some simple conclusions:

1. When we classify families or "spending units" according to annual incomes, a substantial majority fall between $2,000 and $5,000. Somewhere within this range is the center of real economic and potential political power.

2. Included in this middle range are people from all sorts of occupations and social groups.

3. Property ownership in this country is so widely spread in quantity and kind that efforts such as those of Marx and milder species of statists and politicians to portray our society in terms of mutually antagonistic groups are not only false in fact, but inimical to the essential interests of all.

4. Even with respect to the ownership of our vast industrial system, the major premise of statism falls before the onslaught of fact. Ownership of the industrial plant is moving from the hands of the rich and well-to-do to lower ranges in the scale of incomes.

5. The stake of an immense majority of our people in various kinds of savings is very great and vital. Hence, the trend of statist policies toward the appropriation of those savings is a grim threat to that immense majority and not, as politicians and statist propagandists would have it, an "equalization" of wealth and opportunity.

6. Farmers, always identified with the solid, conservative elements in our population, are still essentially tied into the

middle interests. And despite special benefits from the government, they are losing or stand to lose their security through the spread of statist policies.

7. Wage earners are moving rapidly into the middle groups. Their sympathies and ties with other groups are growing stronger, their political behavior shows that they are beginning to realize it. Their true interest is in a free society.

8. The share of the so-called "rich" in the nation's wealth has been melting away over a considerable number of years at a very rapid rate. An immense redistribution has already taken place.

9. I have shown by my statistics of the distribution of wealth why an assertion that "a third of our people are ill-fed, ill-housed and ill-clothed" is and was when it was solemnly pronounced, a gross misstatement that served to divide our people in the interest of political objectives. It is even more inaccurate today. The falseness of such a concept is revealed in the figures of the very government whose political head pronounced that judgment.

Even those who seize the figures showing the large number of people receiving incomes of, say, $2,000 or less to "prove" that such people are unable to sustain a decent living standard are engaged in statistical chicanery. For the Federal Reserve figures on incomes and assets make clear that a great many of those people own considerable property. The percentage of people in the lowest income group—"under $1,000"—who own their own homes is 50, which is higher than the three groups above them and nearly equal to the $4,000–$4,999 group. These home owners have the benefit of relatively free rent, not counted as income. Considerable percentages of this low income group own other types of property, especially "liquid assets." The fallacy in assuming that this group is in dire need lies in failing to recognize that many of them are retired and living on self-made means of security, and that others do not care to work, either because

61

they do not need to or because they are willing to forego earnings for the joy of a lazy life. The latter, as any American knows, are numerous.

10. The fact of rapid and continuous change in the distribution of property and income is outstanding over the past few years. There is no reason to assume that this shift is not continuing at this moment and will not continue in the immediate future. The figures for 1948 or 1949 may already be an understatement of the facts upon which these conclusions are based. But since the constant direction of this change can be assumed, new data will only strengthen the foregoing conclusions.

Who's Who in the Middle Interests

Let us now consider the middle interests in terms of a typical American community, a large village or a small city, and enumerate people and typical organizations.

There are retailers of various sorts, automobile-agency heads, builders, bankers, doctors, dentists, contractors, photographers, lawyers, the publisher of a newspaper, service people such as plumbers, barbers, beauty-parlor proprietors, farm organization officials, utility officials, farm equipment and feed dealers, railroad and express agents, school superintendents, principals and teachers, ministers, rabbis and priests, movie exhibitors, advertising people, managers of manufacturing plants, insurance agents, real estate agents, the postmaster and his employees, organization secretaries, and others.

Then consider the various organizations in such a place. There are the service clubs, women's organizations, locals of farm organizations and 4-H clubs, a chamber of commerce, a junior chamber of commerce, labor unions, veterans' locals, fraternal societies, YWCA and YMCA and affiliated groups.

There are also the many employees of these people and organizations, employees who in many cases identify their interests with those of the rest of the community. There are friends and neighbors.

Then consider how many such typical villages or cities there are in a Congressional district and add those whose business carries them afield, such as salesmen of all sorts.

The reasons why this vast population exercises so little political power are manyfold. In nearly every community people divide party-wise only in local elections. But the great issues that concern us here have little to do with local government. In such communities, divisions on national lines simply destroy the capacity of the people to protect their real interests in the nation. Other reasons for their political weakness, of course, are indifference and ignorance. Indifference may often be the result of a sense of frustration or of helplessness. That is what has been called "the fatalism of the multitude."

The Middle Interests in American History

While all the facts disprove its identity as a class, that great group in our society the members of which are neither rich nor poor has exercised a definitive and moderating role in our history.

From the beginning of our national history in 1789 to the election of 1828, the tone and leadership of our political life was aristocratic, despite the democratic ideas of Jefferson. Jefferson himself was, as Woodrow Wilson put it, "an aristocrat and yet a philosophical radical . . . a patron of the people; appealed to the rank and file, believed in them, but shared neither their tastes nor their passions."

After Jackson, the great land and slave owners of the South dominated the Democratic Party and through it, for the most part, the policies of the Federal government. After the Civil War and until recent times, the influence of great and growing financial and industrial powers was decisive in the Republican Party.

It is not strange that since about 1935 other minorities, awakened to their power to tip the balance in a divided electorate, have been so strong. For many reasons that we need not recite here, it has been altogether too simple for minorities to achieve great, undeserved, and occasionally ruthless power.

Nevertheless, the tone and character of our political life, the generally conservative nature of prevailing policies and legislation have until recently been favorable to the interests of the middle group. Most of our political leaders and statesmen have come from that group. And no political movement or party that a Marxist might call proletarian has ever reached an important national status, although in some states and localities such elements have been powerful and, for short periods, dominant.

The essential political weakness of the middle group lies in several circumstances. It has had a tendency to split its potential between the two parties. This has been especially true since there has been a Solid South. The shopkeeper in Memphis votes for Truman. A shopkeeper in Indianapolis, with exactly the same economic concerns and social outlook, votes for Dewey. A machine member in Chicago and a pensioner in Los Angeles count more than both shopkeepers.

Another factor contributing to the political weakness of the middle group has been the complex, almost indefinable nature of its economic concerns. Politics requires interpretation of these shared concerns in broad, easily understandable terms. It is easy to describe and activate the interests of cattle raisers or cotton growers. But it is not easy to describe the interwoven common concerns and economic kinship of cotton and cattle growers with New England shopkeepers or with

64

skilled workmen in a watch factory in Lancaster, Pennsylvania. Politicians have fished in cloudy waters and have profited by complex relationships.

Since this has been true, the tactic of self-seeking politics has been to split the middle group by appeals and promises to specific minorities. Two of these minorities have been farmers and wage earners. The means for achieving this division has been to stress the factors that set these minorities off from others, rather than the great ties that bind them to others. Demagogues, in appeals to farmers and wage earners, portray their prospective adherents as the very salt of the earth, the foundations of economic life, and the only "indispensable ingredients" in society. By means of cajolery, promises, and plenty of infusion of minority class-consciousness, the substantial middle group has been divided and rendered impotent to unite on the broad issues that might have provided unity and real political power.

"The Forgotten Man"

It is one of the great ironies of American history that at the very outset of Franklin Roosevelt's New Deal the phrase "Forgotten Man" became a major slogan and rallying cry. It so happened that I provided him with the phrase and wove it into an early pre-campaign speech. I took it from a great, perhaps immortal essay by William Graham Sumner, written in 1883. It is well to recall that it was meant to apply by its author, by me, and, I believed, by Roosevelt to the members of a large and substantial group in society, which, incidentally, included all self-dependent farmers and wage earners, as well as many others. I may add, further, that it represented exactly the people I thought the New Deal was going to benefit and exactly the group I am writing about in this chapter.

"Now, who," wrote Sumner, "is the Forgotten Man?"

Sumner defined him as the man who earned his living by productive work, who paid taxes, who accumulated a little capital, who was neither the object of help from government nor the beneficiary of artificial or politically bestowed advantage, who lived up to his contracts, and never asked for favor.

The Forgotten Man is delving away in patient industry, supporting his family, paying his taxes, casting his vote, supporting the church and the school, reading his newspaper, and cheering for the politician of his admiration, but he is the only one for whom there is no provision in the great scramble and the big divide. . . . He works, he votes, generally he prays—but he always pays—yes, above all he pays. . . . He keeps production going on. . . . He is strongly patriotic. . . . He gives no trouble. . . . He excites no admiration. . . . He is not in any way a hero . . . or a problem . . . nor notorious . . . nor an object of sentiment . . . nor a burden . . . nor the object of a job . . . nor one over whom sentimental economists and statesmen can parade their fine sentiments. . . . Therefore he is forgotten.[8]

It was for him that the New Deal was originally conceived. Later, because of political expediency, Roosevelt shifted his appeal to a congeries of small segments of the voting population. The early New Deal ended in an alliance of minorities.

The Nonmaterial Middle Interests

I have described the material interests that should bind together the people who share them in the generation of great political power. By this concentration of attention on material matters, I do not mean to imply that voters are moved only by such things. The economic interpretation of the motives that have made history has been overemphasized in the

[8] William Graham Sumner: *The Forgotten Man and Other Essays* (New Haven: Yale University Press; 1918).

historical and political literature of the past fifty years. It is certainly overstressed in practical politics.

People are moved by many impulses other than those with roots in stomachs and pocketbooks. Human beings are endowed with the sentiments of idealism, loyalty and pride associated with the home, the family, the local community, friends, ancestry, tradition, religion, and patriotism.

These sentiments find expression in thousands of songs, stories, pictures, bits of folklore, associations, memories, and daydreams. They fill a large part of life. To evoke them in others is to give pleasure and to enrich. They make hardships endurable, mistakes tolerable, inconsistency understandable, and even failure bearable. Within them is the heart of political conservatism.

It is hard for the statist to contend with these imponderables. His appeal must be almost wholly a portrayal of the virtues and advantages of change—change to an unknown life, with only promises of new material gains at its center. When he appeals for mass action by the "underprivileged," he pictures the better life of the "privileged" as an emotional summons.

The most potent way to move those who share the middle interests to protective action is to stress that the good life must hold as well as have. It must keep as well as give. It must conserve as well as acquire.

In place of deeply rooted spiritual values, statism proposes a sterile, disciplined, vitamined adequacy. That prospect is a flat plateau of uniformity over which ride the inspectors, regulators, and police of an uninspiring bureaucracy. Socialist jargon is a dry discussion of jobs, subsidies, grants, wage gains, escalators, and pensions.

In the Marxian dream there is no portrayal of the good life. It stresses only the goods of life.

Those whose condition is intolerable, shorn of peace and certitude, can be moved to radical change. But the bitter frustration of the radical takes place after he has effected his redistribution, when he finds that he has made new recruits for conservatism.

The conservative can, if he will, appeal to a thousand priceless values, to loyalties, to pride, to the treasured past, and the best of the present.

A century ago, Benjamin Disraeli appealed to these values in reconstructing a Conservative Party in opposition to a liberalism whose message was largely a compilation of statistics derived from what someone called the "dismal science" of economics. Disraeli glorified institutionalism, which meant to his hearers precious associations of enduring value—the English constitution and its liberties, the church, the great universities, the imperial crown, the bright chronicles of English victories in war and in peace, the great prestige of the tight little island whose flag was raised over the seas and in every continent. He took his appeal from the court of economics to the supreme tribunal of patriotism. And in so doing he staked his whole future on the belief that he could carry with him not only those whose vested interests made conservatism a matter of self-preservation, but the newly enfranchised masses whose deeper sentiments he sought to evoke.

André Maurois writes of the statesmanship of Disraeli: "For him to be a Conservative was not just to uphold with an apologetic smile a Constitution held to be out of date; it was a proud and romantic attitude, the only intelligent one, the only one that loyally took into account the authentic England, those villages grouped around the manor house, that vigorous, obstinate breed of small squires, that aristocracy at once so venerable and so assimilative, nay, history itself." [9]

Disraeli himself said: "This respect for precedent, this clinging to prescription, this reverence for antiquity, which

[9] André Maurois: *Disraeli, A Picture of the Victorian Age* (New York: D. Appleton and Co.; 1928), p. 106.

are so often ridiculed by superficial and conceited minds, appear to me to have their origin in a profound knowledge of human nature."

To him, as Maurois puts it: "A nation is a work of art, a work wrought by time. It has a temperament like that of an individual. The greatness of England in particular is sprung, not from its natural resources, which are mediocre, but from its institutions. The rights of Englishmen are older by four full centuries than the Rights of Man. . . . The duty of a conservative leader was to have the courage to defend the past so far as it was living and likely to live."

Time justified the faith of Disraeli in this appeal to rooted sentiment. Perhaps the present Conservatives might learn from this the doubtful value of attempting to match the promises of the Socialists.

Careful analysis will reveal institutional ties in America just as powerful, though different in kind from those upon which Disraeli based his appeal. These ties are very strong among those related to the economic middle interests. Most important is the American Constitution, the guarantor of a republican form of government, of limited government, of private rights, of the inviolability of the states, and of the authority of the judiciary.

These are not only constitutional principles, but together they make up a great body of tradition to which creeping socialism is a menace. The atmosphere that envelops them is one of freedom, of informed but recognized relationships that cluster around the middle interests, of local self-government, of social and economic custom, of a broad but not unlimited sense of equality, and of a spirit of live and let live, unshackled by law. There has always been in our national character, moreover, an undying distrust of government, of unlimited tenure of office, of prying police and official presumption. Whether this trait has deteriorated is open to question. If so, it is a very dangerous change.

The Middle Interests and National Security

The prosperity, integrity, and political power of the middle groups can be the firm assurance of the prosperity, integrity, and political power of the nation. The ramifications of these interests through the country offer means of stability. The identification of these interests with such concepts as self-help, personal liberty, individual enterprise, and opportunity make the people associated with them the most appropriate spokesmen for the nation. They can be, if they will, the possessors of deserved political power during the long years ahead.

The mobilization of political power in and around these middle interests is the central problem and the urgent necessity of American politics. The philosophy of statism seeks now to split these interlocked interests into minority groups. Such minority groups, the statist believes, can be bought by government and can be infected by the poison of opposition to, and hatred of, other groups. Thus divided, conquest by state power is possible.

The strategy of those who would conserve our free institutions must be to awaken the people in middle groups to a consciousness of their shared concerns and to infuse them with a realization of the peril that confronts them.

Resistance, as I shall show in subsequent chapters, is best mobilized through citizen action, for the moment on the local and district level; and, sooner or later, by national action through a truly national party.

This great middle group is actually united in its economic interests. The great task before it is to find political unity.

PART TWO

TOWARD THE POINT
OF NO RETURN

CHAPTER IV

Origins, Theories, and Motives of Statism

Sources of American Statism

THE PERVERSION OF THE PROGRESSIVE MOVEMENT

In the first years of the twentieth century the most important political movement in America was what was then known as progressivism. It arose from many almost spontaneous uprisings against the excesses of capitalism and protests against the presence of poverty and injustice in the vitals of an incomparably rich nation. Enormous and unbridled concentrations of private property lived cheek-by-jowl with insecurity and need.

In the final decades of the nineteenth century a number of dissenting movements developed, mainly among farmers of the Middle West, the Northwest, and the South. There were Grangerism, Populism, Greenbackism, and other political movements and parties. There were many notable agitators, such as Ben Tillman, Jerry Simpson, and Jacob Coxey. There were writers like "Coin" Harvey and Henry George, and later there were authentic statesmen like Robert M. La Follette, Hiram Johnson, Tom L. Johnson, Hazen S. Pengree, and John P. Altgeld. In Congress there finally arose a

73

group of recalcitrant Republicans led by Victor Murdock, George Norris, and others.

There was William Jennings Bryan, whose life spanned the whole era and whose naïve belief in the power of government to cure economic and social ills was revealed in a series of such proposals as free silver and government ownership of railroads. As Secretary of State, Bryan proposed and secured the adoption of "cooling-off" treaties to cure war. In the twilight of life, still turning to governmental panaceas, he would have cured intemperance by prohibition and atheism by laws against the teaching of evolution. His life was an epic in primitive statism.

This movement of protest, of which Lincoln Steffens was the most colorful historian, challenged the existing order on three fronts. It protested against corruption in government. It sought, through legislation, a larger control by government over economic life. And it sought through government to provide a larger measure of services and social amelioration for the so-called underprivileged.

Theodore Roosevelt, who joined and became the leader of this movement, added a new factor to its program—the enlargement of Federal power. He pointed out that the control of business by government failed because there was a "twilight zone" between Federal and state authority, and he sought to push Federal power into this gap.

The essential character of the progressive movement was therefore a greater intervention by government in private economy and life, and the enlargement of Federal authority at the expense of the states.

No one except the extremists in this progressive movement envisaged or advocated socialism as a remedy. They assumed free enterprise.

There was socialism and "labor" socialism. But the platforms of the Socialist and Socialist Labor parties of those

74

years contain a mixture of proposals for government ownership, easy money, and paternalism of various kinds.

Organized labor played only a small part in these movements of protest. There were great strikes, but these had no
direct political significance. Samuel Gompers, the major labor leader of those times, was as valiant a champion of free
enterprise as was his friend Mark Hanna.

Progressivism in more recent years has moved far beyond
its original scope, assuming that because a small amount of
government intervention proved to be a healthy corrective
for the evils of capitalism, more and more is needed. In this
perversion, more than in an invasion of alien doctrines, lies
our present danger.

WESTERN SEEDS OF SOCIALISM

Mingled here and there with grass-roots progressivism in
the Middle West and Northwest was authentic socialism
brought over by Scandinavian, German, and Czech immigrants. The traditions of the forebears of these excellent people were developed quite independently of those of the British ancestors of earlier immigrants. They did not share the
deep Anglo-American distrust of government. Nor were they
essentially Marxist, for Marxism in Europe did not really get
under way until most of our North European immigrants
had come to America. But in the heritage of these people
there was a deeply rooted antagonism to feudal rulers. The
Norwegians also brought a dislike for the trading classes of
the Norwegian cities.

It is also important to note that these immigrants brought
with them well established practices of municipal ownership
and co-operative buying and selling. The ideals of the free
market and free enterprise were never basic in Germany and
Scandinavia, but were always overshadowed by the centuries-

old "corporation" or guild spirit. Cartels and other forms of regulated markets were taken as a matter of course.

Even in such a stalwart Republican state as Nebraska, municipal ownership of public utilities, especially electricity, is quite general. That state, it may be added, for forty years consistently supported George Norris, the father of TVA.

Later there came great numbers of Poles and other Slavic strains. They had no republican government in their past, only oppression, grinding poverty, and the shadow of great landowners. The more vital minds among them were already aware of Marx.

Volumes might be written on the influence in our life of the collectivist and socialistic thought of various immigrant groups. While all these strains of new Americans have been potent factors in our economic progress, the immensely complex and long-standing influences toward statism which they brought are a part of the background of our problem.

The influence of these Continental ideas has been shown in the preachments and acts of many political leaders in the Midwest and Northwest, and of such groups in that region as the Non-Partisan League, the Farmer-Labor Party and, more recently, the Farmers' Union.

Their influence on economic theory has been noticeable. Thorstein Veblen, the inspiration of many economists, was the embittered son of impoverished Scandinavian parents.

THE MARXIAN INVASION

The voluminous writings of British Fabians have had wide acceptance among educators and other leaders of American opinion. George Bernard Shaw, Sidney and Beatrice Webb, Harold Laski, and others have made thousands of Americans sympathetically aware of socialism.

The influence of John Maynard Keynes, who was not a

Fabian but who believed in compensatory spending, is too well known to need more than a mention.

A considerable number of American economists have also been deeply moved by such Continental writers as Werner Sombart, who rather regretfully predicted that socialism was inevitable. Professor Joseph Schumpeter of Harvard, who was at one time Austrian Minister of Finance, said again and again, and most impressively shortly before his death in 1949, that the trend in the United States toward the welfare state had become too strong to be stopped.

The idea of economic planning by the state was vigorously promoted by Walter Rathenau in a pamphlet published in 1914, "Germany's Raw Material Management." This had its place in the over-all economic planning of the First World War. Ironically, its partial use here became a major factor in crushing Germany in two wars. Four hundred thousand copies of the English translation of Rathenau's pamphlet were sold.

Lenin, suddenly possessed of power, had no plans. Later, he said: "I do not know of any socialist who has dealt with these problems. . . . We need a plan at once to give the masses a shining, unimpeded example to work for."

Rathenau supplied the idea and Communism adopted planning as state policy.

Planning came also to the bewildered British Fabians. And its echoes reached many Americans.

Growth and Manifestations of Statism

THE REVOLUTION IN EDUCATION

There has been, also over the past half century, a profound change in American education. An entire generation has been indoctrinated in a point of view quite unlike that of the youths of fifty years ago. This point of view has affected all learning and literature, but it is sufficient here to note only the aspect dealing with the so-called social sciences, including history.

Our schools, except for a few large universities, before the beginning of this century taught practically no economics, political science, or sociology. History was dominated by a classic tradition, perhaps best illustrated by Bancroft's great work on the United States. That tradition was pervaded by an almost mythological view of America as a sort of preserve guarded by divine concern and dedicated to a Manifest Destiny. Early in this century, with the leadership of Charles A. Beard, James Harvey Robinson, Carl Becker, and others, history was rewritten, with emphasis upon economic and social facts and developments. It was to be expected that this change should be overemphasized, since these new writers were engaged in overwhelming an old and highly entrenched and privileged intellectual order. Their writings expounded plenty of the materialistic interpretation of history. Some of this came from Marx, but it also had roots in more remote philosophers and historians. The new order was almost completely victorious and its viewpoints penetrated the texts not only at the college level but far down into the common schools. John Dewey has been the philosopher and prophet of this movement.

This emphasis on economic and social facts manifested itself in the rise of the so-called social studies in the lower grades, and sociology in higher education. The old "civics," in which the Constitution and governmental institutions were stressed, was almost obliterated in the lower ranges of education. In the colleges the social sciences burgeoned into large departments with many specialized and detailed courses.

Ultimately the great law schools were impregnated by social studies, and courses and research originally devoted to precedent in case-law threw more and more emphasis on economic and social facts. The influence of this trend upon a new generation of lawyers and judges has been apparent in judicial lawmaking.

Not only in the slant of education, but in its services has there been immense change. Under the leadership of the great state universities there has been an enlargement of the range of teachable subjects and an extension of general assistance to citizens. Since this expansion has been most notable in public schools and state-supported universities and colleges, the importance of government in our life has increased.

A large part of this expansion has been a wholesome influence in our life. I note it merely to point up an enlargement of emphasis on government.

Still it deserves to be said that this indiscriminate expansion of education has offered a good deal of opportunity for the wholesale infusion of propaganda into teaching. The forces released in such a revolution involve much special pleading under the guise of free inquiry. Our so-called "social" teaching tends to assume that, since government has steadily increased in importance over a generation or so, "progress" can only consist in a continuation of that trend. In that respect, pioneers like Beard set in motion more than they anticipated, and in some cases they lived to view with great apprehension the perversion of their ideas. This was especially true of Beard.

THE PERVERSION OF THE NEW DEAL

The early New Deal measures, with the exception of the Tennessee Valley Authority plan, were fairly mild reforms. They came from many sources.

In general the early or, as I would designate it, the first

New Deal was merely an extension of the 1912 Progressive Party platform. It seemed in 1932 that we had merely picked up the trail abandoned two decades before. The famous National Recovery Act was an adaptation of the Progressive idea of a co-operative effort of competitors in an industry for wholesome common purposes under the mediating but not the controlling influence of the government. The farm program was created by organized farm movements in the Middle West. The idea of regulating the issue and exchange of securities for the protection of investors was taken from the "blue sky" laws of several states and from century-old British legislation. The Tennessee Valley Plan, the socialistic potentialities of which were not widely realized at the time, came largely from the public-ownership ideas of Senator George Norris. The fiscal policies of Franklin D. Roosevelt were largely hit-or-miss improvisations mixed with plenty of the old inflationary ideas of Bryan and others. Social security plans later were derived from those of some of the states and Britain.

After two or three years some of these measures were extended, not to say perverted, by Roosevelt into a trend that is the source for much of our present danger. After the NRA, there was enacted the Wagner Labor Relations Act, which threw the power of government on the side of labor in industrial disputes and authorized government intervention in organizing labor. The relief program and the carrying on of public works on a modest scale were perverted into a great spend and spend, tax and tax, elect and elect government agency. The farm program, which Roosevelt originally said would not be a burden on the Treasury, developed into an immense structure of subsidies, supports, and guarantees. The TVA excited the imagination of the planners and led to the present effort to create such authorities on a nationwide scale. And the acceptance of deficits, first regarded as a necessary evil, finally, under the influence of the new economics, was regarded as an unmitigated good. Meanwhile, bureaucracy and Federal power grew apace at the expense of the taxpayers and the states.

POLITICAL ACTION GROUPS

Over the past seventeen years many private groups, committees, and associations have been formed and reformed, changing names and officers with great frequency, but always with the single purpose of extending the scope of government. Some of these have been genuine Communist fronts, some have had Communist infiltration; others are simply made up of well-intentioned people who favor special versions of a welfare state. The most permanent residuary survivor of these movements is the Americans for Democratic Action.

AMONG THE BUREAUCRATS

In the early days of the New Deal, I was in a position to see clearly and in detail the great migration of those who came to Washington seeking, and for the most part finding, government employment. The accession of Roosevelt was regarded by them as a political, almost a social revolution. As in all such upheavals, thousands were inspired to participate, either in response to a wholly idealistic impulse to help, or as a means of slaking a thirst for adventure, or for the more prosaic purpose of getting gainful employment after years of more or less impoverished dedication to opposition to things as they were.

These people were a variegated lot. Nonconformity is infinitely diversified. There might be some uniformity in a belief that the country is sick, but prognosis and treatment in politics depend upon personal predilection and character. It is unnecessary to suggest the kinds of remedies and nostrums that were advocated. The point is that nearly everybody who applied for employment sooner or later found it. There was little sifting or investigation, and far too little adaptation of the employee to the job. Those who made the selections, even some Cabinet members, were themselves new to public service. Allegiance to the policies and personality of the President was a test. But this was a poor test, because the Roosevelt policies were themselves an amalgam of many philosophies.

One test was fairly well observed, and the President himself regarded it as important. People were not to be put in charge of matters in which they had lived their lives and acquired their habits of thought and action. Thus, it was believed, private "interests" would be kept from places of privilege and power. One Cabinet member, in seeking to fill a responsible place in his department, told me that he wanted only college professors, for only in them could he find "intellectual honesty." Skills were at a discount. Ideological sympathy was at a premium.

To anyone of even mildly conservative instincts, it was deeply disturbing to witness at first hand the activities of some of these innovators. The possession of power spurred them to new schemes for government action. An abundance of leisure, permitted by the lax discipline of bureaucracy, offered them time for the exercise of fervent imagination.

It was no secret that a great number of these reformers were admirers of the "great Soviet experiment." And some, we now know, were secret agents of Communism.

In my opinion, there is a greater danger in collectivists than in the betrayal of our secrets to foreign powers. The danger lies in what can be done to a nation by public officials who do not believe in a free economy. In Roosevelt's day there were many people working for the government who regarded his reforms as a mere prelude to revolution. "He is only a Kerensky," they were in the habit of saying.

STATISM IN THE STATES

The wide possibilities of independent state action, always latent in the Constitution, were perhaps most fully demontrated by Huey Long in Louisiana. At the height of his regime, he achieved an almost complete dictatorship. The forms of republic that are guaranteed to the states under the Constitution were maintained, but Long's will or caprice was dominant, and great public works and miscellaneous handouts to poor people and communities were the basis of his power. Long, however, was no doctrinaire socialist. He wanted business to remain in private hands and to prosper, for thus he could exact through taxation or political contributions what he needed to consolidate his power. He could do this because he ruled a state rich in resources.

Other states, however, have drifted toward socialism without dictatorship. This has not taken the form of actual control of the means of production. It has come about through the great expansion of social services. The best examples of this are Washington and California. There the advocates of state welfare have persistently worked to eliminate the principle that government concern for personal welfare should stop at securing a minimum subsistence for all. They have largely substituted the objective of equal shares for all. By this I mean specifically the violent opposition to any "means test" in the dispensing of such gratuities as old-age assistance, medical aid, and pensions.

In those states it has been possible to further such ends under direct legislation by a vote of the people. Thus by a simple exercise of suffrage a state is obliged to set up and pay for vast welfare projects, and the assent of governors and legislatures becomes more or less formal. Governor Warren of California, in his budget message in 1949, pointed out that two thirds of the billion dollars required had been voted by the people; the established government could do nothing but find the taxes to pay the bill.

The peril here is that the resources of a state are limited. Ultimately, if people continue to vote money to themselves, states must depend more and more upon Federal grants, and state responsibility and power will be engulfed.

Moreover, in such states organizations with socialist objectives are spawned, supported, and encouraged. The threat of the famous socialistic "production for use" movement is well remembered in California.

RIFTS IN THE CONSTITUTION

The Constitution is a mighty protector of our liberties, but the past twelve years have proved that through its interpretation socialism could arrive in this country without formal amendment. The late Justice Frank Murphy asserted this in the Schneiderman case in 1942.

A wide avenue for socialism is the expression "general welfare," which appears twice in the Constitution. The Preamble lists among the purposes of the Constitution "to promote the general welfare." Much more important, in judicial interpretation, is the expression in Article I, Section 8: "The Congress shall have power to lay and collect taxes, duties, imposts and excises, to pay the debts and provide for the common defense and general welfare of the United States."

For more than a century "general welfare" was very cautiously dealt with both by Congress in its legislation and by the Supreme Court in its interpretations. There is great dispute about what the makers of the Constitution had in mind in phrasing this sentence. Certainly they could not have conceived of its use to permit the Federal government to levy taxes for purposes either clearly within the province of the states or forbidden to both the Federal government and the states.

Jefferson scrutinized this grant of power with grave concern. His opinion was that under it Congress "could do whatever they may think or pretend would promote the public welfare, which construction would make that of itself a complete government without limitation of power." Presumably, he hoped for Congressional restraint if the courts disregarded the Tenth Amendment, a hope since dashed by Congressional majorities that have sought votes in the sacred name of this same Jefferson.

Common sense would suggest that, since the statements among which the words "promote the general welfare" appear all relate to the nation as a whole, "general welfare" means the welfare of the nation as a whole. But instead, we are asked to believe that every little welfare is embodied in this generality. It is easy to see that if every individual or group were to attain all the "welfare" it wants and can exact by voting strength, the nation's solvency—i.e., the nation's welfare—would vanish and all would sink in common ruin. The general welfare of the nation is more than the sum of all individual welfares.

There is also a trend in decisions by the so-called "liberal" judges of the Supreme Court to arrange the rights of life, liberty, and property in an order of descending importance. This trend has been vigorously attacked by some of the judges themselves and by such authoritative exponents of constitutional law as the late Chief Justice Stone and former Appellate Judge Learned Hand. Professor Paul A. Freund of Harvard has clearly defined the dangers of this trend in his little book, *On Understanding the Supreme Court*.[1] Such an interpretation violates the entire body of tradition that the

[1] (Boston: Little, Brown and Company; 1949).

rights of life, liberty, and property are equal and indivisible. The present Court majority makes property a second- or third-class right.

The Declaration of Human Rights of the United Nations, created under the chairmanship of Eleanor Roosevelt, goes a step further. It eliminates property from the trilogy of rights and substitutes "security of person."

Finally, there is the income-tax amendment to the Constitution, which lays no limit at all upon the power of Congress to take the income of individuals and corporations, from whatever source derived.

This brief review of the manner in which the Constitution has been breached in the interest of statism makes it clear that the answer to the trend toward supergovernment cannot come through the courts. It must be expressed politically and at the polls.

THE CAPTURE OF THE DEMOCRATIC PARTY

There is little likeness between the Democratic Party of 1932 and the Democratic Party of 1951. The personnel of its leadership and the nature of its policies have undergone a profound change.

When Roosevelt was nominated, the party stood for a series of traditional principles—the constitutional rights and powers of the states, economical government, reduction of the bureaucracy, and justice in industrial relations. It has gradually been transformed into a Federalist party, a collaborator with labor unions, with an unprecedented bureaucracy, an unbalanced budget as a first principle, and a welfare state as an objective.

An intense struggle within the party has accompanied this change. In the early Roosevelt years the more conservative Northern leaders broke away from the party leadership. Southern conservatives remained nominally Democratic, but carried on their dissent in Congress.

86

The change in policy and strategy by Roosevelt and others was calculated. Labor union leaders, particularly those of the new C.I.O., abandoned the traditional detachment of the Gompers era and moved bag and baggage into the party. A whole battalion of socialistic planners moved into positions of political power in the government. City machines and bosses, little concerned with principle and aware of the vast patronage involved in the government's new policies, learned the jargon of the welfare state and went along. Persistent preference in appointments by Roosevelt raised the more radical partisans to high places.

The most vivid demonstration of the power of the statists was in the Democratic convention of 1948, when over the opposition of traditional Democrats and despite the plans of the nominal leaders of that convention a resolution on civil rights was jammed through.

The party that began with Jeffersonian distrust of government has become a powerful instrument of statism through Federal power.

MACHINE POLITICS ON THE FEDERAL LEVEL

While statists and statism have become more powerful in the Democratic Party, another development has taken place. The immense appeal to minority groups which is possible in a government dedicated to the welfare principle has enabled leaders of the party to weld it into a powerful machine. At the head of this machine, which is centered in the Federal government, is the Chief Executive. Presidents Roosevelt and Truman have been by temperament and training ideally suited to the purposes of this development. The former was not only the shrewdest politician of his time, but a man with a major appetite for power. The latter, while less imperial in his ambitions, conceives of high politics in terms of the lower tones of his Kansas City tradition.

To win elections, such a politician considers it sufficient to exact political service in return for jobs or favors at public expense and also to appeal to the cupidity and prejudices of a sufficient number of minority groups to assure a majority. Promises are made, to be redeemed out of the public treasury, and class is set against class by sly charges and innuendoes.

It seems quite obvious that President Truman rose in politics with no special predilection for statist ideology. Fundamental questions of economic and social reform probably never entered his cosmos. He, like Roosevelt in his earlier years, accepted the order of things as it stood. President Truman is probably mystified when people call his policies socialistic. His speeches are filled with capitalistic platitudes. His economic proposals are carefully coated—no doubt by shrewd helpers—with fulsome assurances of free markets and capitalistic prosperity.

But Truman's preference for machine rule, his alliances with radical minorities, his preference for centralized government, and his belief in the welfare state—all these widen the avenue for the advent of socialism.

For socialism seeks first the control of the machinery of a party and then (through the party) of the government and the nation.

Statist Economics

POLITICS DISCOVERS THE NEW ECONOMICS

Almost any political purpose can be supported by what can be called "scientific economics." It is largely a matter of selecting the appropriate economist or economic theory.

The New Deal was a fortuitous combination of many theories. For a while, none of these gained complete ascendancy.

But after two or three years the Federal Administration turned to more government spending and more governmental intervention in economic life. Doctrines held by an articulate minority of professional economists were found to be useful rationalizations of political policies.

The influence of these economists became clear after 1936. By 1939–40, they were clearly dominant in the Administration, and in the famous hearings of the Temporary National Economic Committee (T.N.E.C.) they had a field day. Their point of view can be summarized in a series of propositions:

1. The economy of the United States has become "mature"—i.e., the frontier is gone and with it free land for an expanding population. The great industries that dominate economic life are also mature—i.e., they need no venture capital, and live off their own earnings. Also—and this is obviously absurd—their plant has been built and new expansion is unnecessary.

2. Opportunity for new and small industries is shrinking, owing to a constant increase (due to inflation) in the amount of capital necessary to start, and owing also to large fixed costs in wages and overhead. Hence, government must finance new industries at very low rates of interest.

3. Since a "mature economy" has arrived and there is a dearth of opportunity for capital investment in big industries, there is a growth in private hands of a "poisonous" supply of savings. This must be "channeled off" by taxation.

4. The most convenient "channel" is taxation to raise money for huge public works, to create employment, and "stabilize" the economy. This is called "compensatory spending."

5. More purchasing power must be created by higher wages. Hence, government influence must be thrown behind labor unions and their demands.

6. In order to enlarge spending quickly to meet the fluctuations of economic activity, appropriations should be made

by Congress in great lump sums for a series of years. The Executive should then have wide discretion as to when and why to spend. This proposal really asks Congress to surrender its power over the purse.

7. Closely related to this is the proposal to give to the Executive power to fix taxes. This is pleasantly called "flexible taxation." It is a broadening of the Executive power to fix tariff rates. This, of course, nullifies the great principle of taxation through representation.

8. Roosevelt toyed with, and cautiously experimented with in at least one budget message, an idea advanced by some economists to arrange the budget by setting up against expenditures the "value" of the public works created. One name for this was an "assets budget." Its effect would be to hide the real state of the nation's finances. Its fallacy lies in its deviation from established principles of accounting, because, for instance, a public work that produces no revenue to liquidate its costs is not a material asset: it is a liability. The fact that such works are good for people is important, but these intangibles cannot be calculated in budgetary figures.

It is easy to see in these "principles" an approach to socialism. The steps are: the suppression of free enterprise; the assumption by the state of industrial financing; the redistribution of wealth through taxation; great spending, sugar-coated by artful but specious changes in budgeting and accounting methods; the acquisition of vast powers by those in charge of government; and, finally, the gradual dissolution of representative government by the absorption into the Executive of the powers of Congress.

THE NEWER ECONOMICS OF THE TRUMAN ERA

The war, with its enormous taxes and spending, Executive discretion, and wide government controls, fulfilled for a time the wildest dreams of the statist economists and little was heard of their peacetime plans and ideas. But with the end of war and the accession of Truman, statist views began to reappear in a modified form. Their first embodiment in legislative proposals was a so-called "full employment bill," which proposed virtual economic dictatorship by the President. This was watered down by Congress to an act, passed in 1946, that gave the President a "Council of Economic Advisers," which was to provide him with an annual report, theoretically a comprehensive account of the economic state of the union but actually what Dr. Edwin G. Nourse, the first chairman of the Council, now regards as a rationalization, in economic terms, of the political purposes of the President.

Since a majority of the President's Council of Economic Advisers were devoted to the economic theories that dominated the prewar Roosevelt Administration, and since the Council has become the center of the Administration's economic thinking, it has been easy, since 1946, to identify the economics behind the President's policies.

Briefly summarized, it is as follows:

1. It assumes not a "mature" economy but an ever expanding one.

2. In the field of agriculture, it calls for price supports and "production payments." The latter are actually food subsidies in indeterminate amounts.

3. If business hesitates to provide private investment, there should be large lending by the Federal government to businesses and would-be businesses to stimulate production and employment. Government should go into businesses of its own, such as iron and steel.

4. Federal deficit-spending is to be accepted not as an unpleasant necessity but as an economic benefit. There will be balancing of the budget, therefore, not in a single year but over an indefinite number of years, which in reality will mean never.

5. Encouragement of labor demands for a high rate of wage-increases.

6. A quasi-corporative economy similar to European patterns consisting of

(a) government "fact-finding" boards, which go beyond mere fact-finding to determining how to distribute the gains of efficiency;

(b) union-managed pension funds;

(c) industries like bituminous coal actually operated by unions with government backing; and

(d) labor-management-government-controlled industries.

7. The adoption of inflation as a permanent policy. Recourse to inflationary methods in the early years of the Roosevelt Administration was justified by the fact that we were in a state of deflation. "Reflation" was the term used to distinguish the recovery effort from one of calculated inflation, with all of its dangerous potentials. Price supports for farmers, higher wages for workers, low, managed interest rates, silver purchases, and deficit financing were the rule. Always in those days there was the assurance that when prices attained a predetermined height, say the level of 1926, these accelerants would be discontinued and stability would be maintained. In the Truman era the second half of the prescription has been dropped.

Thus the economics of the Truman Administration carries on where that of the Roosevelt Administration left off.

THE CULT OF PLANNING

In the British Parliamentary election in February 1950, I was struck by the extent to which Labour Party orators talked of planning. They seldom spoke of socialism and almost never of nationalization. That was because they were desperately trying to win the votes of the middle class. They had also found that their working-class supporters were interested not in socialism for its own sake but in the necessities and amenities of life, such as food, houses, and social services. "Planning" is a good Anglo-American word that means all things to all men except socialists, to whom it is an exact synonym of socialism.

This political hypocrisy in using the word "planning" instead of socialism has been emulated by Americans of the same persuasion and with the same objectives. American statists have revealed their interpretation of a planned economy at great length and on many occasions. In a planned economy there would be set up government committees or authorities to study and plan either the entire economy at once, or various segments of it, and lay down working rules. If these plans are not followed, the government will take over and operate them itself. Planning is therefore not distinct from socialism; it *is* national socialism in its initial stage.

It should be emphasized that government planning has become a reality in Britain. It has not reached that stage in the United States. It is, however, the very heart of the political and economic philosophy of such people of influence as Henry Wallace, Walter Reuther, Rexford Tugwell, Stuart Chase, and George Soule. It runs through the entire program of the A.D.A. It is being assiduously applied within special fields by the bureaus in Washington. It is the basic argument for such projects as the various valley authorities. Its realization as a primary policy of the Democratic Party is inevitable if the left wing of that party retains dominance. Moreover, the necessities of war preparation offer a perfect screen for its extension.

THE MARXIAN PROGRAM

In this review of the characteristics of the statist trends in America, it may be well to keep before us the most orthodox of socialist plans of conquest. The following are the measures proposed by Marx and Engels in the *Communist Manifesto*. It should be noted that these are designed for "the most advanced countries."

1. Abolition of property in land and application of all rents of land to public purposes.

2. A heavy progressive or graduated income tax.

3. Abolition of all right of inheritance.

4. Confiscation of the property of all emigrants and rebels.

5. Centralization of credit in the hands of the state, by means of a national bank with state capital and an exclusive monopoly.

6. Centralization of the means of communication and transport in the hands of the state.

7. Extension of factories and instruments of production owned by the state; the bringing into cultivation of waste lands, and the improvement of the soil generally in accordance with a common plan.

8. Equal obligation of all to work. Establishment of industrial armies, especially for agriculture.

9. Combination of agriculture with manufacturing industries; gradual abolition of the distinction between town and country, by a more equable distribution of the population over the country.

10. Free education for all children in public schools. Abolition of child factory labor in its present form. Combination of education with industrial production, and so forth.

The Seductive Appeal of State Welfare

Since the origins and manifestations of statism are so many and so complex, it follows that those who favor it have many and complex motives.

Some of these are rooted in pure selfishness. People in every party or movement acquire after a while a vested interest to protect and enlarge. There are others who hope for personal betterment or renown in any change in the existing order. They have nothing to lose and much to gain. Others are driven by envy or hatred.

Psychopathology manifests itself in many ways. There is the quest for a faith by people who find conservative religions and patriotism inadequate for their spiritual yearnings. There is the urge within some who are fortunately born or well-to-do to purge themselves of imagined selfishness by turning against their own interests. A well-known psychiatrist has encouraged this means of "deliverance" among his patients. His theory is that by becoming an antagonist to one's "class," one reaches an eminence above that class. There are also persecution complexes, in which the victim imagines that a few "rich, evil men" are subtly seeking to destroy him. The list of such motives for embracing radical causes is very long.

A more important motive of those who embrace statism is the belief, already mentioned, that a capitalist society cannot overcome its defects and must die. Thus, since there has been so strong a trend toward state intervention over the past half-century, there must be a continuation of that trend to complete socialism. A distinguished Republican after the 1948 election said in a tone of resignation that he was convinced that the world was in the grip of a revolution and that he felt it useless to struggle against it. A short time after that, he retired permanently from politics.

Most important of all are those who believe that the ultimate in mutual aid, humanitarianism, and the realization of an abundant life for all can be achieved only by the ministrations of a benevolent government. These people believe, further, that all our traditional freedoms can be preserved in a state exclusively dedicated to those ends. Neither ridicule nor an attack upon personal motives should be used to meet their arguments, for most of them are sincere and unselfish, and within limitations their argument is rationally urged. It is with this belief that we should have a real concern.

The easiest way to describe the grip of the concept of a welfare state on so many warm-hearted Americans is by a brief case history. Herbert Lehman, United States Senator from New York, was for many years a successful businessman. He is a member of an influential investment-banking family. Prior to his entrance into politics, he gave much time and effort to private philanthropic activities. In 1929 he became Lieutenant Governor of New York and, after Franklin Roosevelt's election to the Presidency, attained the office of Governor, which he held for ten years. During and after the war he served the Federal government in ameliorative activities in foreign countries. In 1949 he was elected to the office he now holds.

Senator Lehman deserves his reputation as a benevolent, kindly man. As a statesman, he is neither brilliant, eloquent nor profound. His mental processes are simple; his most successful role has been that of a tidy, energetic administrator.

His instincts made it easy for him to participate actively and vocally in the humanitarian movement in New York politics. Concern for "humanity" was the watchword in the political career of Governor Alfred E. Smith, whom Lehman supported; in the Governorship of Franklin Roosevelt, under whom Lehman served; and in Lehman's own administration.

As Senator, Lehman has become a notable advocate of what he freely calls a welfare state. In his political career he has moved from a belief that the state should have a decent concern for welfare to advocating the theory that the state exists primarily, perhaps exclusively, for the promotion of welfare. He accepts, apparently without question, all the statist implications of that theory. This is shown by his membership in Americans for Democratic Action and his support of the Fair Deal program of the Truman Administration.

This change in the position of a simple and sincere man is significant. For, perhaps without perceiving the fact himself, he has crossed a great divide in economic and political principle.

Because so many hold this belief in a state solely dedicated to human welfare, the advocates of a state dedicated to the satisfaction of innumerable welfares have seized political advantage by posing as the promoters of humanitarianism and the possessors of a monopoly of the sweet spirit of charity. For years, New York State Democrats have sounded the note of humanitarianism and have sought to convey the impression that government before they began electing a succession of Governors in 1918 was cold, ruthless, and indifferent to human needs. A superficial validity is given to their claims, because the years since the turn of the century have been marked by improvements in factory laws and by more adequate care of the delinquent and unfortunate—reforms that would have come under any party.

One expression of this humanitarian theme was raised to the Federal level by President Franklin D. Roosevelt in his acceptance speech in Philadelphia in 1936. He said:

Governments can err. Presidents do make mistakes. But the immortal Dante tells us that divine justice weighs the sins of the cold-blooded and the sins of the warm-hearted on different scales.

Better the occasional faults of a government that lives in a spirit of charity than the constant omissions of a government frozen in the ice of its own indifference.

There is a mysterious cycle in human events. To some generations much is given. Of others much is expected. This generation of Americans has a rendezvous with destiny.

I wrote those words for that speech. They were intended to display a trait in Roosevelt that had endeared him as President to thousands of people who knew him only from his speeches: a genuine willingness to admit mistakes and to try again after such mistakes. The original draft of the speech conveyed a message of national unity and sympathy for all groups. Roosevelt at first wholly agreed with that draft. A day later, he revised the speech and incorporated passages that seemed to be designed to inflame class feeling and bitter antagonisms.[2]

This I believed to be gratuitous and unwise, because the time had come to face a new Presidential term, which was practically assured, with an effort to temper government regimentation and to seek broad co-operation among all groups.

Roosevelt's changes literally destroyed the import of the speech and left only the frame, including the passage quoted above. It was then, after he made that choice, that with no personal rancor I ended my association with his cause and never entered the White House again.

There was a fundamental difference in point of view between us. For to persist, as he did, in the attitude that only the greed and selfishness of some people were denying the decent interests of other people and that only government can defend those "oppressed" people, was to my mind to precipitate devastating conflict and to pervert the moderating role of government.

That speech of Roosevelt's marked the end of one New Deal and the beginning of an entirely new New Deal.

Politicians, following Roosevelt, have learned to use their terms in a manner that Ludwig von Mises calls "a cheap logical trick." He writes:

"They want to render their ideas safe from criticism by attributing to them an appellation that is cherished by every-

[2] The speech as delivered was marked by the expressions "economic royalists," "new dynasties," "concentration of control," "royal service," "privileged princes," "economic dynasties thirsting for power," "new despotism . . . in the robes of legal sanction," "new mercenaries," "privileged enterprise." It said in one place: ". . . throughout the nation . . . individual initiative was crushed in the cogs of a great machine." And again: "A small group had concentrated in their own hands an almost complete control over other people's property, other people's money, other people's labor—other people's lives." And: "Men could no longer follow the pursuit of happiness."

body. Their terminology implies that all opponents are ill-intentioned scoundrels eager to foster their selfish interests to the prejudice of the majority of good people." [3]

Then, when concern for welfare extends to many people and groups, the statist derives the conclusion that the sole provider of this benefit should be the state. For by tradition the term "welfare," especially in America, has meant the care of someone who is unable to care for himself. Thus, the good word welfare has become the captive of statism.

[3] Ludwig von Mises: *Human Action* (New Haven: Yale University Press; 1949), p. 830.

CHAPTER V

Statist Policies

Socialism by Installments

It is certain that socialism by that name and in all its implications will not in the foreseeable future be accepted by the American people. It has never been a popular philosophy in this country. Moreover, traditional socialism has involved so many noneconomic theories and purposes, such as philosophical materialism and opposition to religion and the family, that powerful church groups, notably the Roman Catholic, are its implacable enemies.

The Socialist Party has been tolerated with good-natured indifference, since for many years its voting strength has never been large, and has in recent years declined. Such garden-variety socialists as Norman Thomas, Morris Hillquit, and others have enjoyed a certain popularity, partly because they were regarded as nice fellows and largely because no one believed they were likely to attain their announced objectives. Some, like Mayors Dan Hoan of Milwaukee and Jasper McLevy of Bridgeport, have held public office for years because they have given good government and enjoyed the support of many conservative people. They did not seek to introduce socialism in their cities.

Tests of public opinion, notably one made by Dr. Henry C. Link, show that only a tiny minority of Americans would accept socialism as such. However, Dr. Link's survey showed wide differences of opinion or no opinion at all when people were asked what measures they regarded as "socialistic." A considerable number of people favored measures that they regarded as "socialistic."

Perhaps most of us would agree with these people, for everyone favors some intervention by government, even when that intervention, if generally applied, would be socialism. The test of public policies which should be exacted by those who fear and oppose socialism should be twofold. First, every act of intervention to meet a real need should be proved to be the only possible means of meeting that need. Second, every proposed intervention should be considered in relation to all other kinds of intervention.

When a political regime proposes a whole series of new interventions to be added to many already initiated, we should judge these measures in the aggregate and in their relation to the resources and strength of our free economy. We also have a right to pass judgment upon the motives and intentions of those who propose them. We are solemnly assured by those who favor every measure and trend to be described in this chapter that they are devoutly attached to a free economy and our traditional liberties. But when we consider the aggregate of the policies they favor, we can perceive that such a disclaimer is either insincere or grossly mistaken.

Those who favor all or a substantial majority of these policies ask us to yield so much of our liberty that the ultimate end would be the reality of socialism. Our danger is that we shall accept, on the installment plan, a substitute for freedom.

The Welfare State Absorbs the Welfare Community

RETREAT TO THE PAST

Despite the presence of selfishness, greed, cruelty, malice, domestic strife, and war among us, there yet resides in human beings a deep sense of charity. Human beings do care for each other, and from time immemorial mutual aid has characterized human society. Religions—certainly the religion of the Christian era and its progenitor, the Hebraic faith—have held that concern for others even beyond the confines of blood relationship is a cardinal commandment of the Deity.

For centuries charity was a major concern of organized religion. When all other human agencies failed, the churches were the sole custodians of humanitarianism, as they were of culture.

Poor relief ultimately became a function of government, but its administration was crude, unjust, and inadequate. This defect in state aid gave rise to privately supported agencies of welfare. The current concept of the welfare state, which has been vigorously promoted by Presidents Roosevelt and Truman and countless others, would reverse this trend and return this community responsibility to government, and in large part almost immediately and directly to the Federal government.

The growth of state aid is nourished and accelerated by the abuse of old and revered words, torn from their once established meanings. "Social responsibility" is made to mean the Federal government's responsibility. And "social security" as now used means neither "social" nor "security."

The dangers of a return to government aid are many; a few deserve special mention:

1. The vesting of responsibility for human welfare in government brings politics into the picture. It means the multi-

102

plication of the political devices of unfulfillable promises, half-truths, and irrational appeals.

2. Political "welfare" means the extension of benefits to greater and greater numbers and in greater amounts. These go beyond the meeting of genuine need and ultimately reach everyone as a matter of "right." A "means test," which is the secure check in privately administered welfare, is abandoned as "degrading" and "antisocial."

3. In the vague rhetoric of politics, promises are made to abolish the oldest of human instincts. "Want" and "fear" are to be exorcised by the magic of government action. Unredeemed promises of that sort are not only immoral *per se,* but when unfulfilled they sow the seeds of despair and moral disintegration.

4. To a great extent, political welfare merely takes from people through taxes the means of self-help and returns a part—not all—of those means under the dispensation of a bureaucracy.

5. The immense cost of distributing benefits according to wants instead of needs can break down any economy. Our economic system can afford to supply what people need. But it can never afford all that people want. In a free economy, the wants of people are deliberately stimulated by sales effort and advertising, and in the supplying of wants the economy is strengthened and enlarged. That is not true when wants are met through government grants and taxation.

6. The mounting burden of the welfare state upon the economy is accelerated by a loss in total productivity. There are sharp inducements to older people to abandon productive work for which they are well suited and perfectly capable. There is also the growing number of bureaucrats to administer aid—people who are thus withdrawn from productive work.

7. The moral danger of dependence has been apparent to welfare workers for centuries. The wisest welfare leader I

ever knew incessantly warned his staff that "charity is a narcotic; beneficial in an emergency, deadly as a habit." The delicate application of aid, if guided by this fact, cannot be expected of a great bureaucracy directed from Washington, especially when it is impregnated with the inevitable taint of politics.

8. Bureaucratic and mass administration of aid also tends to stress material values and to neglect all suggestions of self-help, self-confidence, and self-esteem.

The growing cost to the economy is shown in the personal-income estimates of the Department of Commerce, in which there is an item called Transfer Payments. This means payments by the Federal, state, and local governments for direct relief, pensions, insurance, unemployment pay, and all other items for which no work is performed. In 1950 this item was $14,330,000,000. This sum, incidentally, was greater than the average cost of the Federal, state, and local governments in the ten peacetime years before 1941.

It should also be noted that in the very prosperous year of 1950 we were paying $2,400,000,000 for direct relief. This was approximately twenty-four times the amount spent for direct relief in the nonprosperous year of 1930.[1] It was one and a third times what our 833,510 public elementary and secondary school teachers received in 1947. It was nearly two thirds the 1948 cost of public education, including teachers' pay and all other items, including buildings.

THE PENSION MUDDLE

After fifteen years of Federal experimentation, more years of state trials, and a multitude of private plans, the present pension situation is a study in confusion.

First, we have state systems with great variations in the character of assistance granted, the test of need, and the amounts granted. These systems are paid for by the state

[1] See Table C, p. 162.

104

and the Federal government jointly—about one half by each, on the average. The beneficiaries of state systems number about 2,300,000.

Second, we have Federal old-age and survivors' insurance, based on payroll taxes, under which another 2,300,000 get benefits.

Third, there are miscellaneous groups of systems—Federal veteran and military systems; Federal, state, and local civil service retirement systems; the Railroad Retirement system; and many private plans rapidly increasing in number. It is probable that 2,300,000 are getting benefits from them.

Thus, millions of people are to a degree living off the rest of the people through some welfare plan, and the number increases every day.[2] It is true that many or most of them have paid into pension funds, but the future solvency of the funds must be assured by those who continue to work.

The Federal system is neither fair, financially sound, nor honest. The money collected from taxes on payrolls is in excess of the requirements and probably will be for some time in the future. Hence a huge fund piles up, and is "invested" in government bonds. This means that government spends the surplus for other things and incurs a debt for future obligations. The obligations must ultimately be made good by the taxpayer, and in a great many cases that future taxpayer and the beneficiary will be the same person.[3]

[2] The exact number is difficult to determine, since there are a great many who benefit from both government and private plans.

[3] The original tax rates were one per cent for employee and employer. These have been increased to one and a half per cent each for 1950 through 1953. Thereafter, the rates will rise until they reach three and one-quarter per cent in 1970. The fund will amount to $50,000,000,000 by that year. After that the payments are likely to run far beyond receipts under present arrangements. In the August 1951 issue of the *Tax Review,* published by the Tax Foundation, W. Reston Williamson, consultant to the U.S. Social Security Board from 1936 to 1947, said this of the present system: "Frankly, we lack clearly-understood objectives in Social Security. It is a field essentially alien to this country. It has neither been adapted to the United States, nor has a mature statement of its functions appeared to date. There remains today a basic ignorance of its purposes, its ideals, its orientation."

State systems in many cases are immersed in reckless politics. People flock to states with the larger grants, and as their number grows they become a powerful political pressure-group for bigger and bigger grants at lower and lower ages. Demagogues with bigger and bigger promises play upon the cupidity of these people. The burden of state taxation becomes unendurable. Other state services, such as school equipment and teachers' salaries, are squeezed by their plans. The young are literally looted by the old. The young are now denied better education; later, they must pay taxes for the deficiencies of the present system.

Government-aid systems, combined with the growth of private industrial pension systems, induce productive people to retire before they should, compel industries to hire younger employees and make it harder for older people to get work, pile heavier costs on production and thus inflate prices to create a very special "pension aristocracy," and destroy the personal moral obligation of the young to care for their parents and elders.

Private industrial systems on an actuarial basis are possible only in large concerns. They partially immobilize money in trust funds, which will reduce the amount of new productive-venture capital. The worker, moreover, is deluded by these systems because he pays in money of one value and in all probability will get it back at a greatly decreased value, especially if his leaders insist upon a corollary policy of basing wage increases upon the cost-of-living index, which automatically promotes inflation.

GOVERNMENT MEDICINE

While many Federal bills for some form of government medicine on a national scale have been introduced during the past few years, and while several state and local plans have been proposed, the crystallized proposal is in Security

106

Administrator Oscar R. Ewing's 1948 report, *The Nation's Health, A Ten-Year Program*. I use Senate Bill 1679 to describe the general outlines of this proposal, which President Truman endorsed in a lengthy message to Congress in April 1949. Since elections in many states and districts have shown strong public opposition to this plan, it will be amended and sugar-coated in new bills. But as far as the Administration is concerned the purposes are likely to remain the same.

The plan proposes two major extensions of Federal authority in the field of medical care. The first six sections of the bill would provide Federal aid for medical education, research, and hospital and clinical care. It would provide Federal aid to help locate doctors, dentists, hospitals, and clinics in places where there is a shortage of facilities. It would provide aid for state and other health services and also provide some special benefits.

The heart of the plan is the levy of a payroll tax of 3 per cent, split between employers and employees, for general medical, dental, and other care. This money would go into a "Personal Health Services Account." The plan would be operated by a Federal board under the Federal Security Agency. Then states would submit plans for operation on state levels. But if a state failed to do so, the program would be imposed by the Federal board.

Then the public would be allowed to participate in free services. It is estimated that 85 per cent would do so. Then doctors, dentists, nurses, hospitals, and others would be allowed to sign up. Those who would want to stay out could do so and seek patients among the "noninsured" 15 per cent. Beneficiaries theoretically could select their physicians and dentists. The number of patients per practitioner would be regulated. Fees would be fixed and paid by the state agency, with some advisory assistance by practitioners' committees.

Nothing in the bill provides that all the needed money would come from payroll taxes. The name "insurance" is

107

clearly a misnomer, for the additional costs would be paid by general taxation.

In this brief summary, we are concerned with only the socialistic features and implications of this plan.

Its cost would be very high—perhaps from five to ten billions dollars in the first years. Using Veterans Administration figures as a basis, a former Deputy Surgeon General of the Army suggests a figure as high as eighteen billion dollars a year. Presumably, payroll taxes would rise with the need for more money and larger appropriations would be made from general taxes.

No means test would be imposed. All could share.

A vast number of administrators would be required. Opponents of the bill say at least 1,500,000 government employees would be needed.

All sorts of private, religious, and philanthropic activities would be taken over or eliminated.

Practitioners would be burdened with paperwork.

As in Britain, practitioners would be directly encouraged to see more patients than they could adequately treat.

Since grants for education, research, and specialized work would be increasingly dependent on government, drastic and inflexible Federal regulations would prevail.

The sacred privacy of the relation of patient and practitioner would be impaired by access to records by the administrators.

Care for chronic cases, malingerers, and hypochondriacs would stand in the way of acute and emergency cases.

Doctors, dentists, and others would, as in Britain, lose the initiative now prevailing to improve technical skill and responsibility.

Trials of government medicine, notably in the State of Washington and elsewhere, show that costs rise to unforeseen and unbearable heights.

Since the real, determining administration at the top

would be political, such a plan would be subject to irresistible pressures to increase benefits progressively.

In its essentials, the Truman-Ewing plan follows the British system adopted in 1948. In Britain the cost of the health program rose more than 100 per cent above the original government estimate; hospitals were crowded with chronic cases; professional advancement was retarded; and no appreciable effect on general health was notable. The socialists discovered that there were more hypochondriacs than anyone had anticipated.

Ultimately, in the United States, to keep costs within the scope of general tax receipts, iron regulations would be imposed. The modicum of liberty for practitioners and patients would be eliminated and regimentation by government would prevail.

In short, this plan involves an immense and vital extension of government intervention and a consequent invasion of liberty.

Finally, it should be noted that our Federal government is already the largest employer of doctors and the largest operator of hospitals in the country. It spends two billion dollars annually for free care for twenty-four million people.

The Federal Invasion of the States

ROBBING PETER

The American Constitution was designed to preserve personal liberty by several means. Very important among these was the assurance of state sovereignty and, with it, local government. The ascendancy of the Federal government is the deadly enemy not only of the states but of the citizens of the states. For socialism must seek its final objective on a national level.

109

To attain domination, the Federal leviathan must first seize the sources of state and local revenue—revenue that is the life blood of government. The extent of this seizure has already been most alarming.

The Hoover Commission's task force on Federal-state relations points out that in 1890 the Federal government spent 36.2 per cent of all governmental outlays in the nation. In 1946, it spent 85.2 per cent. In 1890 local units spent 55.6 per cent of all government outlays, and in 1946 only 7.2 per cent. The state governments in 1946 spent 7.6 per cent.

The adoption of the Federal income tax marked the beginning of a rapid rise of Federal authority and the decline of state and local importance. Before the Federal income tax was adopted, the Federal government derived nearly all its revenue from customs, liquor, and tobacco taxes. The income tax immediately assumed major importance, but during the First World War the Federal government seized several other sources of revenue, including various admissions taxes, stamp taxes, and manufacturers' excise taxes. Later it added motor fuel, gifts, and estates to its taxable sources. Other sources have been seized as they have been found, always with small regard for the prior possession of states and localities.

This money is not made in Washington. It comes from the states. The sources from which states have drawn their own revenue have been taken by the Federal suction pump. Almost every productive source of taxation, except the property tax, has been lost to most of the states.

The result is utter confusion and overlapping of taxes. The same sources may be taxed several times, and taxpayers themselves have only the faintest notion of what they pay, what they pay for, and whom they are paying.

A large part of the collections of the Federal government comes from such overlapping taxes. And the proportion of the Federal "bite" from these sources is steadily getting larger. In 1934 its share of the taxes from these sources was 63 per cent. In 1946, it was 91 per cent.

Since all governments—Federal, state, and local—follow the Donnybrook slogan, "Hit the heads you see!" obvious sources are hit hard, and more difficult but fair sources are neglected.

Since the greatest growth of Federal power has taken place in the two wars and in the depression, it is easy to predict that in the great crisis created by the threat of Communism this absorption of local sources of revenue will continue at an increasing rate. States are at a great disadvantage in this competition. The Federal income tax is all-powerful. Moreover, an individual state has the handicap of trying to avoid driving individuals and businesses to other states that have more favorable taxes.

The grave danger of all this is that the state and local governments, which are close to the vital needs of the people and are under close observation by them, will become less competent to perform their proper functions. These protective divisions of our nation will wither for lack of nourishment.

TO PAY PAUL

Along with this progressive seizure of state and local sources of revenue, and on the overworked theory that under modern economic conditions the problems of government override state boundaries, the Federal government has stolen from the states many of their traditional powers and functions. Assistance to the aged and unfortunate, highway building, the regulation of business and labor, the control of elections and primaries, the enforcement of criminal law, and many other activities of the states have been partially taken over by Federal authority.

Under a constant enlargement of Federal jurisdiction

111

made possible by a more and more "liberal" interpretation of the Constitution by the Supreme Court, almost very aspect of competition and private business and labor is now subject to Federal law. Consequently, state legislation in many of those fields has become meaningless. Regulation has loosed upon the states a horde of Federal bureaucrats who have little sympathy for local customs, preferences, and protections, and who are responsible only to Washington. This condition has grown much worse during the war and in the subsequent cold war.

Great Federal enterprises for defense and related purposes have grown up, with payrolls so large that local communities have become increasingly dependent upon them. This has seriously impaired local independence.

Federal power has grown immensely through grants-in-aid to the states. Through such grants, the Federal government now influences or controls 75 per cent of state activities. Under the pretext of successive crises—the depression, the war, and the cold war—the size and variety of these grants have grown at a tremendous rate. Fifty years ago, only $3,000,000 was paid out of Federal funds to the states. By 1912, grants had risen to $5,255,000. From then on, the march began in earnest, in part because the Federal income tax with its unlimited power over incomes became operative, and in part because of the great requirements of the First World War. By 1920, the figure was $33,188,000. With the coming of the New Deal, the pace increased until, in 1941, grants had reached $836,682,000. Under President Truman's Administration, these grants have risen until in 1950 the sum was nearly $2,234,700,000. This is the most graphic way of describing the deterioration of a great constitutional system.[4]

[4] The alarm of states because of the threat to them of the unlimited Federal income tax is well shown by the adoption by many state legislatures of a proposal for a Federal constitutional convention whose mandate would be to place a limit on the Federal income tax rates.

There has also been a parallel and consistent decline of local self-government through the increase of state grants to cities, counties, and other small units of government. In five years, state grants to localities have increased by a third.

A special evil in the development of Federal power under President Roosevelt was the habit of by-passing the states in extending aid to cities and other local units of government. In the administration of relief under Harry Hopkins, this was a calculated political objective.[5] The Federal machine thus made a close alliance with city machines through the granting of relief money, to the political advantage of both.

Where money goes the bureaucrat follows. Money means power. And power begets control.

This trend, if continued, will ultimately erase local self-government and reduce the states to the status of mere agents or provinces of the Federal government. The balanced system created by the Constitution will be gone, and national socialism will have eliminated its most formidable barrier.

VALLEYS OF AUTOCRACY

It is not without meaning that our planners and statists so deeply revere the memory of the late Senator George Norris. For it was Norris who offered to the eagerly receptive Franklin Roosevelt the basic idea that became the Tennessee Valley Authority. That immense project, which was in reality a comprehensive adventure in state planning, was only partially completed when Roosevelt and Norris proposed an application of the same idea to practically every major river valley in the nation. This extension of the TVA idea has been an Administration policy ever since.

Bills to set up regional authorities for the United States as a whole have been introduced regularly since 1937, when President Roosevelt sent to Congress a message recommend-

[5] Hopkins admitted this to me in 1935.

113

ing a series of authorities for seven watershed regions. Most comprehensive was H.R. 894, sponsored by Representative Rankin in the Eighty-first Congress. It is hard to determine who is behind the Rankin bill, for seemingly those in power in our government would prefer to introduce bills for regional authorities one at a time, rather than impose a plan for the entire United States.

In the forefront are the plans of the Administration for a Columbia Valley Administration and a Missouri Valley Authority. Bills for their creation have been perennials in Congress for several years. Extensive hearings have been held, and vigorous government propaganda has been carried on, mainly by the Interior Department.

The plan of a valley authority involves the creation of a government-owned corporation, with a small board of governors appointed by the President for long terms. To this corporate body are transferred properties of the government, including dams, plants, irrigation projects, and many other public works. The authority is then vested with very broad powers to administer these and to build more. Congressional appropriations are made, but through extensive business operations the authority also accumulates large sums of its own.

The statutory powers of the governing board of the TVA and of the proposed CVA and MVA are so great that state and local governments lose or would lose many of their traditional functions. Governor Arthur Langlie of Washington was guilty of no great exaggeration when he said that a CVA would reduce his state to a "territorial" status.

The major business of such authorities would be the production, distribution, and sale of electric power. With government money behind them and no taxes to pay, they could by competition practically destroy private power-companies. Under their wide powers, they could buy private companies and either run them or resell them to co-operatives or other public agencies. Through their arbitrary power to allocate costs, they could, and in the TVA they do, saddle the Federal government with disproportionate costs for the so-called non-reimbursable purposes of dams, such as navigation and flood control.

Local governments, shorn of tax resources, would have to come, hat in hand, to the authority for doles in lieu of taxes.

The authority of states over their water and land would be invaded, and long-standing systems of water law would be set aside.

In effect, a valley authority is a supergovernment with sharply limited responsibility to Congress and practically none to the states involved. By the sale of electricity, of water for irrigation, and other benefits and services—practically all below cost and at the expense of general taxation—a vast paternalism would emerge in the Columbia and Missouri valleys as it has in that of the Tennessee.

A valley authority is a great adventure in paternalism. Under it, local control of government dies, the public is subsidized, private property is absorbed, and the springs of free expression and education are polluted by government propaganda. Private wealth and property end in public monopoly.

CIVIL RIGHTS BY FEDERAL ACTION

It would be a denial of the principles under which we live to say that all Americans, regardless of race, color, religion, or national origin, should not share established political and economic rights and privileges. Among these are equal protection of the law—notably in the criminal law—participation in the political process by voting and holding office, and freedom to secure employment and participate in economic life. The manner in which these rights and privileges should be secured, however, is a highly debatable subject in Congress and elsewhere.

This question is raised by the proposals made in the Tru-

115

man Administration's civil rights program. That program was made specific by the President's Committee on Civil Rights, which made its report in 1947. It was submitted with full approval and recommendations by the President early in 1948.

Since this subject goes back into nearly a century of our history and since a great mass of legislation has been introduced, with interminable debate, in Congress and the states, it is best to limit our discussion to the specific proposals of the President's Committee, which were:

1. The establishment under the Federal government of new facilities to enforce Federal laws and to supplement state criminal-law administration.

2. The extension of Federal criminal jurisdiction to what would amount to the power to police the prosecuting and police officers of the state. The most notable feature of this would be an anti-lynching law.

3. Federal laws designed to remove restrictions upon voting in primaries and elections.

4. Federal laws designed to prohibit discrimination in private employment and in government services. A feature of this recommendation is that the Federal government would enforce nondiscrimination not only by direct action but by withholding Federal funds.

For the purpose of this book, it is unnecessary to review the constitutional questions involved or to consider the practical political-party problems raised. We are concerned with the need and effect of Federal intervention when either state and local powers are involved, or with questions that properly lie outside all government concern.

As in most subjects in which government intervention is sought, several vital questions are raised by these proposals:

Are all the alleged "rights" stated by the President and his

116

commission in truth "rights" that a government such as ours has an obligation to enforce?

A great deal of looseness attends the discussion of "rights." Equality before the law and protection from crime is a right. Voting and office-holding are not rights *per se*. They are privileges or "offices" extended to qualified people. And the authority to establish such qualifications is for the most part a state matter. No one has a "right" to public or private employment.

If we grant that the "rights" involved are genuine, do the facts regarding the denial of those "rights" justify Federal compulsion?

The facts with respect to the failure of criminal-law enforcement in the Southern states—even the facts assembled in the report of the President's Committee—show a situation no more serious than that which exists generally in the nation. On the subject of the failure of law enforcement, I speak from an experience of a dozen years in the study of law enforcement.[6] There exists and has existed for years incompetence in law enforcement in many parts of the nation, notably in some Northern cities, just as serious as that which prevails in Southern states. The very figures of the President's Committee show that lynchings, once a serious problem, have declined to two or three a year. In 1945 and in 1947 there was only one. There have been many more murders, for which no one was punished, in many a small Northern city every year than there have been lynchings in the United States. Police brutality, of which the Committee complains, exists wherever police are incompetent, corrupt, or politically controlled. The Committee complains of the injustices in evacuating Japanese residents on the West

6 See my *Politics and Criminal Prosecution* (New York: Minton, Balch & Company; 1928); *Our Criminal Courts* (New York: Minton, Balch & Company; 1930); and *Tribunes of the People* (New Haven: Yale University Press; 1932).

Coast during the war. But that was done not by the states but by Federal authority, and it was upheld by the Supreme Court.[7]

In the exercise of voting and other political activities, there has been a rapid trend toward admitting Negroes to equality.

As for employment, specific figures cannot be depended upon, for the matter usually lies in the mental attitude of employers.

Government Intervention in the Free Market

THE FARMER ON THE DOLE

If the proposal of the Truman Administration known as the Brannan Plan has served no other useful purpose, it has brought thinking people to a realization that, unless some method is found to restore agriculture to a permanently self-sustaining basis, there is nothing ahead for the American farmer but well-kept serfdom under an all-powerful government. The Brannan Plan, with all its socialistic implications, has become the warning and the threat of the future.

In the beginning of the New Deal, there was the so-called domestic allotment plan, with restriction of free production, and subsidies of some hundreds of millions a year raised in large part by a processing tax. After the Supreme Court invalidated that plan, the same end was sought by soil-improvement payments.

The war brought a demand for expansion rather than restriction. Parity had not been reached in the preceding plans, but in 1942 a guarantee of 90 per cent parity was given for a period that would have ended in December 1948. With elec-

[7] The opinions in this case, *Korematsu* v. *U.S.* in 1944, were by Justices Black and Frankfurter.

118

tion just ahead, however, Congress voted a new plan embodying flexible supports. President Truman, despite his signature on this new, makeshift law, vigorously attacked the Congress that passed it for its ruthlessness in reducing the farmer's income.

And then, not long after the Truman election in 1948, came the Brannan Plan.

Since the Brannan Plan has been changed from time to time to meet or seem to meet valid criticism, it is not possible to state exactly what it is at any given moment. Moreover, the nation has moved toward a war footing since the plan was created, and many of the basic assumptions of the plan have changed. Also, it has received many direct repudiations at the polls, and a great majority of Congress is now opposed to it. Its chance of passage seems remote.

However, its main outlines undoubtedly indicate the trend of statist thought in the agricultural field, and it will no doubt be proposed again in an amended form.

The essentials of the Brannan Plan are:

The guarantee of an agricultural income at a level fixed at the average of the first ten of the past twelve years. This would perpetuate the high prices of the war years 1942 to 1945.

Perishables and nonperishables would be treated on different bases.

Nonperishables would be supported at the fixed level by a series of marketing quotas and acreage allotments. Large farms would be discriminated against.

Perishables would be allowed to find their levels in the market. But the government would determine a fair value for these and make up the difference in money to the producer. This would, in substance, be a consumers' subsidy.

The Brannan Plan represents an extreme effort to extend artificial supports for farm products at an enormous but indeterminate cost to the Treasury. It also would impose upon the farmer a heavy yoke of regulation, backed up by provisions for jail sentences. There are sixteen pages of penalties in the bill embodying the plan. Ultimately, under such well-paid regimentation, the agricultural interests of the nation would occupy a privileged place in the economy. The effect upon the ingenuity and enterprise of the farmer would be enervating. And resentment would rise among other elements of the population, who would be paying for the benefits.

Meanwhile, in order to administer this regime of subsidies and benefits, the bureaucracy would be greatly enlarged.

THE FEDERAL GOVERNMENT IN BUSINESS

In the many economic enterprises other than agriculture, the Federal government has moved well past mere regulation and into competition—direct or indirect—at a rapidly increasing rate in the past two decades. This, of course, is not merely a threat or a promise of socialism. It is socialism growing by progressive steps, under the pressure of persons and organizations whose purposes and point of view are for the most part antagonistic to the ideal of the free market or who frankly do not believe that any important part of a free economic system can survive.

The best recent survey of Federal business enterprise is that of the Hoover Commission. In summary, it says:

There are about 100 important business enterprises which the Federal government owns or in which it is financially interested. These concerns engage directly or indirectly in lending money; guaranteeing loans and deposits; writing life insurance; the producing, distributing, and selling of electric power and fertilizers; the operation of railways and ships; the purchasing and selling of farm products; and the smelting and sale of metals.

The government's direct investment in these enterprises is in excess of $20 billion, and there are further authorized commit-

120

ments to supply about $14 billion of them. In addition, the government guarantees directly and indirectly about $90 billion of deposits or mortgages, and the life insurance written by government agencies approaches $40 billion.

The Hoover Commission, with no authorization to consider the wisdom of these government activities, merely stated the facts and suggested means of administering existing activities. However, even in their limited field the members of the Commission differed very sharply, and a third of the text of the report is devoted to dissenting opinions. The more conservative members followed Hoover. Members and former members of the Administration, Senator Aiken, and Democratic members of Congress dissented.

These Federal business enterprises, set up at various times and for varied purposes, present a picture of utter confusion. Their only common characteristics are that they narrow the field of a free economy, they are expensive to the taxpayer, and they offer a wide opportunity for the intrusion of politics into business life.

The activities of these business enterprises present a bewildering variety. They not only compete with private enterprises but they compete and conflict with each other. Some of them are means of subsidizing their clients. Most of them are subsidized by the government. There is little means of determining their efficiency, because of the lack of clear accounting and reporting. For a long time some of them by-passed Congressional appropriations by direct borrowing from the Treasury.[8] Most receive unfair tax-exemptions. Some invest their surplus in government securities, thus compelling the government to pay interest on its own investments.

However, one fact emerges from the history of this growth

[8] Congress, by the 1945 Government Corporation Control Act, attempted to get this situation under control by requiring certain government corporations to submit budgets for its consideration.

of government business enterprises. Sponsors seldom say frankly that government can do the job better. Always, there is some idealistic or humanitarian objective, such as public health, the amelioration of the condition of the "under-privileged," public welfare, national defense, full employment, or succor for the unsuccessful.

These multitudinous and immense business enterprises not only directly pre-empt the field of private opportunity, but, individually and collectively, they present a threat to all the rest of the economy by competition, tax advantages, or some other form of influence.

There is no indication that the invasion will ever be halted by its instigators. The various proposals of Presidents Roosevelt and Truman, of the supporters of these Presidents in Congress, of statist-minded organizations that have consistently supported the Federal Administration in elections over the past few years, all show an intent to move government, especially the Federal government, further and further into business.

For example, there was the famous Full Employment bill, sponsored by President Truman in 1945 but greatly watered down by Congress.

More recently, there was the Economic Stabilization bill, introduced by Representative Brent Spence in February 1949. The Spence bill would have authorized the President to build new plant facilities "to help achieve the quantity goals for designated essential materials." It was in line with the authority asked for in this bill that a few weeks after its introduction President Truman arbitrarily decided and made public his decision that the steel industry was behind the quantity goals that he had fixed, apparently in his own mind. Hence, he threatened to put the government into the steel business.

Senator Murray of Montana and seventeen of his colleagues sponsored a bill in 1949 that was a fairly good specimen of what statism would do if it could summon the votes in Congress. It was called the Economic Expansion bill and was an amazing miscellany of economic planning, government-in-business, and pompous rhetoric. It proposed that the President should determine the amount of investment to attain "one half to three-quarters of a million" new jobs a year and a three to four per cent increase in national production. Then the President should ascertain whether private business would provide these and, if not, bring government spending programs to Congress to supply the deficiency. The bill would start all this with an authorization of $11,000,000,-000 in loans, $3,300,000,000 in additions to various revolving and emergency funds, and several hundred millions in new expenditures. Such determinations and planning are not possible under any economic calculation. But under a spurious assumption, the government would undertake a vast expansion of government business activity and spending. That, of course, was what the sponsors wanted. The proposal shows the strength of statism in the Senate alone, for nearly twenty per cent of its members lent their name to this monstrosity, and there is little doubt that the President knew of the proposal and tacitly approved it. It is an indication of what may be proposed after the current rearmament program is over.

The detailed proposals of this and the original 1945 Full Employment bill are too long to be set forth here. The general purpose, however, was to level off the economic cycle by Federal action, to "guarantee" full employment, to set up new government business in competition with private business, and to subject the nation's economy to government planning and direction. There would be government price-and-wage fixing, production quotas, and government inquisition into the private books, records, and trade secrets of private business. Except in name, these proposals all follow the lines of the orthodox socialist plans of the British Labour Party.

It will suffice here, for the purpose of illustration, to select two fields of government-in-business—the Federal government as a banker, and the government in the utility business.

THE GOVERNMENT AS A BANKER

The extent of the Federal government's activity in lending money and guaranteeing other loans is described in detail in the Hoover Commission's report on *Federal Business Enterprises* and in the Hoover task force report on *Lending Agencies.*[9]

The following is a comprehensive summary of the size and ramifications of the banking business of the Federal government according to the Hoover Report:

There are 40 agencies in the Federal Government engaged in lending, guaranteeing, and insuring (other than social security and pension agencies). Nine of these agencies, with loans outstanding, have either ceased lending or are in liquidation.

As of June 30, 1948, the Federal Government had an investment of over $12.5 billion in these agencies and had further commitments to supply them over $9 billion. Loans guaranteed by Federal agencies amount to about $8.5 billion; and the value of deposits insured by Federal agencies amounts to something over $80 billion. Life insurance written by Government agencies totals approximately $40 billion.

Some of these agencies have obtained more than $2 billion of capital from private investors.

At least 35,000 employees in 300 offices and branches of these agencies are paid by the Federal Government.

Some of these activities are legacies of depression and war; some are permanent fixtures in our economic system for expanding and securing the channels of credit; and some were created to effect social rather than economic objectives.

[9] The latter was largely the work of Price, Waterhouse and Company, certified public accountants.

The danger abundantly revealed in Federal lending is in loans or guarantees made directly to individuals or private companies, except in such emergencies as a deep depression or war. It requires little proof to realize that lending to private persons or companies in nonemergency times is a direct invitation to political chicanery, corruption, and gross favoritism.

Jesse Jones who, despite pulls and pressure from the White House down, steered the RFC for years, believes "that neither the White House nor Congress is competent to lend money." He said further in a memorandum to me in 1950:

Banking by Government should only be done on a strictly nonpartisan basis and it is difficult with salaries paid by the Government, and meddling by Congress and the White House, to get competent men to do the lending. It is impossible to keep politics out of Government lending. All members of both houses are available to their constituents to make appeals for them. They cannot very well decline, and most of all, the party in power apparently cannot keep its hands off. The directors of the RFC or any Government lending agency cannot ignore the authority that appoints them. It resolved itself, largely, to a case of out-managing a situation. Some years ago a friend asked me to go deer hunting with him in the Rio Grande Valley. It was a little early in the season and there had been no cold weather and I asked him if he were not afraid of rattlesnakes—To which he replied: "You can always out-manage a rattlesnake!"

In 1950 and 1951 the Fulbright Senate subcommittee created a national sensation by its revelations of favoritism, gross incompetence, and some acts at least closely bordering upon criminal activity in the granting of loans by the Reconstruction Finance Corporation. This agency, created in 1932 under President Hoover, fulfilled an excellent function in a depressed time. It was also used during the war to make loans for worthy defense purposes. But it also extended its operations to direct lending of all sorts. Many, if not most, of these loans were clearly not in the public interest. Some of them were made under direct political pressure, and some revealed shockingly bad business judgment.

Greater than the danger of favoritism, corruption, and incompetence is that of distorting the economic system through vast government holdings in many lines of business. Socialistic policies are extended through the use of government credit. Government money is used to foster unfair competition with private companies that the Administration may decide to punish. Companies can be told to accept the money and expand certain lines or else their competitors will receive it. Vast business properties could be owned by the banker-government.

A prominent New Dealer has admitted that government lending at low rates of interest will end in the government owning "most of the productive resources of the country." This assertion by a well-known and high official of the United States government merely underlines the intent of statism to control first the credit and then the productive enterprises of the nation. As we have seen, such "centralization of credit in the hands of the state" is the fifth point of the Marx-Engels program in the *Communist Manifesto*.

FEDERAL GOVERNMENT IN THE ELECTRIC UTILITY BUSINESS

In thirty years the proportion of the electric power supply of the United States generated by Federal plants has grown from a negligible amount to more than ten per cent. Since the ownership and operation of this vital business is the prime objective of statist policy, let us see when this growth has been most rapid. The following percentages indicate the shares, in various years, of the total installed capacity in kilowatts which were supplied by Federal plants: [1]

[1] These figures are from the statistical bulletin of the Edison Electric Institute for 1950.

Year	Federal Per Cent of Total
1920	Negligible
1930	0.7
1940	4.9
1945	10.1
1950	10.0

There was a slight decline in the percentages during the four years after 1945 because of the postwar expansion of private plants, but the upward movement is again under way. Of all additions to capacity in 1951 and 1952, the Federal share will be 14.7 per cent. At the end of 1952, the proportion of total capacity will reach 11 per cent.

This increase is due not only to the capacity of the Federal government to spend vast sums on this development, but to the fact that partially hidden subsidies are used in the competitive field and private companies have been absorbed by government.

Since falling water seems to be a free source of electric power, the public, stimulated by government propaganda, is led to believe that hydroelectric power is cheaper. This proposition needs to be qualified in a number of important respects. It is true that in locations like Niagara Falls, British Columbia, and in parts of the Pacific Northwest, where there is an assured water supply and favorable topography, hydroelectric power is more economical, even where it must be transmitted over long distances. In places like California, New England, and the Southeastern states, where there is favorable topography but a limited and sometimes irregular water supply, a combination of steam and water production is most economical. In other locations, where low-cost fuel is available, steam is usually cheaper than water power. And where there are concentrations of population and industrial plants, steam is generally the only source available to meet the demands of the market.

The joker in the claims for government power is the element of subsidy which is invariably involved. When the Federal government builds great multiple-purpose installations, there is an arbitrary allocation of cost to flood control, navigation, and irrigation. The first two of these are paid for by the Federal government and are within its constitutional authority. In earlier days irrigation was supposed to be paid for by water users. But for reasons that could only be explained by a long discourse on the mysteries of government bookkeeping, there has been an increasing trend toward subsidizing agricultural water-users.[2] Thus, if the allocation to flood control, navigation, and irrigation is higher, the alleged cost of power will be low. And it is not difficult to show that the allocation to these nonreimbursable purposes has generally been excessively high.

In many instances also there is no charge for interest on money spent, although the taxpayers of the nation must pay interest on the money borrowed by government. There is also the loss of tax revenues to local governments when government plants grow and private, taxpaying plants are eliminated or prevented from growing.

A good example of how subsidies distort the picture is provided in a publication of the Department of Conservation and Development and the Public Service Commission of the state of Washington. It makes this comment concerning further hydroelectric development on the Columbia River:

If the total cost of the balance of this program, excluding costs chargeable directly to flood control and navigation, is charged to power together with the cost of transmission, the cost of electric energy delivered to the principal load-centers in the Puget Sound area and on the lower Columbia River will be about 6 mills per kilowatt hour. The cost of producing an equivalent amount of electric power by the operation of modern steam electric genera-

[2] See pp. 131–6.

tion stations located in the load centers would be identical within the limits of accuracy of the calculation.

If this be true in two states like Washington and Oregon, which have little or no natural supplies of coal and oil but fine water-power resources, what must be the situation in places where coal and oil supplies are near and abundant? The drive for public power-projects is continuous and powerful. There has been developed in the Interior Department a vast propaganda machine for the preaching of the doctrine of public power and vast new developments in harnessing the waters of every river valley. The cupidity of states and local communities is aroused by glowing pictures painted of great Federal projects. There is log-rolling in Congress by representatives of these states and communities, and project after project gets under way.[3]

The Federal government has not only been intent upon a policy of gaining ascendancy in the field of producing electric power, but it has given great stimulus to public ownership in the retail sale of power. It has constantly sought new business by underselling to cities and other communities private producers of power at costs that amount to a subsidy, but its policies of preference have offered other advantages that aid the growth of municipal ownership. In 1951, according to the Edison Electric Institute, twenty-one per cent of electric customers in the United States were receiving service from public bodies, co-operatives, and other agencies having such preference under Federal law. In some states (Nebraska, Tennessee, Mississippi, Washington) more than half of all customers were thus served.

[3] The great Central Valley of California has been the scene of a constant effort of the Federal government to gain ascendancy for public power. In that area the state of California, the Federal government, and the Pacific Gas and Electric Company achieved for a time what seemed to be a workable balance between public and private power. That balance has been constantly threatened in recent years.

The manner by which such preferences have been given is a most interesting example of the twisting of legislative language to attain an end not contemplated when the law was passed. In 1906, a reclamation law was passed which said that the Secretary of the Interior might lease surplus electric power from irrigation projects "giving preference to municipal purposes." The records show no indication that this was intended to give preference to municipally owned utilities. But the precedent that was inferred by public-power advocates has been woven into a large number of Federal laws relating to the sale of electric power from projects built during the past two decades.[4]

The intent of these laws was further extended on the authority of Secretary Ickes of the Interior Department in 1946 by a directive to his subordinates. It said that they should not merely wait for a preferred customer to come forward and offer to purchase the power, but "Active assistance, from the very beginning of the planning and authorization of a project, shall be given to the organization of public agencies and cooperatives in each project area." Thus the old intent of the law of 1906 was first extended to the giving of preference under the New Deal; and then under the Fair Deal the Department of the Interior was to go into the business of organizing public agencies and co-operatives to receive the preference. That is one example of the progress of statism in forty years.

While the great hydroelectric installations of the Federal government represent most of its investment in the utility

[4] An example of the effect of this was pointed out by Representative George A. Dondero in the House on May 14, 1951. He said: "It has been estimated that 11 per cent of all the power customers in Michigan could be classified as preference customers. If the Bureau of Reclamation built a huge multiple purpose project in Michigan, only 11 per cent of Michigan's customers would be entitled to this power. Although 89 per cent of the customers had, through their taxes, contributed to the building of the project, they would be denied any benefit from the project because they happened to patronize the wrong power distributing concern."

business, the Rural Electrification Administration is its major activity in reaching customers directly. This enterprise when it was established was regarded as a sound and beneficial form of government aid. Private companies were unable, for economic reasons, to reach into sparsely settled rural regions, and government provision of transmission lines for retail sale was regarded as a legitimate subsidy that might so increase the prosperity of agriculture as to increase substantially the economy of the nation. When Federally produced power was not available, reasonable arrangements were made to buy power from private companies. At this time, about half of the power used by the REA comes from private companies.

The REA and the co-operatives with which it is associated have not been content with such arrangements, however, and the inevitable burgeoning of government business has been rapidly proceeding. Co-operatives have been building their own generating plants, not because private power has been unavailable, but because they claim it is cheaper to build for themselves. The apparent economy thus claimed is, of course, not because of the preferences above noted but because of the tax exemption of co-operatives. The latest development consists of plans by the REA to tie many smaller co-operatives together in super-regional co-operatives under the direction of the REA administrator. The REA would then encourage the building of competitive plants by government loans for generation and transmission. Ultimately, the REA would be a gigantic monopoly serving two to three million customers.

EXERCISES IN BOOKKEEPING

The reclamation policies and activities of the Federal government that have now assumed such great importance in the national economy and such a heavy charge on public funds originated in the basic Reclamation Act of 1902. That Act was designed to make more land usable to farmers and thus to open horizons of opportunity which had been foreclosed by the exhaustion of the supply of arable public land. It provided that the Federal government would build dams, canals, laterals, and other works to provide irrigation for the prospective users of nonarable land. Users were to repay the costs of the Federal works over a period of ten years and, after that repayment had been made, these works should belong to the users. As time went on, it was found that the costs of the projects were increasing and that land needed more help. Consequently, in 1914 another act was passed that extended the time of repayment to fifteen years on newly irrigated land and also permitted existing contracts more time for full repayment of balances due. In 1922 another Act was passed that provided for co-operative arrangements among farmers to deal with the government in the making of contracts. Irrigation districts were to be set up in which there should be water-users' associations. The period of repayment was extended in 1926 to forty years. In 1949 a development period of ten years was added, which further lightened the burden of repayment.

However, in the course of these years, notably at the time of the building of the Hoover and Grand Coulee dams, the generation of electric power became a very important element in reclamation projects. This offered a new and very productive means of contributing to the payment of large projects. Moreover, those who wanted to lighten the costs to irrigationists found other means to share costs. This was recognized in a notable Act in 1939, which provided for the allocation of costs among various purposes for which projects might be used. Included among reimbursable purposes were not only irrigation, but power, municipal water supplies, and a number of other items. There were also included non-reimbursable purposes such as navigation and flood control.

This, of course, greatly increased the so-called "feasibility" of projects whose cost was mounting very rapidly.

Moreover, in a number of specific projects Congress, with the eager collaboration of the Bureau of Reclamation, had inserted in the law further extension of time for repayment, from fifty to sixty-eight years. In the Central Arizona Project now before Congress, the time for repayment has been lengthened to seventy-five years. The general policy of repayment, however, remains the financial framework of Federal reclamation work.

Throughout, the principle has been followed that repayment for irrigation shall be for cost without interest.

At the time of the 1902 Act, it was planned that a considerable part of the money for projects should be derived from the sale of public lands. These revenues went into a Treasury account known as the Reclamation Fund. Later, this fund was augmented by a part of the proceeds of oil and other mineral royalties. There has also been a generous series of loans to this fund from the General Fund of the Treasury.

In recent years, notably in the past decade, projects both for irrigation and for power have offered smaller and smaller prospects for repayment. Costs have risen to an immense degree, sites with firm supplies of power-producing water are less and less promising, and land for irrigation offers less and less prospect for profitable production. Hence, the Bureau of Reclamation, anxious to enlarge its activities and its authority, and communities eager for Federal expenditures have sought more and more ingenious means to justify new projects. Elaborate calculations of project values and justifications have been portrayed, such as benefits to wild life, revenues from people seeking recreation, benefits to navigation and flood control, and the opening of new sources of taxation. Most of these when carefully examined reveal a plentiful amount of wishful thinking as well as some dubious bookkeeping craft. Slowly the policy of reclamation has

133

shifted into wholesale subsidies at the expense of the generality of taxpayers.

The most notable of these exercises in bookkeeping, as well as the one that, if not checked, will ultimately be a grave national problem, is an effort of the Department of the Interior to use in new multipurpose reclamation projects an item known as the "interest component" as part of the subsidy provided out of power revenues. As the Federal law now stands, the selling price of electricity from government projects must be enough to cover several "components." These are charges for amortization of the principal invested, for interest on this investment, for operation and maintenance, and for replacement. On Bureau of Reclamation projects the rate charged for power must include these "components" plus such an amount as is necessary to help put water on the land for irrigation. This is a subsidy paid out of power revenues. The "interest component" is fixed at three per cent on the power investment. The intent of Congress was that this three per cent should be returned to the Treasury to pay interest on the money borrowed for the project.

By 1944 it was found that all the devices mentioned above to make projects feasible in the face of mounting costs were inadequate. Hence, in that year the Solicitor of the Interior Department rendered a strange opinion, which is now regarded as law by the Bureau of Reclamation although it has had so such recognition by Congress. This was permission to put this "interest component" into the Reclamation Fund as part of the subsidy to irrigation. Legislation has not been passed to authorize this interpretation by the Solicitor of the Interior Department. Efforts of members of Congress to restate the original intent of Congress have been introduced, but because of the violent opposition of the Interior Department these have failed of enactment. That is where the subject now stands.

The trick in this is that the Treasury and the taxpayers of

the nation will, during the period of repayment, be compelled to meet the interest charge on the investment in projects from sources other than the power income from projects. And this charge will be compounded. Unless this practice is prevented by legislation or by some opinion overruling that of the Solicitor of the Interior Department, billions of dollars will go into the Reclamation Fund, and interest charges will fall on the taxpayers. Meanwhile, vast sums will be spent in subsidies for projects that have no chance of paying for themselves.

Another bookkeeping device, closely related to this use of the "interest component," that the Bureau of Reclamation has been zealously advocating is what is known as basin accounts. A basin account would involve the pooling of revenues from all projects in a great river basin, such as the valleys of the Columbia and its tributaries. This pool or account would be a source from which money could be appropriated for all sorts of projects, including irrigation works. Such accounts would have two functions. The first would be to enable the government to sell power at a standard rate all over the area, regardless of the varying costs of power from the several projects involved. Power produced at high cost from plant A would be pooled with power produced from low-cost B, and an average price established. The second function of such an account would be to provide subsidies for irrigation projects that develop no power or are wholly unfeasible from an economic point of view.

The result of the establishment of basin accounts would be to blur the situation over a great area, to make it difficult for the public, and indeed for Congress, to determine the economic value of projects, and to permit a wholesale subsidization of agriculture in all the irrigation activities involved. It would also add great power and authority to the Bureau of Reclamation. With more and more users of water and of electric power living in whole or in part on subsidies,

135

it is easy to see what would happen to personal liberty and to local self-government in such an area.

If a specific need for the production of a certain type of food or fiber can be demonstrated, and a specific area presents the best possible place to produce that necessity, the issue of a subsidy for a specific irrigation project should be squarely faced by Congress. The proliferation of miscellaneous and hidden subsidies is a certain means of establishing many privileged groups who would be living off the earnings of many others. Moreover, the political dangers of such government subsidies are quite obvious.

GOVERNMENT AID TO CO-OPERATIVES

The beginnings of the co-operative movement in this country can be traced back to European origins. It has been said that the shape and methods of the movement came from the so-called Rochdale enterprise in England, more than a century ago. The Scandinavian countries offer many prototypes.

The idea is so simple that it would certainly have developed among any people seeking cheaper and more effective methods, first of marketing products and next of purchasing their requirements as consumers.

A sizable part of our economy is now occupied by co-operatives of various kinds and the trend is growing.

The more important co-operatives in this country fall into seven categories: farmers' marketing co-operatives; farmer's purchasing co-operatives; city consumer co-operatives; city producer co-operatives; service co-operatives; dealer-owned co-operatives; and super-co-operatives at the wholesale and manufacturing levels.[5] There are, in fact, co-operatives the members of which are not individuals at all, but privately owned corporations.

[5] I am not concerned here with mutual insurance companies.

136

The fields in which co-operatives have reached their greatest importance are agriculture, dairying, fruit growing, and oil producing and refining.

The great growth of co-operatives in the consumer field in various European countries has not been paralleled here, largely because under private business we have developed economies in distribution and sales through mail-order houses, chain stores, and manufacturers selling to a national market.

Government reports in 1947 said that there were in this country 32,246 co-operative organizations, with 20,971,934 members. Business volume in 1945 was $7,182,185,001. Co-operative associations handle very big businesses in many diversified lines. The greatest sugar refinery in the world is co-operatively owned. Dairying co-operatives handle 75 per cent of the milk sold in the United States. Other co-operatives market 55 per cent of the citrus fruits, 40 per cent of the butter; 20 per cent of the livestock, and 10 per cent of canned fruits and vegetables. Co-operatives manufacture and sell an almost limitless range of articles. There are also the credit co-operatives, including the many varieties of farm co-operatives planned with government aid, and the rural electric co-operatives.

The immense growth of co-operatives in the past three decades has unquestionably been principally due to the exemptions and privileges accorded them by the government. They have been specifically exempted from the anti-trust laws and the regulations under the Securities Exchange Commission, and have preferential treatment under such government enterprises as the Tennessee Valley Authority. New bills providing for other valley authorities specifically name co-operatives for preference in purchasing power properties.

But the most important privilege that co-operatives enjoy is in taxation. These exemptions have caused violent controversy, stimulated by private businesses that have been placed at a serious competitive disadvantage.

The enthusiastic support of these present and prospective privileges by the more socialistic elements in our government points to a problem that goes to the foundations of a free economy. More ardent proponents are frank to say that the co-operative movement is destined to supplant the whole capitalistic system of profit and loss. It has been hailed by the American Socialist Party as a genuine means of achieving its objective of an economy based upon common ownership of the means of production and distribution. This extreme view, however, is not accepted by the more moderate leaders in the co-operative movement itself.

There is nowhere any disposition to destroy co-operatives as such. They have performed a valuable service in the lives of many millions of people, and, with a fair balance of advantages with private business, they can be a part of a free economy.

The essential danger is that co-operatives will depend upon an ever growing government for competitive privilege, and for what really amounts to a subsidy from the taxpayer.

The unfairness toward and the danger to private enterprise is especially notable when co-operatives move into fields only remotely related to the original purpose for which they were created. No reasonable person can quarrel with the propriety or fairness of a group of dairymen pooling their individual businesses in the marketing of their product, even to the extent of owning and operating a large fleet of trucks for that purpose. If, however, such a co-operative establishes a manufacturing enterprise for the purpose of selling trucks to all sorts of businesses, and thus moves into competition with manufacturers in that same business who enjoy none of the exemptions of the co-operative, a wholly new problem of competition is involved. Such a business should then be placed on the same legal footing as its competitors. And in every case the public should be protected against monopoly.

Intervention by Regulation

ADMINISTRATIVE ABSOLUTISM

In the past sixty-odd years there has grown up, especially in the Federal government, what President Franklin D. Roosevelt once called a " 'fourth branch' of government for which there is no sanction in the Constitution." He was referring to the mass of administrative commissions and boards created to regulate this or that and to deal with private interests without consideration for those judicial forms and protections which are the essence of liberty.

As long ago as 1937, President Roosevelt's Committee on Administrative Management had this to say of this conglomerate mass of regulatory agencies:

Commissions . . . are in reality miniature independent governments set up to deal with the railroad problem, the banking problem, or the radio problem. They constitute a headless "fourth branch" of the Government, a haphazard deposit of irresponsible agencies and uncoordinate powers. . . . There is a conflict of principle involved in their make-up and functions. . . . They are vested with duties of administration . . . and at the same time they are given important judicial work. . . . The evils resulting from this confusion of principles are insidious and far-reaching. . . . pressures and influences properly enough directed toward officers responsible for formulating and administering policy constitute an unwholesome atmosphere in which to adjudicate private rights. But the mixed duties of the commissions render escape from these subversive influences impossible. Furthermore, the same men are obliged to serve both as prosecutors and as judges. This not only undermines judicial fairness; it weakens public confidence in that fairness. Commission decisions affecting private rights and conduct lie under the suspicion of being rationalizations of the preliminary findings which the Commission, in the role of prosecutor, presented to itself.

The major dangers in these commissions were that they not only gathered evidence but presented it and then judged it; that there was little opportunity for judicial review of their decisions; and that there was, until 1946, no real Congressional determination of what constitutes fair standards of procedure.

The defense of administrative absolutism is based, according to Roscoe Pound, the great former dean of the Harvard Law School, upon "ideas of public law imported from Continental Europe," which, of course, are the expression of vast state power.

The danger in this irresponsibility of bureaucrats was thus described by Woodrow Wilson forty-two years ago:

I can see no radical difference in principle between government ownership and government regulation of this discretionary kind.

Regulation by commission is not regulation by law, but control according to the discretion of government officials. Regulation by law is judicial, by fixed and definite rules, whereas regulation by commission is an affair of business sense of the comprehension and thorough understanding of complex and various bodies of business. There is no logical stopping place between that and the actual conduct of business enterprise by the Government.

After years of effort, the American Bar Association secured the passage of the so-called Logan-Walter bill, which was designed to correct the evils of these commissions. It was vetoed by President Roosevelt. Finally, in 1946, an act was passed defining and limiting the powers of administrative tribunals. It remains to be seen how fully the Federal courts will give this act the interpretation it should have.

A sinister tendency that has been gaining ground in government agencies has been to step beyond the limits of regulation and to usurp the power to dictate business policies and judgments. A good example of this trend is found in the history of the Interstate Commerce Commission, a senior and highly regarded member of our group of Federal regulators.

The fundamental role of the ICC was originally judicial and legislative—judicial in its authority to determine the respective rights of carriers and of shippers; legislative in its delegated power to protect the public in interstate commerce. But for a long time the ICC has tended to enforce its own judgment upon railroads, in what essentially are matters for the railroads themselves to decide.

The lawful province of the ICC is to see that rates are "just and reasonable." But the commission hastened to interpret this authority as extending to guessing—and that is the proper word—"the probable effect of increases . . . upon the future movement of traffic." Note the distinction here. The determination of "just and reasonable" rates should rest upon current rates, earnings, and valuations. The exercise of business judgment about the future belongs, in a free economy, to management.

The judge thus doffs his robe and dons the prophet's mystic garb. Crystal balls are added to the statistical paraphernalia of the commission.

It deserves to be noted further that many faults of the railroads which have hampered their competitive development have been indirectly the result of too much and too detailed supervision by the ICC. The deadening effect of such control, however sympathetic it may be, is like that which appears when a child has been too closely cared for and regulated by an oversolicitous parent. The effect upon the railroads has been a plentiful measure of bureaucracy and red tape in the railroads themselves. Stagnation is the inevitable product of too much guidance.

141

FEDERAL CONTROL OVER INDUSTRIAL RELATIONS

Labor unions are a proper and inevitable part of a free economy. Union organization enables the individual to bargain for his services on equal terms with aggregations of stockholders and management.

In the past few years unions have gone far beyond this. With the hearty encouragement of Presidents Roosevelt and Truman, they have entered into close alliances with one party. Thus they limit their freedom and that of their members. Their funds have been lavishly used for and by that party. Such identification with a party will either result in the creation of a labor party—which would mean a party dedicated to the interests of a single group—or the subordination of labor to the party machine. In either case, labor's liberty is curtailed and in the long run destroyed.

Still more dangerous to the liberty of labor is the extent to which, under the Wagner Act of 1935, the traditional functions of free labor to organize and to bargain were taken over by government. This was a dangerous extension of Federal power over not only labor but all industry.

Socialism is the deadly enemy of free labor and free unionism. That has been shown in every European country which has embraced national socialism or Communism. The British Labour Party, originally conceived to be the means for labor's emancipation, has now become a means for the gradual absorption of labor's liberty into a supergovernment. The legal provisions by which this subjugation has been made possible should carry a sound lesson for American labor.

The identification of unions with one party and with the political administration in control of government is not only a threat to labor's liberty but it perverts the nature and functions of government itself, in a manner inimical to the interests of the nation as a whole. In this situation government is no longer regarded as the agency of all interests, above and detached from specific groups. The impartiality of a common government is the essence of a free state.

ANTITRUST CONFUSION

Nobody favors monopoly in anything, even in goodness or in good intentions. Private as well as governmental monopoly is the deadly enemy of a free economy. The common law has from time immemorial prohibited monopoly and any custom, procedure, or practice fostering monopoly. The states have by statute outlawed monopoly, and in 1890 the Sherman Act applied the old common law against monopoly or "restraint of trade" in the Federal jurisdiction. The Clayton Act of 1914 broadened and clarified the Sherman Act and exempted labor unions from its application.

But despite the clear intention of the law, its application has been the subject of utter confusion. For sixty years there has been no clear definition of the nature of those trade practices or that degree of the possession of the market which might constitute monopoly. The Sherman law and its amendments are so vague and confusing that compliance and prosecution have been hit or miss. The real purpose of the law, the maintenance of free competition, is not mentioned in the act. Under court definition, it is even unlawful for competitors to agree among themselves upon a code of fair practices intended to protect and preserve competition.

To clear up the confusion and to provide an administrative means of policing and warning business, the Federal Trade Commission was established in 1914. The purpose of this agency was excellent, but its labors have resulted in even greater confusion. Over the years it has issued orders declaring more than 2,200 business practices to be illegal. The result is that almost every business is at all times violating one or more of these, whether it knows it or not, and stands in danger of prosecution.

143

Other acts have been passed that further complicate the problems of a business that tries to comply with the law. A business that, following the intent of the Sherman Act, cuts prices to undersell a competitor may be subject to prosecution under the Robinson-Patman Act. But if, in compliance with the Robinson-Patman Act, it keeps its price level with its competitor, it may fall afoul of the Sherman Act.

A group of companies might be told by, say, the Secretary of the Interior to co-operate in some activity for purposes of meeting an emergency, and later find the Attorney General prosecuting them for "conspiracy." This actually happened in a very important case involving a number of oil companies.

Attempting to stumble out of the confusion, the Department of Justice has devised the strange plan of the "consent decree." This plan is really an effort to fix with certainty what a company can or cannot do and to have a court approve the result. Under it, a suit is brought against a company or a group of companies in an industry, thus presenting the issue to a court. Then with the consent of the defendants the court approves a set of specifications with respect to what defendants will or will not do in the business issue involved. This in substance requires a defendant to plead guilty when he thinks he is innocent. It is an illogical, ineffective method of law enforcement.

The dangers of the reigning confusion in the administration of the antitrust laws are threefold:

First, legitimate business can have no clear idea of the practices it may use in legitimate competition.

Second, the power of government to prosecute can be used for what really amounts to official blackmail. Government powers of prosecution are so broad and vaguely defined that zealous "reformers" can use them to compel private business to conform to arbitrary and even fantastic ideas of business conduct.

Third, the vagueness that shrouds a definition of "good"

144

or "bad" business provides a perfect weapon for demagogic attacks on all private business.

THE ATTACK ON BIGNESS

For three quarters of a century the more extreme attacks on private business have concentrated on big business units. Over all those years they have provided excellent political ammunition. The antagonism of the consuming public can be aroused because of the seemingly great profits made by large companies. The sympathy of small competitors is enlisted. And the relatively few votes involved in overhead management are politically expendable.

To be sure, during a large part of this period bigness could properly be associated with notoriously unfair competitive practices. There was, in fact, a "trust" problem, for which the remedy was and is the enforcement of fair practices and the prosecution of monopoly.

The late Louis D. Brandeis has been cited by some current reformers as authority for the proposition that all business bigness is bad, and there is some proof of this belief in the title of a collection of his papers, *The Curse of Bigness*.[6] There is, however, no justification of the title in the text of the book. His complaint was against monopoly and unfair practices, not against bigness as such. He asserted that a business may be too small or too large to be efficient. He was too much a statesman and too much a believer in free enterprise to assert that it was a proper function of government to attempt to enforce efficiency. In at least one of his dissenting opinions he recognized that the public, through its legislature, might place a handicap upon a big business in behalf of small units. But in general his views have been distorted by those who would lay the heavy hand of government upon bigness itself.

[6] (New York: The Viking Press; 1934).

An effort by government to apply a Procrustean measure to business size would introduce drastic regimentation. Government would have to cut down big companies in line with some arbitrary scale and build up small ones with various sorts of aid. Government would thus forcibly redesign industry.

To this end, we already have Federal policies directed toward subsidizing small businesses with loans below the interest rate of the free market. Government's judgment of the business prospects of small enterprises is substituted for the judgment of private moneylenders. "Competition" is subsidized by help of various sorts to favored businesses and companies. Most important, since 1936 there has been in corporation taxes a progressive principle that penalizes large businesses.

Thus, efficient businesses—little and big—are taxed to support government-favored businesses. This is an authentic process of leveling. And meanwhile, prejudice against big companies is constantly built up by the demagogic utterances of sponsors of supergovernment.

An excellent weapon in the hands of such sponsors has been a recent dissenting opinion of a minority of the Supreme Court, which proclaimed this strange doctrine: "Size in steel is the measure of the power of a handful of men over the economy. That power can be benign or it can be dangerous. The philosophy of the Sherman Act is that it should not exist."

It should be noted that if two more judges had agreed with this interpretation it would be the law of the land.

This doctrine comes down to saying that whatever the behavior of large companies may be, their possession of the possibility of monopolistic power should be considered a substantial violation of the Sherman Act. They would thus be liable for the potential power to do wrong, despite the lack of evidence of any act of wrongdoing.

146

It would be like arresting a man at a red light because, though he stopped, he could have driven his car through.

Expropriation

TAXATION AS AN AGENT OF POWER

The second of the means specified by Marx and Engels in the *Communist Manifesto* to bring about a socialist society was the use of taxation on incomes and inheritances. In the 1880's Professor Adolf Wagner, noted socialist writer on taxation, outlined in detail how the state could be transformed by taxation. His formula was to disregard the principle of taxation for revenue and to fix rates for the purpose of effecting a redistribution of income and wealth. European socialists have generally advocated heavy taxation rather than direct expropriation. The result, of course, is the same.

The British socialists were unable to raise tax rates much higher after they came into power after the war because the burden of taxation, at a rate of approximately 40 per cent of the national income, was at the point of diminshing returns. But they substantially kept taxes at the wartime levels, and then used the money for benefits, subsidies, and socialist reform. This has had the effect of strifling private investment and plant renewal, paving the way to nationalization. And it has compelled persons and businesses whose incomes were practically eliminated to use their capital for subsistence.

Nothing in our Constitution prevents such expropriation under the power to tax incomes and inheritances. Thus, the jealous regard for the rights of property in some of the provisions of the Constitution is nullified by the simple terms of the Sixteenth Amendment. And it is ironic that this Amendment was initiated and finally enacted through the efforts of old-fashioned liberals.

147

Of course, it was assumed that this great power could safely be vested in Congress. That, however, was not the assumption of the framers of the Constitution, who wisely sought to check all government, including Congress. Nor was it the assumption of John Marshall, who wrote the classic warning that "the power to tax involves the power to destroy."

We have learned the folly of our trust. Inch by inch, Federal taxation has invaded not only private property, but those tax sources which are the life blood of state and local government. It was a notorious fact that an objective of the prewar New Deal was the limitation of all incomes to $25,000 a year. Harry Hopkins was in the habit of frightening his opulent friends by telling them that the intention of the New Deal was to limit them to $17,500. How he arrived at this figure is not clear. It is clear, however, that the limit of $25,000 was earlier specified in the platform of the Communist Party. In 1942 a $25,000 limitation was actually established by Executive Order. Later it was repealed.[7]

For a long time, the Federal income tax was essentially a

[7] The Communist Party platform for 1928, as published in the *Daily Worker* for May 26th of that year, contained, under Tariff and Taxation, the following plank: "Graduated income tax, starting with incomes above $5,000 a year, and increasing gradually, so that all incomes over $25,000 per year are confiscated."

Following the adoption of the Price Control Act of 1942, President Roosevelt said in a message to Congress in April: "I therefore believe that in time of this grave national danger, when all excess income should go to win the war, no American citizen ought to have a net income, after he has paid his taxes, of more than $25,000 a year." The next day this statement was substantially repeated in an address to the nation. On that day the *New York Times* attributed the inspiration of this statement to the U.A.W.-C.I.O. After the passage of the amendments to the Price Control Act in October, 1942, the President issued an Executive Order containing the following provision:

"7. In order to correct gross inequities and to provide for greater equality in contributing to the war effort, the Director [Economic Stabilization Director] is authorized to take the necessary action and to issue the appropriate regulations, so that insofar as practicable, no salary shall be authorized under title III, section 4, to the extent that it exceeds $25,000 after the payment of taxes allocable to the sum in excess of $25,000. . . ."

In April 1943, Congress in Public Law 34 invalidated this provision in the President's Executive Order.

148

class tax. Large segments of the population were exempt, notably those farmers who themselves produced much of their own subsistence, and millions of small-income earners. And the tax has always been stiffly graduated so that the rich would bear the costs of the government.

The great danger to free institutions comes from the use of the taxing power to achieve purposes other than the collection of revenue; to curb, regulate, or destroy. More recently, this has been called the use of the taxing power for "social objectives."

There is now no restraint upon this power, nor is there any effective constitutional safeguard against its misuse. Legislative use of this power usually produces the hypocritical assertion that the purpose is "revenue," and the Supreme Court, tongue in cheek, blandly accepts this excuse.[8]

Professor Harley L. Lutz, in his book *Public Finance*,[9] offers the following objections to this use of the taxing power:

1. It violates the true conception and purpose of taxation, which is to gather revenue, and in using this indirect means of regulation and reconstructing social and economic life, proceeds largely by guesswork.

2. The questions of benefits and ability, so essential to real taxation, are impossible to answer when the purpose is regulation and discrimination.

3. The administration of such taxes creates very complex problems requiring the building up of enormous bureaucratic machinery.

4. When this form of taxation is used to regulate the character of industry, there appears the same incompetence of government that characterizes all socialistic planning.

An excellent example of this misuse of taxing power is the

---

[8] A very interesting example of the application of this dangerous principle was inserted in the Guffey-Vinson Coal Act, which was enacted after the invalidation of the Guffey Act by the old Supreme Court. The new Act was upheld in 1940.

[9] (New York: D. Appleton-Century; 1936).

149

tax on undistributed profits, once formally adopted at the insistence of President F. D. Roosevelt and later repealed. It still exists, however, for use by the Treasury in the famous Section 102 of the Revenue Code. This tax forces upon corporations the business judgment of the Treasury in the maintenance of reserves against emergencies. Another example, already noted, is the tax exemption of many co-operatives. Another would be the application of the progressive principle to corporation taxes, with the intent to penalize bigness.

Taxation for purposes other than raising revenue weakens the real capacity of government to collect necessary revenue. It destroys the essential sources of government income, represses initiative, prevents the creation and growth of new businesses, and weakens the whole economy. It creates for a time the intoxicating atmosphere of getting something for nothing, but ends in a lower standard of living for all. And it fosters the growth of a collectivist society.

DEFICIT FINANCING

Deficit financing has been endured, then pitied, then embraced. Until the end of the First World War, the Western nations generally regarded a budget deficit as a disease to be avoided, and if caught to be cured as soon as possible. In the early days of the German inflation, however, it was accepted as an evil less serious than unemployment. Even Lloyd George in 1922 suggested that, despite the traditional soundness of England's fiscal policies and despite the clear evidence that inflation impoverished the great middle classes, the avoidance of unemployment was paramount. But now we know that the German inflation was no cure for unemployment, that it ultimately whetted the appetite of people for easy salvation through the state, and that ultimately the Germans sold their liberty for national socialism and jobs.

Two distinguished visitors who saw Germany in 1920 when it was under the spell of this delusion came away infected and built elaborate rationalizations for deficit spending in other countries. These were Professor Irving Fisher of Yale and John Maynard Keynes. Fisher later came to be well known in America as the advocate of a flexible dollar and in early New Deal days was busy in Washington peddling his wares to members of the Administration—notably to President Roosevelt.

It was Keynes, however, who became the prophet of the new economics. His theory of compensatory spending won great authority. He also sold his ideas to President Roosevelt. Since then others, like Alvin Hansen of Harvard, have developed extensions of Keynesianism with new and seductive elaborations and terminology.

Deficits in the Federal government are, of course, met by borrowing. Some money is borrowed directly from the "public," that is, from individuals who buy bonds and put them away. This method merely takes money from the savings of individuals, who then cannot use it for spending. The government spends it, however, and the effect of inflation upon the whole process depends largely upon what this money is spent for. If it goes into things that are not in short supply, it has little inflationary effect. If not, it becomes just as great an inflationary force as if the individuals themselves had spent it.

But the government borrows most of its money from the banks. It brings to the bank, not assets, such as an individual does when he borrows, but its bonds or IOU's. The bank puts these away and books them as assets. The bank then puts the amount of the "loan" down as a government deposit and the government draws checks against it and spends the money. This new money is added to the nation's existing supply, and from present indications it will not be withdrawn from circulation for many years—perhaps never. The effect is inflationary, for it means more outstanding money against the same supply of goods.

Deficit spending is not only a direct creator of inflationary evils, but it has a profound bearing upon the vital safety of popular government. The Federal Administration of the 1930's, inspired by the sophistries of the "new" economists, used the resources of public credit with little restraint by Congress. The Federal debt almost trebled in those peacetime years. It is reasonable to believe that many of the experiments in which government indulged in those years would not have been attempted or endured if they had had to be financed by taxation. That was, to a degree, a surrender of self-government. More than sixty years ago, a great American economist, Henry Carter Adams, in his *Public Debts* offered the following warning on this point:

As self-government was secured through a struggle for mastery over the public purse, so must it be maintained through the exercise by the people of complete control over public expenditure. . . . Any method of procedure, therefore, by which a public servant can veil the true meaning of his acts, or which allows the government to enter upon any great enterprise without bringing the fact fairly to the knowledge of the public, must work against the realization of the constitutional idea. This is exactly the state of affairs introduced by a free use of public credit.

Even more serious than the impairment of responsible government is the plain question of integrity—perhaps we might say collective integrity.

There is a great difference between a government bond and an obligation issued by a private corporation. The latter has a definable and measurable material value behind it. The buyer pays his money and accepts the certificate. He acquires a legal right to take property if repayment is not made according to the terms of the obligation.

A government's bond, on the other hand, is not backed by owned property. Governments produce no wealth. They hold the wealth of certain kinds in trust, and they have the power to seize wealth through taxation. Their promise to pay in a bond can only be fulfilled by the taking of wealth from those who have it. The purchaser of a bond cannot even depend upon the known integrity of those who at the moment possess the power of government. He must trust that those who will possess that power in the future will have the honesty to pay. And if the purchaser looks back over the centuries he must know that he is taking a very serious risk. For history provides ample evidence of the lack of integrity of governments. By repudiation of debts, by induced inflation, and by various sorts of conversion, governments have traditionally escaped the payment of their obligations.

Moreover, in selling bonds to get the money for some current expenditure, governments are promising to compel someone in the future to part with his property to pay for something that he has not enjoyed. Deficit financing pledges the future for the benefit of the present.

All sorts of specious arguments are advanced by extravagant governments to justify deficit financing. One of the most fraudulent is that "government debts are harmless; we owe the money to ourselves." But actually, a government pledge is not between vague collective entities like "ourselves" and "themselves." It is between the government, acting for all the people, and a specific person who has parted with his money. Moreover, it is not even a pledge between people now living. It is a pledge to people now living that other people will pay in the future. If "we owe it to ourselves," we shall sometime have to "collect from ourselves," and that will be very painful.

In the complex fabric of modern finance, our Federal government achieves a large part of its deficit financing by forcing the banks to take the obligations and to pay for them in depositors' money. In this process another fraud is perpetrated, in the form of manufactured money, which, as I have pointed out, induces the further expropriation of values by inflation.

THE BLIGHT OF INFLATION

It is hardly necessary to discuss here the causes, nature, and effects of inflation. The people of this country have had a postgraduate course in that branch of economics for two decades.

There still prevails, however, a tendency to mistake symptoms for causes. The most common symptom of inflation is the rapid and erratic rise of prices. In its first phase, the supply of money is increasing and passing from hand to hand faster than the supply of goods and services available for purchase. In many political movements in the past, such as "free silver" and "greenbackism," the remedy for all economic ills was said to be an increase in the supply of money.

But inflation is largely due to psychological rather than economic causes. Fear of the scarcity of certain goods and services appears, and there is a scramble for those goods and services. That is the second phase of inflation.

The third phase—and the deadly one—appears when there is a widespread fear of the purchasing power of money. People then indulge in a generalized rush to spend money for goods. This is called the flight from money.

The second phase is marked by a fear of scarcity of goods; the third, by fear over the value of money.

There are of course very great perils in the first and second phases, which the United States has endured for many years, notably since the end of the Second World War. The policies of our Federal government since the early 1930's have generally been directed toward the stimulation of inflation. Deficit financing, low managed-interest rates, the stimulation of

154

drives for higher wages in certain favored lines dominated by powerful unions, and higher and higher food prices have all contributed. Since from 80 to 85 per cent of the cost of living ultimately depends on labor costs, a policy that favors an automatic increase in wages based upon an increase in living costs assures ever increasing prices. At times, government has caused a rush by irresponsible predictions of scarcities. Many restrictive controls and tax measures adopted in the Roosevelt Administration were inherently inflationary. For example, the check upon short selling greatly reduces the corrective influence of a downward pressure in the stock market during an inflation. Higher capital-gains taxes are inflationary. People are more reluctant to sell during an inflation, and thus there is removed a downward pressure on prices.

The plain fact is that generally in the Roosevelt and throughout the Truman Administration there has been deliberately planned and stimulated inflation. War actualities and fears have provided ample means for this purpose.

The objective of this drive has been inherent in political strategy. It is to provide greater and greater scope for the expansion of spending and bureaucracy, while promoting the enrichment of some at the expense of others—always because there are more voters among the "some" than among the "others."

It is already apparent that even if the great spending for war materials and mobilization had not reached its present stage, the present Federal Administration was determined upon inflation as a means of paying for its program of statism. President Truman, speaking in Pittsburgh in September 1949, made this announcement:

The selfish interests [a phrase repeated 22 times in the speech] say we can't afford these programs during a boom because that would be inflationary. They say we can't afford them during a recession because that would be deflationary. They say we can't afford them during a war because we are too busy with defense, and

155

we can't afford them in time of peace because that would discourage business. So according to the selfish interests, we never can afford them. But the truth is—we can't afford *not* to put these programs into effect. We can afford them, we ought to have them, and we will have them.

Dr. Edwin G. Nourse, the President's top economic adviser, after a long struggle for his principles, accepted this speech as his repudiation and shortly after resigned his office.

The President's budget proposals in 1951 lend additional evidence that inflation is a settled policy. Expenditures for the full welfare program and other nonmilitary purposes were recommended. The proposal for new taxes to avoid a deficit was a political maneuver, because the President must have had small reason to expect Congress to raise taxes as much as he requested.

The Administration screens the dire reality of inflation with what Jules Abels calls "Couéism" or "the virus of euphoria," in which a number of techniques are used: [1]

"The hortatory technique," which gives glowing pictures of ever widening, dynamic progress; "the prod or gadfly technique," which consists of telling people that they had better go along or be ruined; "the underwriting technique," by which government offers guarantees to business against loss; "the social welfare technique," in which people are reconciled to loss of savings by promises of pensions and other forms of assistance; "the mass purchasing power technique," by which it is said that, with more and more spending, everybody will have more to spend.

It may be added that in thus inducing people to believe that the mad progress of inflation may be good for them, the forces of statism postpone for a long time public realization of the ultimate reckoning.

[1] These are listed by Abels in *The Welfare State* (New York: Duell, Sloan and Pearce; 1951), pp. 70-2.

156

CHAPTER VI

The Reckoning

The Material Costs

WELFARE, UNLIMITED

The famous dictum of Jeremy Bentham that the objective of human effort should be "the greatest good of the greatest number" has been used as a screen for the most egregious errors and deceptions. In generations of politics it has been used to suggest that the greatest number can profit only by expropriation, at the expense of a smaller number. It is not only difficult, if not impossible, to determine what "good" is and to identify those who make up the "greatest number," but Bentham's dictum rules out the true concern of the state, which is the sum of all.

The good of a greater number sometimes may best be preserved by protecting the good of a smaller number. The philosophy of the early New Deal constantly stressed the indivisibility of interests. Roosevelt likened the nation's economic system to a "seamless web," a phrase borrowed from Pollock and Maitland's great *History of English Law*.

The early New Deal, still clinging to the concept of an economic "seamless web," recognized that some individuals and some minorities must be protected from the "vicissitudes" of life. This protection would be a distributed burden and would not impair the operation of a free economy.

The later New Deal and the Fair Deal have energetically torn the "seamless web" by singling out some interests for favor and others for disfavor. Occasionally, special favors for special welfares are justified by the claim that these welfares are essential to the whole, the general welfare. Secretary of Agriculture Charles F. Brannan prefaces his disquisitions on his plan by arguing that the prosperity of agriculture is an essential factor in general prosperity. This postulate is correct, but he fails to show how an indeterminate monetary benefit to one group can indefinitely promote the general economic welfare.

The progressive increase of favors became a means of perpetuating political power. Agricultural benefits would, under the Brannan Plan, be moved upward beyond the old parity formula and be based upon an entirely new calculation. The early New Deal first encouraged private housing enterprises by mortgage guarantees. Then government undertook mass housing projects for people with very low incomes. Ultimately, there emerged the idea of building for "middle-income" people.

Finally the state-of-many-welfares becomes a mechanism for taking from those too weak to resist and giving to those strong enough to control. The masters of such a state speak only in promises and only of material benefits. They neglect national unity, mutual forbearance, and common patriotism. Instead of promoting the general welfare, they promote alliances of powerful groups, in endless conflict with other groups. The state becomes a vending machine where votes are inserted and money pours out.

The pursuit of welfare finally ends in the progressive increase of benefits, with no end in sight as long as political office can be held.

HOW MUCH SOCIALISM CAN WE AFFORD?

The British economist, Professor A. C. Pigou, in his *Economics of Welfare* speaks of the "national dividend," which is to be nicely divided among outright provisions for welfare grants, for the sums necessary for the rehabilitation and expansion of the productive plant, for national defense, and for the maintenance of the bureaucracy.

American politicians and reformers assume that the productive forces of the nation will accommodate themselves to the progressive strain imposed upon them, and therefore little or no limit is placed on plans for increasing the load. In recent years they have expanded their plans by appropriation of larger and larger parts of the "national dividend" for economic and military aid to foreign nations. These expenditures have already reached an enormous total, and the end is not in sight. The purposes vary from support of foreign currencies to undefined indeterminate enterprises in developing the resources of backward areas—President Truman's Point Four.

The arguments in support of huge governmental expenditures for multitudinous purposes assume that the sources of real wealth can be indeterminately expanded. Figures are used that have only shadowy meaning because of the progressive deterioration of the value of the dollar.

The possibility of the expansion of our real wealth is outside the realm of theory or good intentions. The most reliable measure of our national increase of wealth is national productivity. Between 1899 and 1939 our increase in real productivity averaged 2 per cent a year per man-hour. Since 1939, the average rate has been 2½ to 3 per cent. There can be no miracles in this increase in the national product. It must always depend on the slow development of natural resources, the rate of inventive and scientific progress, the supply of manpower, the capacity of management, the capital available for plant renewal and enlargement, and other factors.

Productivity is also affected to an important degree by psychological elements—optimism, daring, and the hope of profit and prestige. These are sheared away by state paternalism.

The relative values of these psychological elements, however, are subject to wide differences of opinion. In the political interpretation of human impulses, speculation and wishful thinking enjoy their greatest latitude. The statist places a high economic value on the assurances of personal security. In freedom from "want," he says, there is an elevation of spirit that moves mountains. He assumes that material security makes free men, and that men thus "free" will labor diligently for the sheer love of labor.

But, he promises, there will also be freedom from labor and much more leisure for the amenities and for cultural pursuits. The magical machinery provided by state research will minimize the part that human action takes in production. Mrs. Roosevelt once commended the quaint views of a theorist who anticipated a life in which labor occupied only the years between the early twenties and the early thirties. During the rest of life, the packages of maintenance would be delivered to the door.

Productivity, which is the source of national wealth, depends upon human effort. Leisure, a late beginning of life's work, and an early retirement reduce productivity. The pensioner's quest is toward pushing the age of retirement down to 62, then to 60, and even lower. Quite obviously, more and more would be living off the efforts of fewer and fewer, unless, as Mrs. Roosevelt's theorist contends, a man or woman can create a life's nest egg in a few years after maturity.

But in seeking security for some the government impairs the security of many more. Savings, whether privately acquired or gathered and "kept" by the government, are declining in real value because of the very policies that exalt the theory of personal security. We have seized the capital of the past and have denied future security to those who have put aside funds to assure it.

In determining how much socialism we can afford, we must realize that we are not dealing with fixed and unchanging forms and boundaries. The statist trend gathers momentum from the very forces that it generates.

The socialist creed holds that "each should receive according to his need and each should give according to his ability." Neither ability nor need are static factors, to be measured with mathematical finality. "Needs" grow to "wants," and "ability" must be measured against a progressive disinclination to give. Without incentives, "ability" declines and dies.

PROBABLE COSTS

In the years since 1945, the Federal Administration has proclaimed in bold terms its plans for the welfare state. This has stirred the minds of millions of serious people with a growing apprehension of implications and costs. Meanwhile, another great shadow has loomed over the nation—the threat of war and the need for war preparation. The vast cost of this preparation, which has risen from a few billions to more than sixty billions annually, and which promises further increases into an indeterminate future, makes it impossible to calculate other costs of government or the means of meeting those costs or the future capacity of our economic system to sustain them.

The reality of a world war, however, would shatter all estimates and prognoses.

But even with what would now seem a moderate expenditure for arms, the additional cost of statism endangers the future of a free economy.

161

TABLE C, WELFARE RECEIPTS

These items are included in Personal Income by the Department of Commerce and called Transfer Payments. No services were performed for these payments in the year paid.

(In Millions of Dollars)

Payments by Federal, state, and local governments for direct relief, pensions, unemployment insurance and other welfare payments. Direct relief and military pensions are shown separately.

	Direct Relief	Military Pensions	Other	Total Paid by Government *	Paid by Business †	Total Welfare †
1930	$ 105	$ 468	$ 437	$ 1,010	$534	$ 1,544
1931	176	548	1,300	2,024	649	2,673
1932	317	571	527	1,415	737	2,152
1933	558	456	440	1,454	659	2,113
1934	745	382	425	1,552	641	2,193
1935	954	418	423	1,795	594	2,389
1936	635	433	1,858	2,926	594	3,520
1937	787	434	630	1,851	567	2,418
1938	965	446	994	2,405	429	2,834
1939	1,024	462	1,026	2,512	451	2,963
1940	1,013	476	1,199	2,688	431	3,119
1941	985	474	1,158	2,617	502	3,119
1942	956	476	1,223	2,655	495	3,150
1943	929	491	1,046	2,466	505	2,971
1944	939	649	1,503	3,091	506	3,597
1945	986	1,013	3,648	5,647	532	6,179
1946	1,177	1,693	7,993	10,863	557	11,420
1947	1,478	2,181	7,470	11,129	674	11,803
1948	1,727	2,297	6,522	10,546	739	11,285
1949	2,169	2,389	7,052	11,610	742	12,352
1950	2,360	2,467	9,503	14,330 ‡	752	15,082

* Federal, state, and local governments.
† Pensions paid by corporations and other businesses not included.
‡ This is more than the average annual expenditures of the Federal, state, and local governments for all purposes in the 10-year period ended December 31, 1940—much of which was from borrowed money.

The rising costs of welfare since 1930 not only show the present burden our economic system bears for nonproductive purposes, but indicate what the future may bring—or rather, take. According to L. Robert Driver, the payments in 1930 by Federal, state, and local governments for direct relief, unemployment insurance, pensions and other expenses, including military pensions, were $1,010,000,000. In 1950, they were $14,330,000,000.[1]

The sum in 1950 was nearly double the amount of corporate dividends paid in that year. It was more than the farm income of that year.

"Welfare," as now interpreted by statist philosophy, includes almost every activity of the government except armament, foreign gifts and loans, service of the debt, and a few other items. As we have seen, the Supreme Court has interpreted "the general welfare" as an almost unlimited sanction for Congress to expand these activities. Any effort to figure the ultimate costs must fail, because the ultimate is hidden in the mists of conjecture.

If we try to make such an estimate with the measuring rod of a good standard of living, we shall fail for several reasons. We cannot describe what will be deemed a good standard of living, because wants will continue to increase long after present needs are satisfied. And those wants will be satisfied as long as political pressures, political promises, and political expediency decree that they will be satisfied. As long as it is politically rewarding to enlarge the range of benefits, politicians will assume that the benefits are economically feasible. Inflation must be the ultimate answer.

Nevertheless, despite the tendency of needs to expand into wants, we can make a rough estimate of what "welfare" will cost by comparing the present living standards of millions of Americans with the "standards" oratorically and officially held as adequate or necessary. For example, if we were to add $1,000 a year to the incomes of the 9,600,000 families now reported to be living on $2,000 a year or less, the cost would be $9,600,000,000 a year.

The President's Council of Economic Advisers, before the Korean War, estimated that the cost of the Administration's social insurance program alone, when fully achieved, would

[1] Table C, prepared for me by Mr. Driver, shows these payments by years.

be $25,000,000,000 annually. But they included only pensions, survivors' benefits, assistance to disabled and unemployed, and government medicine. Immense sums must be added for housing, veterans' care and benefits, agricultural help, great reclamation and power projects, and made-work. There must also be added loans for helping business and direct expenditures for government in business. There will be rising costs for such old, permanent parts of government as the Congress, the courts, and the diplomatic service, in which the effect of inflation will be felt. Finally, and most important, there will be the costs, direct and indirect, of keeping the boom going.

It has been estimated that special taxes on payrolls alone for old-age, medical care, unemployment, workmen's compensation, and sickness insurance would reach 23 per cent in a few years. These charges will be largely passed on in the form of inflationary rises in the prices of manufactured products.

Government planning of public works, however necessary some of them may be, always encounters a grave hazard. Plans are made on the basis of current costs. They go to Congress for consideration, which involves delays of months or a year or two. When authorized, they may not be started for some time and may not be finished for years. Meanwhile, in an inflationary period costs rise. It has become almost the rule that in recent years great reclamation projects have ultimately cost two, three, or more times the estimates. Thus, we can never be sure even within approximate limits what the spending obligations of the government really are.

Figures that justify the high cost of the welfare state generally assume a high rate of prosperity. Most of those costs will rise sharply in any depression years. And the capacity of the economic system to sustain them by taxation will be sharply lowered in such a period.

Any determination of the kinds or rates of taxation necessary to support the statist's dream of a welfare state is impossible, because, as I have shown, we cannot tell what the costs will be. We are told by President Truman and his economic advisers that their progressive demands for more spending will be met by increases in the national income and wealth. We are told about a national income of a trillion dollars in the year 2000. This estimate of our future wealth is so staggering that we are expected to believe that we can afford the costs of almost any possible adventures in government.

Since such an estimate is made in future dollars whose value is indeterminate, it is not possible to relate it to what we know of productivity. Even if the most favorable view is taken of past progressive increases in productivity, there is no sound or plausible reason to expect that the national product can survive the drain of constantly enlarged government benefits and other forms of government spending.[2]

If inflation should continue at the rate established in the twelve months after the outbreak of war in Korea, the Truman trillion of national income would be realized in 1967. If in our calculation we should use the increase of wholesale instead of retail prices, the trillion would be reached in 1963. This takes into consideration only the level of production and services of 1950. If that should increase, the trillion would be realized sooner.

THE ILLUSION OF REDISTRIBUTION

Since government cannot by any magic formula yet devised create wealth—only money, the pliable token of wealth —the course of the statist is to shift income from one to another.

But a redistribution of income can by no means meet the costs of plans now proposed by the Federal Administration.

Treasury figures on incomes show conclusively the inade-

[2] This point has been developed on p. 159.

quacy of individual incomes to meet future costs of the Federal government. Let us take those figures for the year 1948, when President Truman unfolded for the electorate the specifications of his Fair Deal.

If in that year the Federal government had taken every dollar remaining in incomes over $500,000, the additional revenue would have been only $284,000,000, which would run the government in 1952 for just 34 hours. If it had taken everything remaining in incomes over $50,000 the additional revenue would have been only $4,080,000,000—enough to run the government for twenty days in 1952.[3]

A tremendous redistribution of income has taken place over the past two decades, and any further extension would probably injure those who would receive as well as those who would give.[4]

Huey Long might say if he were alive: "But I would tax the corporations." That is also a great illusion. Beyond a certain point, probably far below present corporate rates, additional corporate taxes are passed on in the price of the goods produced. They fall upon consumers.

The statist is like the operator of a shell game who deceives the spectator by moving the pellet from one shell to another and by shifting the position of the shells themselves. His hand must be quicker than the eye. The statist's calculations must be more rapid and deceptive than those of the payers and payees.

When the government pays the cost of maintaining old people, it must convince younger people that they are relieved of that burden themselves, and it must assure those who are growing older that they need not save. But somebody

[3] Similar figures for other income groups were: Over $300,000, $466,000,000 —enough for two and one fourth 1952 days; over $25,000, $8,880,000,000, or enough for 43 days; over $10,000, $20,793,000,000, which would last the government exactly 101 days in 1952. These figures assume 1952 calendar year's expenditures of $75,000,000,000.

[4] See the conclusions on this point in studies by the National Bureau of Economic Research and by others, summarized on pp. 58–9.

pays the cost and pays for government, too. When government imposes higher and higher payroll taxes, it pacifies the worker-contributor by imposing a larger tax on the employer. The employer calmly accepts the tax and passes it along to the consumer in higher prices.

Nothing is created. In fact, less is produced than before, because incentives to work longer hours and more years and to work more efficiently and to risk money in new enterprises are gone. All that is done is to redistribute in complex ways and with deceptive appearances whatever wealth there is.

THE DEATH OF RISK

There is no such thing as certainty in a free economy or, in fact, in any economy that the world has known. It cannot be assumed in economic life that every owner of capital will seek the safest investment. Such an assumption denies not only the lessons of experience, but the plain facts of human nature. The spirit of risk, adventure, and gambling is forever on the prowl. The ages have taught men that mortal intelligence cannot calculate, weigh, and balance all the factors that affect the course of events and hence that mortal eyes cannot peer with certainty into the future. Men have also learned that some of them possess more of foresight and of daring than others and that rewards come from the exercise of these qualities. Hence, there is competitive struggle in which quick decisions, risk-taking, losses, and gains prevail. All that this contest demands is freedom of choice.

In the infinite varieties of human nature and temperament, some will possess more daring and imagination than others. A few, perhaps a small minority, will be moved to risk money, time, and energy by the venture that promises not the smallest possible loss but the greatest possible gain. Among this minority are the greatest failures and the greatest successes. But generally when one fails another profits by that failure. And the net is progress, production, and the making of wealth.

Investments are made in the face of known uncertainties in the marketplace. No one deliberately chooses a bad investment. What makes an investment bad is the appearance of factors that were not or could not be anticipated.

Statists have prated for years about how "idle dollars make idle hands" and derive from this generalization the theory that government must forcibly seize—or "channel," as they put it—"idle" capital and invest or spend it through the government.

There could be no greater fallacy. For there is no "idle" capital except the dollars hidden in the mattress or in the ground. There are degrees of "safety" in investments, and there are many people to whom temperament or responsibilities dictate caution. But their capital is entrusted to others, and the very laws of survival demand that it eventually be set to work. And this capital affects economic life; it affects the volume of production, prices, and profits.

The newer the enterprise, the greater are the risks of investment in it. Here is where the venturesome man enters the picture.

The more complex and the more productive of wealth our economy becomes, the greater must be the investment in dollars per wage earner. It has been reliably estimated that the average investment necessary per wage earner is $10,000 a year. That means that $6,000,000,000 of new risk-capital is needed in the United States every year.[5] But statism reduces, discourages, and destroys essential risk-capital. The incomes of those who have traditionally supplied it have been the prime objects of expropriation by taxation. The average income of people in that group after taxes has been reduced approximately 75 per cent in twenty years. And since what they now have left after taxes barely meets and in many cases

[5] Abels: *The Welfare State*, p. 127.

168

is less than their cost of living, their margin for new investment has practically vanished. Moreover, since many are now paying their living expenses out of capital, their old investments are shrinking, too.

A wry reaction to this by many people is that they cannot feel sorry for those well-to-do people who must live on smaller incomes. That reaction is, of course, heightened by the political incitement of class feeling over the past few years. But nobody needs to feel sorry for the people who now have large incomes. They will live and live well. What has been accomplished by leveling them is the destruction of what they hitherto contributed to those economic ventures which make national wealth, and create new businesses and more jobs. The statist has missed his victim and injured the very people he professes to help.

Since tax resources are inadequate to support a welfare economy, the next recourse of the politicians who support it must be the deadly harvest of inflation.

There is no escape so long as the trend toward the welfare state continues. The final chaos and ruin of inflation would be bound to come. Values would be meaningless in terms of money. There would be a flight from money to things. Government credit would collapse when no one would buy bonds. Financial institutions could not survive the fall in value of their securities. The past would be pillaged by the ruin of savings. The future would be buried in debt and confronted with the almost insuperable task of reconstructing a financial and industrial system.

The Nonmaterial Costs

PLANNING FOR THINGS ENDS IN PLANNING FOR MEN

John Jewkes, a brilliant British economist, offers this conclusion in his book *Ordeal by Planning:* "The modern plan-

169

ning movement sets out, with good will and noble intentions, to control things and invariably ends up by controlling men." [6]

Professor Jewkes may be straining a point in attributing good will to the entire planning movement. We can waive the issue of motives, but it is true that personal and property rights are so closely bound together that the denial of one leads immediately to the denial of the other.

When planners mask their purpose under the term "national" or "social" planning, they do not point out that the real plans are, after all, made by human beings who are in public office by political skill or charm or sham. Authority is in the hands of, and plans proceed from, the brains of people who generally have little knowledge of economic life. The single will of the governing person or groups makes the essential decisions; and in a nation where the externals of popular government prevail, the rules of politics rather than those of economics prevail. Our own blundering experience with such partial planning as price-and-wage control and economic mobilization should teach us this fact.

The tragic lack of competence of political figures to grasp the realities of the economic institutions that they undertake to direct was well illustrated when the socialist government in Britain took over the coal industry. The Minister of Fuel and Power confessed: "I have been talking about nationalization for forty years, but the implications of the transfer of property have never occurred to me." The Parliamentary Secretary of this man had only this to offer: "It is not for me to say . . . the precise criteria which should be applied to measure efficiency, but it is a subject which would repay thought and some of us are thinking about it."

Such "thinking" as these people might apply to an economic problem would, to say the least, be fruitless. They have never known the economic process from the inside, and

[6] (London: Macmillan & Co., Ltd.; 1949).

their thinking would in any event be frustrated by their basic prejudices.

Of course, we may assume that all kinds of technical and economic information is at the disposal of a government. But even if we further assume that government planning can organize and grasp the outlines of this material, the government still has no reliable means of economic calculation, because the normal activities of a free market do not prevail in a planned economy. A first-year medical student may profit from the dissection of a cadaver, but he cannot practice medicine until he learns about the behavior of living people. When there is no free market to determine prices, there is no way to measure values. If government devises means of having people act under regimentation only as if they were buying and selling, the reality of values is not present. People cannot play market as children play soldier in the front yard or fisherman in the bathtub.

Coercion, therefore, is indispensable to planning. The planner must make people work where he decides they should work. He must determine what workers must do. He must direct the flow of income and the use of property. He must eliminate the consumer's freedom of choice. He must impose these restrictions on freedom or he cannot plan, for he is dealing with a massive, complex, and interrelated organism.

Ultimately, those freedoms which the socialist piously promises to preserve are gone. A planned economy cannot be operated by a parliamentary body where votes determine hundreds of subsidiary decisions. The sanctity of the dwelling must be violated. Jewkes points out that Prime Minister Attlee admitted in 1947 that "seventeen Ministries have power to authorize inspections involving the entry into private houses and premises without a search warrant." Obviously, the gentle stream of planned decisions cannot be ruffled by judicial intervention. In the end, freedom of speech itself

171

falls a victim of atrophy, because there is nothing left to be determined by public opinion.

THE MORAL CLIMATE OF STATISM

At least four of the initial assumptions of statism lead to stark materialism, domestic tensions, envy, and hatred. These assumptions are:

That the basic purpose of the state is to supply the individual with more of the material means of life;

That political power is attained by the promise of those benefits;

That political power is further assured by creating envy and hatred among social groups—in short, class feeling;

And that since the national government is to be the source of benefits, the loyalty of the individual must be to that source, rather than to his immediate neighbors and local institutions.

The foregoing assumptions of statism have in recent years become more and more evident in our public life.

The literal application of the assumption that the state exists only for material ends is obvious in the speeches and propaganda of politicians now in power and of statist political-action organizations. The traditional spiritual values are mentioned only in the form of more or less irrelevant catchwords, mainly as material for perorations and slogans.

Reckless promises are made by politicians, with all the politicians' callous assurance that if their promises cannot be fulfilled the blame can be cast on the stubborn opposition, and that the same promises can be renewed from time to time.

Since the beginning of the great expansion of state power and indiscriminate benefits, the fissures of class and group prejudice have been widened. Unpopular minorities have been pilloried for purposes quite similar to those for which dictatorships abroad have reviled religious and racial groups. After the great depression, the businessman was used as a target for demagogues, just as was the Jew in Nazi Germany and the kulak in Soviet Russia.

With the source of benefits reserved to Washington, there has been a weakening in loyalties to the neighborhood, to fellow workmen and employees, and to local government.

There has been ample evidence in the past four or five years that as the size and power of the Federal political machine have grown, shady practices have appeared in high places. Corruption will appear wherever money accumulates and responsibility is difficult to place. These evils and their revelation have their corroding effect far down the line in the private lives of citizens. An immature college boy who is approached by a gambler with a proposition to throw a basketball game might well be moved to evil by the reflection that the newspapers every day tell about offices sold for cash and bad government loans arranged through influence.

It must be underscored that these changes in the moral climate are due in the main to the materialistic postulates of statism. For even if the material objectives of statism can be obtained, the plenty that might miraculously result would be the beginning, not the end, of the good life.

But the greatest blow to morality is the self-evident fact that the promised plenty is not attainable under socialism. Thus, the appeal is not only created for ends that are not the best objectives of life, but its pretensions are themselves fraudulent.

THE TWILIGHT OF LIBERTY

From time to time I have referred to the losses of personal liberty through the progressive adoption of statist policies. In this chapter of reckoning, despite some repetition, a number of those losses should be summed up.

The farmer has paid for his benefits by successive surrenders of freedom. First, he accepted restrictions on his acreage. Then, as he exercised his remaining freedom to intensify the efficiency of his production, "marketing quotas" were established—a further denial of freedom, for which he received a cash return. Under the Brannan Plan he would surrender still more freedom in return for cash benefits. That plan would compel a limitation on the size of his farm or he would lose the benefits. It would substantially permit government to tell the farmer what to plant.

All government policies in soil conservation and irrigation have tended to force farming into units of a specific size. The farmer whose property holdings grow because he succeeds and buys more land finds the hand of government bearing down harder and harder. The ultimate under such policies would be farms of standardized size, crops within specified limits, assured but limited profits, and even the loss of choice in what the farmer might raise.

The farmer's financial affairs, including his credit and his debts, have to a degree moved within the jurisdiction of the bureaucracy.

Finally, he is told by President Truman that since his prosperity is considerable, he would be most ungrateful if he should vote against the political regime "responsible" for the improvement.

The worker's freedom has been restricted by the government's alliance with his leaders. His income has grown, but his liberty has diminished. His ambition to excel other workers finds impediments in union discipline, featherbedding, and make-work practices. His livelihood becomes dependent on good standing in the union because his leaders hold over him the threat of the loss of his seniority, pension rights, and other benefits. The penalty for recalcitrance is expulsion from the protective custody of the union. Moreover, since power has passed from local to national and international

174

unions, largely through the operation of Federal law and political alliances between union leaders and Federal politicians, the card-carrying member is ruled from afar and by persons whom he has never seen and over whose right to office he has precious little control. If he and his fellow members in a local take independent action, the whole group may be expelled or merged with another larger and more obedient local.

Even his political rights have in some instances been ruthlessly suppressed. Locals or the officers of locals have been summarily punished for supporting candidates opposed by the national union. Money collected in dues has been contributed to political parties or used by the political-action adjuncts of national unions by national union leaders. Members are asked for donations for political purposes in a way that is hard to refuse.

The businessman hardly needs to be reminded of the growing limitations on his freedom. The shrinkage of risk capital through taxation is met by inducements to become the debtor of a government bureau. Government lending agencies often dictate in matters of business judgment. Masses of regulatory laws, many of which have outlived their purposes, impose the yoke of bureaucrats on businesses. Companies are told that they must or must not expand. Political decisions arbitrarily favor some businesses at the expense of others.

The citizen's right to keep or dispose of his savings has been greatly impaired by taxes and the inflationary spending of the welfare state. Stockholders, too, large and small, have received less and less of the proceeds of the businesses in which they have invested.[7]

Higher education in privately endowed institutions, long the true sanctuary of freedom, suffers from the invasion of statism. The income of such institutions is squeezed by heavier and heavier taxation of former and prospective support-

[7] See p. 48.

175

ers. Government grants for this or that are eagerly accepted by desperate trustees and administrators.

The president of one of our great universities told me recently that in another generation the great majority of privately endowed colleges and universities will either become dependent on government aid or pass out of existence. At the moment, gifts are forthcoming from friends who made their money in past years. But the children of those friends may, like the meek, "inherit the earth," but not their fathers' money.

Experience under the G.I. Bill of Rights, a fair and just measure in itself, is pointing the way to free government-paid scholarships for everyone. There has also been a heavy draft of college instructors and officers for government work of all kinds or for projects that supplement salaries. A consequence of this has been an infusion, into the teaching of these people, of propaganda favorable to more and more government.

In the lower schools the trend toward Federalism is already apparent in the proposal for Federal aid to education. However this might be hedged in words to leave state and local schools free, it is idle to deny that where Federal money goes, control will follow.

Other cultural and welfare institutions are driven to seek and accept government bounties because of the drying up of philanthropic money. The vast social security setup is gradually shaping the policies and methods of all private social welfare work. Inevitably, the notable professional associations, schools, and agencies of social work which have hitherto built up technical standards and ideals will be dominated by government workers who can scarcely be uninfected by the bureaucratic virus of statism. The ideal of the welfare state is, of course, to absorb all private charity except perhaps a few oases protected by powerful religious groups.

Since the growth of statism means that more members of

medical, legal, engineering, and related professions must turn to the government for employment, the freedom of those who adopt those professions is steadily restricted. The number of lawyers required to administer the vast bureaucracy that has grown up in the Federal government since 1933 is very large. Likewise, great numbers of accountants, publicity men, engineers, and many other professional people have been swept into government work. The Truman Administration's plan for government medicine would almost immediately take into government service a substantial majority of doctors and dentists and related technical men. The person who works for the government enjoys measurably the right to quit and go into private business or employment. But as the area of government expands, the great attribute of liberty—the right to choose the place and nature of one's job —is steadily narrowed.

In the final end of statism everyone would work for one authority. There would be no other means of earning a livelihood. And the inflexible rules of civil service would prevail.

Under such conditions, a choice between political parties, if there were more than one party, would be merely a question of degree and of personalities. If a nation once accepts statism as a way of life, the drab choice, if there remains a choice, is between one or another set of masters. But when a political regime gets its hands on the administrative devices of an all-powerful government, it will use those means to keep itself in office.

President Roosevelt said in his Annual Message to Congress in 1936: "Our resplendent economic autocracy . . . realize that . . . we have built up new instruments of public power. In the hands of a people's government this power is wholesome and proper. But in the hands of the political puppets of an economic autocracy such power would provide shackles for the liberties of the people."

Those "instruments" are much more numerous and more

powerful now. They are in other hands. They are in the hands of a "resplendent" political machine.

It is hard to see, despite the protests of such socialists as Clement Attlee, how the ultimate of socialism can be but one party and, in that party, one master.

Free speech might theoretically remain. But the power and vitality of expression would slowly ebb in a society without wide freedom of choice. Public debate might prevail, but it would be without bite or purpose.

In Britain, where government has a strong hand in the administration of the Church of England, there were evidences under the Attlee government that strongly socialistic ministers of the Gospel were assigned to strongly Conservative parishes. Thus, along with the Lord's word there were scattered among the faithful overtones of the great doctrine of "fair shares."

Finally, under growing government, the invasions of privacy multiply.[8] Hosts of inspectors and others are at large, checking the citizen's whereabouts, peering at his business records for one reason or another, and flooding him with government directives and propaganda. These invasions of liberty are inevitable. The terms of statist philosophy demand them.

The moral and spiritual implications of a paternal state under the external forms of free institutions were vividly described by Alexis de Tocqueville in his comments on American institutions in the 1830's. This is his prophecy, which may yet be fulfilled:

I think, then, that the species of oppression by which democratic nations are menaced is unlike anything that ever before

[8] The invasion of the regulators under one of our welfare measures is thus described by a member of a New York law firm: "A girl from the Wages and Hours agency spent a day and a half in our office interviewing each of our women employees to see if she was fairly treated. Our girls get a minimum of $65 a week. Our office boy gets $45 for a 32-hour week. This is $1.40 per hour. But we were forced to post a sign in our office that no one on the premises can work for less than 75 cents an hour."

existed in the world; our contemporaries will find no prototype of it in their memories. I seek in vain for an expression that will accurately convey the whole of the idea I have formed of it; the old words *despotism* and *tyranny* are inappropriate: the thing itself is new, and since I cannot name, I must attempt to define it.

I seek to trace the novel features under which despotism may appear in the world. The first thing that strikes the observation is an innumerable multitude of men, all equal and alike, incessantly endeavoring to procure the petty and paltry pleasures with which they glut their lives. Each of them, living apart, is as a stranger to the fate of all the rest; his children and his private friends constitute to him the whole of mankind. As for the rest of his fellow citizens, he is close to them, but he does not see them; he touches them, but he does not feel them; he exists only in himself and for himself alone; and if his kindred still remain to him, he may be said at any rate to have lost his country.

Above this race of men stands an immense and tutelary power, which takes upon itself alone to secure their gratifications and to watch over their fate. That power is absolute, minute, regular, provident, and mild. It would be like the authority of a parent if, like that authority, its object was to prepare men for manhood; but it seeks, on the contrary, to keep them in perpetual childhood: it is well content that the people should rejoice, provided they think of nothing but rejoicing. For their happiness such a government willingly labors, but it chooses to be the sole agent and the only arbiter of that happiness; it provides for their security, foresees and supplies their necessities, facilitates their pleasures, manages their principal concerns, directs their industry, regulates the descent of property, and subdivides their inheritances: what remains, but to spare them all the care of thinking and all the trouble of living? . . .

After having thus successively taken each member of the community in its powerful grasp and fashioned him at will, the supreme power then extends its arm over the whole community. It covers the surface of society with a network of small complicated rules, minute and uniform, through which the more original minds and the most energetic characters cannot penetrate, to rise above the crowd. The will of man is not shattered, but softened,

179

bent, and guided; men are seldom forced by it to act, but they are constantly restrained from acting. Such a power does not destroy, but it prevents existence; it does not tyrannize, but it compresses, enervates, extinguishes, and stupefies a people, till each nation is reduced to nothing better than a flock of timid and industrious animals, of which the government is the shepherd.[9]

[9] Alexis de Tocqueville: *Democracy in America* (New York: Alfred A. Knopf; 1945), Volume II, pp. 318–19. The title of the chapter in which this appears carries an ominous warning: "What Sort of Despotism Democratic Nations Have to Fear."

PART III

A ROAD AWAY FROM SOCIALISM

CHAPTER VII

Progress with Liberty[1]

Socialism Is Not Inevitable

Back in high school days, in every debate on socialism, we heard the stock argument that socialism is inevitable. It went something like this: Over the years government has been taking over an increasing number of activities—schools, water supply, road and bridge building, and other services that have hitherto been private activities. This expansion of government has been necessary because of the increasing complexity of life. There has been a drift of people toward cities, where life is more complicated and people need more protection and assistance. Since this drift will continue, the expansion of government will go on toward ultimate socialism.

In this reasoning, the relation between cause and effect is assumed. It is also assumed, and without justification, that the alleged cause will continue to exist and that the same effect will follow.

[1] In this chapter I suggest how a number of objectives for which statist solutions have been proposed can be gained by measures that do not endanger our liberty. I follow the outline of Chapter 5, in which I presented a number of examples of the statist trend in contemporary policies. But in each case I seek to show how the dangerous implications of those policies can be avoided and the desirable objectives achieved.

In making these suggestions, I claim no originality. I have gathered ideas from many sources. The test is whether these proposals would assure a fair measure of government service at a cost tolerable to our economic system, and preserve our republican government, individual liberty, and opportunity.

In America belief in the inevitability of socialism has been strengthened by the ponderous learning and thinking of such foreign writers as Sombart, Schumpeter, and Harold Laski. American facts have been twisted to fit the theories of such writers.[2]

There is a dangerous fallacy in accepting an economic conclusion based upon the observation of foreign facts by foreign observers. Marx, Engels, and their school found the materials for their conclusions in European and Asiatic life in which classes were crystallized, resources were scanty and undeveloped, labor was in long supply, capitalism was absent, uninspired, or stagnant, and in which political absolutism reigned on every side. Marx during his life simply could not foresee the prodigious growth of production under capitalism which was to be diffused into higher standards of living for the worker. Sombart knew little of the New World; Schumpeter was unfamiliar with his adopted America. Laski knew little of the America that existed outside the lecture rooms where he expounded his ideas.

The theory of inevitability has no historical, logical, or experimental proof in America. It has no better basis than the warning of the old temperance lecturers that one drink or two of ardent spirits leads inevitably to a hobnailed liver and a drunkard's grave. Or than the contention of some pacifists before the First World War that the complex nature of modern civilization made a major war impossible.

The trend of the future is by no means predetermined by the trend of the past. But in following that theory foreign scholars have even ignored the historical facts of their own countries.

As the eighteenth century opened, the state was almost supreme in the affairs of men. That century ended in a tremendous tide of revolution in which individual freedom was exalted over the established claims of government.

[2] See pp. 76, 77.

184

Ludwig von Mises challenges the myth that socialism is inevitable, in this way:

There was, for instance, in the course of ancient Greco-Roman civilization a tendency toward an interregional division of labor. The trade between the various parts of the vast Roman Empire intensified more and more. But then came a turning-point. Commerce declined, and there finally emerged the medieval manor system, with almost complete autarky of every landowner's household.

Or, to quote another example, there prevailed in the eighteenth century a tendency toward reducing the severity and the horrors of war. In 1770 the Compte de Guibert could write: "Today the whole of Europe is civilized. Wars have become less cruel. Except in combat no blood is shed; prisoners are respected; towns are no longer destroyed; the country is no more ravaged."

Can anybody maintain that this trend has not been changed?

But even if it were true than an historical trend must go on forever, and that therefore the coming of socialism is inevitable, it would still not be permissible to infer that socialism will be a better, or even more than that, the most perfect state of society's economic organization. There is nothing to support such a conclusion other than the arbitrary pseudo-theological surmises of Hegel, Comte and Marx, according to which every later state of the historical process must necessarily be a better state. It is not true that human conditions must always improve, and that a relapse into very unsatisfactory modes of life, penury and barbarism is impossible. The comparatively high standard of living which the common man enjoys today in the capitalist countries is an achievement of laissez-faire capitalism. Neither theoretical reasoning nor historical experience allows the inference that it could be preserved, still less be improved under socialism." [3]

Thus Mises disposes of the historical basis of the argument for the inevitability of socialism. There is also a conclusive way to dispose of the argument for its inevitability here in

[3] *The Freeman*, Vol. I, No. 10, February 12, 1951, p. 301.

the United States. That way is to show how every reasonable objective of those who seek to improve our society can be attained without resorting to socialistic methods.

The Twofold Challenge of Statism

The program of American statists could not have won the acceptance that has been accorded it, except for a challenge that conservatives find difficult to answer. It is that there were glaring defects in our national policies in the many years of conservative government.[4] There were injustices to correct and needs to be fulfilled, and any government should have faced them resolutely. The statist claims, and wins support for his claim, that he is attempting to alter those mistaken policies to correct evils and to meet needs as well as he can. At least, he says, he is doing something.

The most perceptive analysts of Franklin D. Roosevelt's New Deal agree that its portrayal of defects in the economic and social order were keen and for the most part accurate. Roosevelt, like many other reformers, knew there was something wrong and he knew, somewhat vaguely, where it was wrong. He was not so successful in seeing what was wrong. He was still less successful in applying remedies, for his remedies often aggravated the disease.

[4] I have used the word "policies" here advisedly, rather than the word "principles." For in the years of conservative government toward the end of the nineteenth and the beginning of the twentieth centuries there was nothing seriously wrong in principle with the disposition of the Federal government to give business a more or less free rein and to respect the constitutional province of the states. Some tariff protection was needed, but there was no justification for the manner in which tariff bills were written or for the excessive rates that were established. The Congress, backed by and limited by the Supreme Court of those times, was reluctant to invade the province of the states in the regulation of business and in social legislation. The Sherman Anti-Trust Act was sponsored by a stalwart conservative acting upon sound principle. The evils and excesses of the period lay in the failure of government to exercise its corrective powers effectively and in the extent to which self-interested exploiters of freedom of enterprise influenced government.

It was quite characteristic of Roosevelt that he stressed objectives rather than methods. Somehow he, Truman later, and their articulate subordinates have always tended to assume that, because their objectives met public acceptance, their methods must not be called into question. This tendency, so common among reformers, is in reality an application of the proposition that the end justifies the means. But bad methods can as seriously damage an economy as bad intentions, perhaps more seriously, because the public is deluded by political jargon into confusing ends with means.

The challenge by Roosevelt, Truman, and other exponents of salvation-through-government to "show us a better way" has been difficult to answer, because critics have been of many kinds and of many points of view. They have exhausted themselves in negative criticism, bitter denunciation, and personal vilification. And many have been of the let-us-alone-and-do-it-to-somebody-else variety. Opposition candidates have weakened their case by grave concessions of principle to please this or that special interest or party faction. Hence, statism has succeeded in portraying its opposition as a house divided against itself, barren of constructive ideas and possessed only of a passion for the power and perquisites of office.

This challenge can be met by frankly recognizing that the conservative must, in stressing the imperative need to preserve the tested principles of the past, remember that change and progress are possible within the framework of those principles. In making the choices that lie before us we should recognize that, since sovereignty rests with the people, popular needs and aspirations must freely be taken into account. Finally, much as we may deplore some of the established activities of the state, they are realities too substantial to be swept aside. Let us see, therefore, what can be done to encourage progress within the limits of those realities and in the safe spirit of preserving our essential liberty.

We need not only to keep principle in mind, but to create workable proposals for change.

General Principles

THE ESSENTIALS OF INDIVIDUAL LIFE

One of the soundest approaches to the making of public policy is to start with what are sometimes loosely called the people's "wants," but which should be called the legitimate aspirations of individuals.

Franklin Roosevelt in the depth of the depression in 1932 approached his New Deal in that way. "What," he asked, "is it that people want?" His answer was "work and security," which, as a purely political appeal, did well in an unhappy time.

Work and security, however, fall far short of the sum of human aspirations. The Negro slave before the Civil War had plenty of work, and his security was zealously protected by his owner. The free life demands opportunity and faith and mutual confidence and love of community, state, and nation.

To contribute to all these should be the abiding concern of statesmanship. In a free society people share a quest for a better life, rather than enjoy the assurance of a determined share of material means. It is the job of the statesman to bring to the aid of the individual all that the state can do, without restricting the area in which the individual may do what he can for himself to satisfy his legitimate aspirations.

WANT AND NEED

However successful may have been the Roosevelt appeal to the "wants" of the individual, there was in it either a calculated deceit or a misuse of the word. That was true not only in his appeal in 1932 but years later in his famous "freedom from want." For want is far from synonymous with need.

It is conceivable that a rich, orderly, and humane state can meet the demonstrated need of every individual. But nothing in the world can meet the wants of man. The dynamic force in a free society is the enlargement of wants and the eternal striving to satisfy them. Giving the individual the opportunity to strive to satisfy his wants should be the cardinal purpose of free institutions.

THE DESIRABLE AND THE POSSIBLE

In politics, where immediate success is attained by saying what people can be made to believe, rather than what is demonstrably true, accent is generally placed on the desirable rather than on the possible.

An "objective" that is presented as an ideal, distant or difficult to achieve, should be plainly labeled as such. The extravagances of political oratory often obliterate the distinction. The duty of honest statesmanship is to measure, so far as is humanly possible, the possibilities of reform.

Perhaps once in a generation a statesman takes the course of blunt truth. Churchill was able to do that in the dark days of the war. Grover Cleveland had that habit.

The conservative in these days needs to remind himself of that honest course. He cannot match the statist in the portrayal of the ideal life, for he is defending a life that is too well known to be depicted as ideal.

THE ECONOMIC OBJECTIVES OF A DYNAMIC SOCIETY

To secure those national values which may truly be said to contribute to the general welfare, a few simple objectives might well guide the conservative leader, be he in government, in business, in organized labor or elsewhere.

The first is to increase the national wealth by more production. That means a higher standard of living. It is attained by encouraging those who would start new productive businesses, by increasing the span of the working life of all, by keeping at a minimum the number of unproductive people, by increased efficiency through mechanization and inventions, and by increasing capital and keeping it at work.

A second objective is to stabilize economic life as much as is possible, avoiding inflationary excesses and deflationary stagnation. This requires not necessarily "full," but abundant, continuous employment.

The third objective is to seek a more equitable distribution of wealth. This objective cannot be met solely by the heavy hand of law and government. In fact, the effort of statism to achieve a greater equality of wealth more often results in the equality of poverty. Modern industry has learned that steady employment at high wages is best for all concerned.

The cardinal error of statism, best illustrated by the Labour government of Britain, is that the second and third of these objectives has been pursued to the neglect of the first. The three are interdependent. All are essential to progress.

MEASURABLE AND TOLERABLE GOVERNMENT INTERVENTION

Since a conservative must at the outset accept realities, he must recognize the fact of some government intervention in private affairs.[5] We already have a generous measure of intervention—a strong government with many controls, innumerable regulations, and large supports for various segments of the economy. These may or may not have been initially de-

[5] See Chapter II.

sirable, but they have become adventitious props—some of them enfeebling—and they cannot abruptly be removed without danger of disaster.

The conservative ideal should be the exercise of great care and discretion in imposing new forms of government intervention and also a constant effort to reduce the area already occupied by government.

In cutting back the area of government intervention, a first task is to encourage the taking over of more responsibility by private agencies and associations. For example, it is clear now, after several years of regulation by the Securities Exchange Commission, that the stock exchanges themselves can take over a large measure of self-regulation. There should be constant revision of laws and of administrative machinery to permit self-discipline to grow.

Moreover, in setting up agencies of government, there is great need to see that one does not work at cross purposes with another. The best example of confusion is in our anti-trust laws, where a business in avoiding the violation of one law runs squarely under the proscription of another.[6]

The method and spirit of administering government intervention is all important. Those who would exercise the power of government must themselves believe in freedom.

Rational and Workable Personal Aid

THE PRINCIPLES

1. Whatever relief is provided for those in need, through government or private channels, must come from a common source—the productivity of the nation. The sustained health of that source must be the measure of all aid, as well as the measure of our general standard of living. When government takes from that source, less remains for the standard of living

---

[6] See above, p. 144.

191

and for private aid. The argument that taxation is an equitable means of distributing the burden of aid is potent. But it must be balanced by several other considerations. One is the efficiency of government and another is the fairness of the necessary taxes. Another is the danger of destroying a sense of obligation in those who give. Privately given aid has a value for both those who give and those who receive.

2. Government aid is a return to a system utterly discredited in the past. The occasional surviving "poor houses" and "poor farms" are reminders of that past.

3. Personal aid includes much more than items of material subsistence. It should create personal, neighborhood, and community responsibility, self-help, self-esteem, and human dignity. These nonmaterial values are likely to be neglected in any government activity.

4. Since the task of administering aid as a means toward the development of self-help is a delicate and highly specialized process, it cannot be done wholesale. It cannot be standardized on a large scale. It should operate within the personal relations of the community and the neighborhood. The kindly but watchful neighbor is the indispensable protection against abuse. The absence of this personal relationship was a glaring defect in the Roosevelt-Hopkins emergency relief and Works Progress Administration of the 1930's.

5. In the development of privately supported and directed community welfare over the past generation or more, there have been developed a highly trained profession of welfare workers and a body of more or less scientific knowledge. These should not be sacrificed or impaired by the invasion of a government bureaucracy, however vigorously that bureaucracy may pretend to be the exponent of high professional and scientific standards. Politics and mass administration can and do prevail under a system of government aid, however nobly conceived and plausibly defended.

6. Under free institutions there has been much more care of the unfortunate. It is demonstrable that in the days before the rise of modern capitalism those who had a claim upon the sympathetic help of others were known as the "poor" and the problem as "poverty." The "poor" were regarded as wretches unable to help themselves and wholly unnecessary to society. It was not only more blessed to give than to receive, but the giving had more value because it raised the giver in the estimate of society and of God. The receipt of the gift involved only the incidental lengthening of the life of an unneeded member of society.[7]

Productive capitalism has provided an opportunity for employable "poor" to become earners. The enlightenment of our times now speaks in terms of lower or higher incomes. The objective of direct help is to build self-help.

Where there are the greatest masses of the destitute, there is almost none of modern capitalistic enterprise. It is not too much to say, as does Ludwig von Mises, that the plight of these people is caused not by capitalism but by the absence of capitalism. Under the American way of life, an increased population does not necessarily create new problems of support; it provides new labor to build wealth. Mises points out that people are no longer helpless because they are poor, but poor because they are helpless.

Not only is inequality of income inevitable; it is the essential incentive to create and succeed. Basically, this incentive creates the surplus out of which it is possible to care for the genuinely unemployable. True welfare, therefore, has a vital stake in the preservation of economic liberty.

OLD-AGE SECURITY

The responsibility of providing at least partial means for old-age security has been thrust upon the state and Federal

[7] See *Human Action*, p. 832.

governments. One reason for this has been the great increase in the average span of life. Some form of Federal action was probably inevitable and would have been taken by any party in power. Let us assume, therefore, that some government provision for old-age security is a conceded objective. The present problem is to provide a way of attaining it that is fair, that does not impair personal liberty, and that does not, through a crushing tax burden, endanger the economic system itself.

The first step in escaping from the morass into which we have wandered is to rationalize the present Federal social security system. That system is neither flesh nor fowl. It is not based upon honest actuarial principles. At the moment, it collects more than it pays out. But, since it neglects the principles followed by any insurance company—principles that, it might be added, are enforced upon that company by government itself—its promises and potential obligations are far beyond its resources.

On any rational scale of judgment, the social security system is actually far in the red. To meet its obligations at some future time, perhaps not so many years removed, the government must reach into general tax revenues.

We should accept, in principle now and later actually, the policy of pay-as-you-go or, as one observer has put it, owe-as-you-go.

We should continue the contributory payroll tax for some time, if for no reason except to impose some tax on those who will ultimately benefit. It should be recognized that in the end all must pay for those who receive pensions and that the cost of pensions is a continuing charge on the economy. When that happens, and when the fraudulent but now prevalent assumption that people pay directly for their own benefits is abandoned in the name of honesty, Congress should see that pension costs are bearable.

That should mean that no one would receive pensions as

194

a matter of right. The basis should be one of need. Every incentive should be provided to retain the productive value of people over 65. If science has produced more health and years of life, there should be a corresponding payment in productive work into the sum total of the national product. Those who provide for their own security, who have means of their own, or adequate property, should not enjoy government aid. And children and other morally responsible relatives should share in the support of those who have in past years provided for them. Abhorrent though it may be to shallow exponents of statism, there should be a needs and a means test for every individual who receives government benefits. This should apply in the states as well as in the Federal system. It does not of course apply to the right of an individual to draw out the money, with interest, that he has contributed in taxes for a future pension.

Vital, active citizen groups of taxpayers should counteract the pressure of pensioners' groups and lobbies.

Government can do little to cure the weaknesses in industrial pensions now exacted under collective bargaining. Experience alone must be the savior there.

The problem is political, economic, and moral. If we do not overhaul our present systems of government aid the future will face chaos, unbearable taxation, the bitter awakening of deluded beneficiaries amid inflation, government bankruptcy, and the loss of liberty under repressive government.

CO-OPERATIVE, NOT GOVERNMENT MEDICINE

The sponsors of government medicine base their arguments on two premises—first, that competent medical services should be made available to more people; and, second, that medical facilities, methods, and the products of research should be expanded. They then offer their plan as a solution.

195

The answer to this is that both these objectives are being approached with the expansion of co-operative private efforts under a minimum of government aid.

To discredit present private efforts, the sponsors of government medicine have advanced several "proofs" that are either irrelevant or false.

The figures the sponsors present for deaths that better medical care might have avoided include deaths by accident, by cancer, by heart disease, and by other causes that could hardly be prevented under the government plan. They also used draft-rejection figures to prove the health deficiencies of Americans. These are most unreliable to prove such a point, since two thirds of draft rejections were for reasons with which medical facilities have little to do.

Sponsors also ignore the amazing progress over the past generation in the control and eradication of disease. Arbitrarily, they say that we should have more doctors. But we already have more doctors per capita than any other country except Israel,[8] and the relative proportion is increasing.

It is untrue that only half of our people can afford voluntary health insurance. This is denied by the Federal government's own figures of personal incomes. And any fair-minded observer would deny the subtle class appeal in the President's statement that adequate medical service can be had only by "the upper-income classes."

Common sense demands that we consider present progress and evaluate against it the clear denials of liberty in the alternative proposal for government medicine—always re-

[8] Paul de Kruif pointed out, in an article in the June 1951 *Reader's Digest*, that reputable medical schools have increased their freshman classes by a number equivalent to the opening of fifteen new medical schools. He also makes the important observation that we cannot judge our needs merely by counting doctors' noses. The immense strides in medical treatment, particularly in the development of the wonder drugs, have enabled each doctor to treat many more patients than he was able to in the past. For instance, a drug that can shorten the length of an illness from five weeks to five days obviously frees the doctor for the care of more patients.

membering that government intervention would destroy present voluntary efforts.

Everyone recognizes that as our society becomes more complex, as our population increases, and as medical science becomes more specialized, we need group practice, more hospitals, more specialized clinics, and more prepaid care. Those needs are rapidly being met.

The Blue Cross hospital plan started in 1929. It now has more than 41,000,000 members. It is growing every year. There is also the Blue Shield medical plan, which covers 22,000,000. More than 20,000,000 are now covered by other voluntary medical plans. It must also be noted that the unions are tending to include some sort of medical benefits in collective bargaining. It can confidently be expected that at least 90,000,000 people will soon be protected by some form of co-operative medical care.

In addition, we already have a very extensive system of government medicine for veterans, their dependents, and others. The Hoover Commission reported in 1949 that the Federal government at that time was already giving medical care to 24,000,000 beneficiaries. Of these, 18,500,000 were veterans. And since then the Korean War has brought its casualties and liabilities. More than forty Federal agencies rendered medical service in 1949, at a cost of $2,000,000,000. Of this expenditure, only 15 per cent went for public health, research, training, and administration. The rest was spent for direct medical care.

This immense expenditure for government medicine to which we are already irrevocably committed should be considered before we rush pell mell into free government medicine for all. The $2,000,000,000 that we are already spending should be compared with the entire cost of government medicine in Britain, which has in the past two years been about $1,100,000,000 in terms of our currency.

When it is asserted that millions are still left outside

private voluntary plans, the private practitioner, who is the traditional means by which Americans have had medical service, is forgotten. Co-operative plans are comparatively new. Millions have not heard of them. But the great majority of these millions are protected by the devoted care of their own doctors. Presumably, there are many who have had little or no need of a doctor. But they know that when they do, someone can be found to help. Any American can think of countless acquaintances who are content to depend upon their family or neighborhood physicians when they are needed. Their freedom to do this is a very real thing, as is the devotion of tens of thousands of physicians, often unpaid and unrequited. The idea that this relationship should be reduced to a routine of government is repugnant to every consideration of self-reliance, of self-inspired charity by the physician, and of freedom itself.

Presumably, many people should be taught, mostly in the schools, the virtue of prevention of illness and of early seeking of medical care. Also, the singlehanded efforts of practitioners should be supplemented. But something must be left to education, the forming of habits, and learning by experience.

Several bills have been introduced in Congress to extend Federal medical aid to states. The Taft-Smith bill would create a national health agency to administer most of the nonmilitary, nonveteran health agencies and to distribute Federal funds to states to broaden medical facilities and to provide medical and dental care for those unable to pay the whole cost.

There is the Hill bill, to provide government aid to maintain membership in voluntary plans for those who are unable to pay for it.

There is also the Flanders-Ives bill, which goes nearly all the way with the Truman-Ewing plan in Federal grants to medical education, hospital construction, and aid to local

198

public health services. It provides subsidies for voluntary plans, which would enable a very large proportion of the population to enroll.

All these alternative plans are designed to extend adequate medical care to a greater number of the population, without the wholesale government intervention involved in the Truman-Ewing proposal. There is little to choose among them, if it is to be granted that Federal aid should be extended for any purpose beyond aid to medical education and hospitals. In all of them, as in other aspects of Federal aid, there is some danger of growing Federal power. Here, as elsewhere, it would be wiser to return to the states some of their appropriate sources of taxation and thus enable them to meet their own health problems.

There confronts the nation no health crisis that requires a drastic break from the tradition of private and co-operative medical care, supplemented by Federal, state, and local aid for research, education, and building. The immense strides in medical coverage by private plans and in cheaper and better remedies deny not only the presence of a crisis, but the likelihood of any crisis in the foreseeable future.

Indispensable and Indestructible States

THE PRINCIPLE

The basis of the American constitutional system is a strict limitation upon the national authority and broad protection for the rights and powers of the states. Many provisions of the Constitution make this clear. The Tenth Amendment in the Bill of Rights restated this principle as an added measure for state security.

Practical experience and economic and social change have not impaired the wisdom of this general principle. It is essential now to reconsider current Federal-state policy against that background. Jefferson wisely included in his enumeration of proper government powers "mutual relations," which in modern terms means government activities in which state and Federal authority have joint responsibilities. We recognize three groups of functions—first, Federal; second, state; and third, joint Federal and state.

The major Federal functions clearly authorized by the Constitution are: foreign affairs; maintenance of armed forces; veterans' services and benefits; regulation of ships, waterways, railroads, and airplanes; immigration; interstate commerce; bankruptcy; patents; trade practices; monopolies; banking and the sale of securities; operation of the postal service; collection of Federal taxes; debt services; atomic energy; and so forth. There are a number of other current activities under Federal administration and control: support of farm prices; old-age and survivors' insurance; certain lending and insurance corporations; and the protection and regulation of labor affecting major and essential industries whose operations overlap state lines.

State and local responsibilities should include: general civil and criminal law, including property law; general police protection and law enforcement; fire protection; administration of elections; education; public health services; most highway construction; care of the delinquent and unfortunate; employment security and employment aid; housing; and slum clearance.

These activities, which cost nearly $10,000,000,000, should remain within the jurisdiction of the states. Any Federal concern for them should mainly be in the restricted realm of research, advice, and limited emergency aid.

Joint responsibilities should include: the construction of some highways and other public works serving national as well as state purposes (for example, airports, flood control, irrigation, and improvement of rivers and harbors); conservation of natural resources; and agricultural research and information.

THE STATES, OUT OF BONDAGE AND OFF THE DOLE

The first step toward a restoration of balance between Federal and state authority should be a reallocation of the sources of taxation. Such a reallocation should be planned by a joint commission composed of (a) members of Congress; (b) governors and state officials; (c) citizens jointly appointed by (a) and (b). The Federal Executive should have no part in this reallocation.

Some of the principles that might guide such a reallocation were well stated by a Hoover Commission task force, which considered Federal-state relations. Sources appropriate for state and local taxation should be:

1. Sources widely and evenly distributed over the whole country.

2. Forms of business, wealth and income of a nonmobile nature.

3. Sources in which receipts are obtained in connection with the regulation and enforcement of state laws (or local ordinances).

4. Sources related to special benefits, privileges or protection received from the states or their subdivisions.

Taxes suitable for Federal use would be, according to the task force:

1. Those which permit a high progression in taxation.

2. Sources highly concentrated in a few states.

3. Forms of business wealth and income of a highly mobile nature.

While no specific prescription can be laid down here for such a reallocation, a number of examples may be suggested. The Federal government should retain all customs duties, alcohol and tobacco excises, manufacturers' sales taxes, a flat rate on individual incomes much less than is now levied, the corporation income tax, payroll taxes for old-age and survivors' benefits, and a few specific levies such as railroad payroll taxes for unemployment and retirement.

The states should exclusively have death and gift taxes, gasoline and lubricating-oil taxes, retail sales taxes, limited individual income taxes, business and severance taxes, and payroll taxes for unemployment benefits.

Local units should exclusively have property taxes, various admission and amusement taxes, retail sales taxes where states do not use them, and various licenses and fees.

A single example will show how Federal encroachment through grants-in-aid could be avoided by reallocation. We have had much agitation for a $300,000,000 grant for education. If the Federal government would turn over all amusement taxes to the states and/or localities, they would have from that source approximately $450,000,000, plenty for education and other purposes without Federal control.

Such a reallocation of taxes is the most important means of preserving our Federal-state system.

To insure the security of state authority, a drastic reorganization of Federal grants-in-aid is required, as well as the reallocation of sources of taxation.

In stating the principles that should guide such a reorganization I cannot do better than to quote the specifications laid down by the Hoover Commission task force:

1. National grants should be available for public services only if the service to be performed is national in character, or if it is one in which there is a definite and measurable national interest.

2. National grants, where and when available, should be made for broad categories of public services.

In the interests of efficiency and economy, and to preserve a larger measure of state initiative, the states should be permitted the discretion necessary to adjust their activities to meet particular needs and situations.

3. Grants-in-aid programs should be based, in all cases, on close co-operation between the national and state governments. In no event should the national government attempt to deal directly in grant programs with the political sub-divisions of the states or with individuals.

4. National supervision of the administration of grant programs should be restricted to initial approval of over-all plans, post-audit of expenditures, and technical assistance and guidance during operation.

5. The present patch-work of grant-in-aid programs should be systematized, with provision for co-operative planning, appraisal, and administration on a continuing basis.

6. Definite, specific machinery should be established for implementing Federal-state relations in the development, operation, and administration of co-operative, intergovernmental programs.

A recommended first step is the establishment of House and Senate committees of the Congress, or, preferably, a joint Congressional committee on Federal-state relations charged with the duty and responsibility of studying the over-all situation and determining initially the needs that exist and the extent of the program to meet such needs.

Companion to this, some agency in the executive branch of the national government, perhaps the Bureau of the Budget, should concern itself with achieving balance in the administration of the several grant programs.

It should be added that all grants-in-aid should be based on the demonstrated needs of states. They should be given only after there have been determined by an economic formula the resources, population, and special requirements of a state. The demonstrably poorer states then might draw somewhat higher per capita grants. Then the grant should be made to the state in a lump sum—a sum for a group of services, not for a specific purpose. This would enable the state to determine the purposes to which the money is to be devoted. If a state prefers to spend more on schools and less on roads, or more on hospitals and less on poor relief, it should make these decisions itself. Congress should require audits and accounting of the sums granted.[9]

INTERSTATE CONTROL OF NATURAL RESOURCES

Like many of the proposals for more Federal intervention, the concept of Federal valley authorities has a desirable objective. There is need in a great river valley for some over-all planning and development. One project, be it a dam or an irrigation area or a system of interconnected power lines, must be considered in its relation to other valley projects. Herbert Hoover as Secretary of Commerce, in 1926, made a notable speech outlining the need for the constructive planning of water use. His vision was later realized in the Boulder Canyon project. The TVA operation and the Columbia and Missouri valley proposals are a perversion of that idea.

Comprehensive planning, construction, maintenance, and administration of resources should be by a joint action of Federal, state, and private agencies. In resisting the efforts of the Federal administration to take plenary authority over their natural resources, the states have persistently urged the use of the interstate compact that is authorized by the Constitution. A number of specifications follow, of how this might be done: [1]

1. Corporate authorities should be created, through interstate compacts, in which the Federal government would be one of the parties. The powers of such agencies might in some cases extend to whole river basins and in others to portions of those basins. In some places the contract might be made between a single state and the Federal government.

---

[9] The creation of such an economic formula as is here suggested is quite possible. It has been done by state governments in allocating aid to counties. It has also been tried in a modified form in some Federal programs.

[1] I have elaborated these recommendations in a small book, *Valley Authorities*, published by The American Enterprise Association, New York City, in 1950.

2. The first task of such agencies should be broad planning, in which the expert services of the Federal government, the states, and appropriate private agencies and corporations should participate.

3. The Federal government should play an important role not only in planning but in construction. The Hoover Commission's recommendation that the Interior Department have this responsibility is sound. Competition between that Department and the Army Corps of Engineers should be eliminated.

4. The Interior Department might construct some projects under authorization and appropriations by Congress, with generous contributions by the states and private corporations.

5. There is no reason why a state-Federal authority, properly incorporated, should not raise all or a large part of the money for the reimbursable projects by bond issues. At the 1950 Governors' Conference, Governor Driscoll of New Jersey forcibly urged this upon his fellow executives. If these projects really will pay for themselves, as their exponents assert, the bond market is the place for the test. Governor Driscoll suggested that, considering all the factors, including interest rates and the inflationary effect of deficit spending on the economy, it might be much cheaper to pay for these projects by selling the necessary securities to the public.

6. A major issue is whether dams and other great projects belong to the Federal government or to the states where they are located. The water and the land that they are built to improve belong to the states. The improvements should also belong to the states, either individually or in such compact groups as I suggest. Federal money, when advanced to pay for them wholly or in part, is a loan that should be repaid.

A proper policy to assure such permanent ownership should be based on the proposition that in paying for such projects the Federal government lends engineering skill and money for the reimbursable projects and for the reimbursable parts of multiple-purpose projects. It should pay all the costs of flood control and navigation. There should be repayment, with interest, for what is loaned. The states, with the Federal government as a partner, should create the corporate body through a compact to hold these improvements as owner, to administer them, and to provide for their payment.

7. The interstate-Federal compact creating such agencies should provide an impartial method of allocating costs. This might be done by a group, some members of which should be appointed by the President and an equal number by the governors, or, if legally possible, by the Supreme Courts of the states.

8. In the economic activities of such a co-ordinated agency there should be no settled policy of preference for public versus private water distribution or electric-power production and distribution.

9. Tax policies should be worked out in compacts by which fair allocations of contributions by states can be made. States might well make such contributions if there were returned to them tax sources now arbitrarily held by the Federal government.

10. The interstate compact, without Federal participation, can be used by two or more states to provide a means of developing projects involving more than one state. The New York–New Jersey Port Authority is a very successful example of this. It is in fact a new agency of government with wide powers created by agreement between two states. It builds and operates bridges, tunnels, and terminals.

11. In spite of many efforts to create a firm national policy concerning the conservation and development of our national resources, Federal activities in this field are a study in confusion, bureaucratic ambition, statist influences, tricky

bookkeeping, economic extravagance, and log-rolling in Congress.[2]

A new Federal Administration should face this problem with determination upon a fresh start. It should determine at the outset that its policy should look toward a free economy and away from government monopoly and control. A temporary national commission should be formed, the purpose of which should be the creation of national policy toward the conservation and development of natural resources. The initiative for the creation of such a commission might come from the President, the Conference of Governors, or from Congress. Members of the commission should be appointed by the President and the Conference of Governors— perhaps an equal number by each. Members of Congress, Governors, or other public officials should not be members. It hardly needs to be added that the members of this commission should be of proven ability, experience, and distinction.

Among the problems for which this commission should seek a definitive answer should be (a) a proper criterion for the feasibility of public projects, with reference to economic need, costs, and national rather than local advantage; (b) the financial burden of such works in relation to the tax burden they would impose; (c) a proper method of apportioning costs among the various purposes for which they are built and among the sources from which payment for them should be drawn; (d) the manner in which such works and projects should pay for themselves, including the number of years over which repayment should be made and the bookkeeping involved in such repayments; and (e) the relationship of public projects to such private enterprises as electric utility companies.

These and many other issues might well be resolved on a

[2] See pp. 126–36.

high level by such a commission, which because of its eminence could be a powerful factor in the necessary education of the public nationally; for the greatest danger now is that the complexity of these issues obscures them from all except the initiated and the selfishly interested. The general philosophy laid down by such a commission and the patterns of action suggested might well be a determining factor in future activities of the Federal government, the states, and private enterprise.

CIVIL RIGHTS THROUGH REGIONAL ACTION

The constructive approach to the problem of civil rights should be through regional rather than Federal action. In the preceding section I have indicated the use of interstate compacts as a substitute for Federal valley authorities. A different form of regional action is needed in protecting civil rights, because the necessary corrective measures are not suitable for a formal compact. Action within each of the individual states is necessary.

An important development in regionalism has been a long succession of meetings of groups of Governors, promoted by the Council of State Governments. At these meetings during the past few years problems common to groups of states have been discussed, and decisions have been made for parallel action by the several states concerned. Then the Governors have returned to their respective states with proposals for legislation and administrative action. There have been regional conferences of governors from New England, from the Far West, from the Middle West, and from the South.

Something more than a meeting of governors is called for in approaching the problem of civil rights, since it goes far beyond formal legislation. State legislation is required in the enlargement of voting privileges for Negroes. There may be some justification for state legislation in setting up advisory commissions on employment practices. But the widening of employment opportunities should be initiated privately by business and employers generally. The suggestion of "anti-lynching" action is irrelevant, because, as I have pointed out, lynching is now practically nonexistent and mob violence requires effective criminal law enforcement by state authority.

Civil rights involve social, educational, religious, economic, and political influences and authorities.

The President could make a contribution to the solution of this problem, through calling a general conference of Southern leaders, including Governors, members of Congress, educators, clergymen, businessmen, and others, and place the question before them. If he will not take this constructive action, such a joint endeavor might be initiated in some other way.

Toward a Free Market

STABILITY FOR AGRICULTURE

Principles. The Federal government's first effort toward agricultural aid was to encourage free farming by parceling out its publicly owned land. Then, to aid in the marketing of crops and to encourage general settlement of the West, railroads were subsidized with grants of public land, and with money. Following that, the Federal government limited its help to agriculture to research, information, and education. It was assumed that with such aids as these a free market would prosper the farmer.

It was not until a large segment of American agriculture felt the grip of distress after the First World War that further government aid became an issue. The chief argument for this aid was not the repudiation of the ideal of a free market, but the assertion that the farmer did not and could not enjoy

209

the advantage of a free market. The slogan was "tariff equality," which meant that, since those who sold goods to the farmer were protected by the tariff, the farmer himself should have equivalent protection for his product. He bought, he claimed, in a protected market and sold in an unprotected market. And he was constantly endangered by surpluses and ruinous prices.

He also complained bitterly about the terms and conditions under which he secured credit. He paid more, he claimed, for the money he needed for his business than did the people who made the things he had to buy. His agitation for inflation over several decades was a sincere effort to improve both his price and his credit situation. It lacked foresight, because when prices rose and money became cheaper, his economic situation remained relatively the same.

Finally, after years of effort, farm leaders secured the various benefits and special legislation that have marked the past twenty years. Meanwhile, many factors other than government benefits have contributed to the improvement of the farmer's lot, and the farm problem has ceased to be an emergency. There is time now to evaluate the experience of past years, to consider the wisdom gained by those leaders who have been closest to the farmers, and to set down principles for guidance in the future.

Some of these principles are:

1. A free market should still be the ideal in agriculture as well as in other parts of the economy.

2. It is necessary to take account of the limitations that government has placed upon a free market in agriculture, and to work toward the removal of these government stimulants and benefits, within the framework of existing legislation.

3. The present improved status of the farmer is very largely a result of mechanization, education, communication, and other products of a free economy. It is not, except in a

minor degree, due to government intervention. Hence, the farmer has a vital stake in the preservation of a free economy. He cannot, except at his own peril, contemplate a further enlargement of the power of government.

4. The farmer's real interest is in expanded rather than in restricted production.

5. Contrary to the advice of false political leaders, his interest is in the control rather than in the acceleration of inflation.

6. The farmers are a minority group. Any policy that puts him at the mercy of a national political party, or of the government, places him in great peril. For, once he is wholly dependent on government benefits, he might by a sudden turn toward economy be the victim of chaos and ruin. This warning has been repeatedly emphasized by Allan Kline, president of the Farm Bureau Federation, and by other notable farm leaders.

Politics, however, is concerned with votes rather than with agricultural security and stability. It seeks to place the farmers of the nation in a privileged and hence a vulnerable spot. Their true friends are those who point out their common concern with all other groups in the nation.

Elements of a Program. The following propositions are designed to suggest how the foregoing principles might be carried out, not only by government, but by all private agencies and individuals concerned with agriculture. They take into consideration not only the long and, we hope, normal years beyond the current national emergency, but the special conditions that are now confronting agriculture:

1. To attempt the abrupt removal of price supports would be not only impractical but politically impossible. Hence, the trend of legislation should be toward more flexible supports at conservative levels. Discretion in applying these supports probably must be left with the President and the Secre-

tary of Agriculture, but every effort should be made by Congress to enforce a strict responsibility of the Administration and to eliminate political manipulation of such supports. Within reasonable limits the removal of supports should be progressively guided by a timetable fixed by Congress.

2. It is also desirable that government continue reasonable and relatively inexpensive marketing aids to push farm products that are in long supply and to hold back others in short supply. This calls for no extensive regimentation.

3. Marketing agreements in which producers act co-operatively under the sponsorship and supervision of the Secretary of Agriculture are legitimate means of increasing price stability. Since those agreements, however, extend to agriculture privileges strictly forbidden under the antitrust laws, the public should be offered some safeguards against unreasonable price levels.

4. There is no reason why, even under a price-support system, a multiple or two-price system should not be recognized for some crops. Thus producers of certain crops could divert to secondary uses a surplus raised at their own risk. This would benefit all concerned.

5. Crop insurance to protect farmers against crop failure is sound, but it should not be used as a means of sustaining prices. If it is not worked out on a self-sustaining basis, it is merely another subsidy.

6. Consumer subsidies should be limited to stamp programs in periods of serious unemployment and to school-lunch programs.

7. Practical encouragement and limited incentives should be offered by government to develop scientific methods for the storage and transportation of perishables.

8. The conduct of research, the dissemination of information and the promotion of agricultural education, which are

the traditional services of Federal and state governments, should continue.

9. The expansion of the industrial use of farm products, notably in the production of alcohol, should be encouraged. The advocates of "chemurgy" have probably been overenthusiastic in stressing its importance but, with the development of more economical means of conversion, it should promote greater stability in agriculture.

10. There has been an alarming growth of government control of farm credit. This trend should be reversed and cooperative credit agencies should be developed under government supervision rather than control. Private credit-agencies should also be encouraged to take over most of this responsibility.

Beyond these specifications, the government cannot safely extend its control and support of agriculture. Above all, the farmers must realize, as their more conservative leaders realize, that their prosperity and stability depend essentially on their own efforts as individuals, as members of their organizations, and as citizens of the nation. "The farm program," says Allan Kline, "never makes farmers prosperous. It takes a whale of a lot more than that. It takes efficient production, high production per man, the appropriate use of capital, keeping up with the research that goes on, soil management and animal husbandry and what have you. . . . It is impossible to have a high standard of living unless it is earned."

CREDIT WHEN AND WHERE CREDIT IS PROPER AND NECESSARY

Principles that should guide the Federal government in a withdrawal from indiscriminate, incompetent, and dangerously socialistic lending through its many banking agencies are these:

1. Government should lend to private agencies and insti-

tutions only in periods of great emergency, such as deep depressions and wars.

2. At those times, loans should be clearly in "the public interest"; they should contribute to the safety and stability of the nation and the entire economy. When loans are made, the granting and administration of them should be competent and free from favoritism and corruption.

3. Government loans and guarantees should always be made to an intermediary private agency, such as a bank, rather than directly to the beneficiary. Thus, there would be interposed between government and borrower a private business-agency equipped with business experience and judgment.

4. Loans by the Federal government to states, cities, or other units of government for such purposes as the San Francisco–Oakland Bridge should anticipate self-liquidation and be justified by public, not private, necessity.[3]

PUBLIC POLICY AND PRIVATE RISK CAPITAL

Much of the pressure for government lending comes from those anxious to provide working capital for new enterprises that are unable to get loans on long terms for what are essentially business risks. This is largely the problem of small business.

The difficulty such enterprises face is due to a number of causes, most of which have originated in the very government that now proposes to do the lending itself:

1. A major source of risk capital in the past has been supplied by individuals with surplus money to invest in small, new, sometimes hazardous enterprises. They have assumed that perhaps one out of several such risks would develop and make back what they would lose on others. As we have seen,

[3] A number of more specific principles and suggestions for government lending are made by the Hoover Commission task force on lending agencies. They should guide Federal policy.

much of this source has now dried up because of heavy taxes on large incomes.

2. Risk capital has been withheld from such enterprises because of the reduction of the prospect for profits, on account of heavy taxes.

3. The great bulk of accumulated savings has quite properly been put in such safe, conservative investments as insurance, bonds, and utility stocks.

4. Because of this, government has properly placed strict limitations on the investments of banks, insurance companies, and other related lending agencies.

5. It is true that large, established corporations take risks from time to time in the development of new lines of manufacturing. An example of this was the development of nylon by the DuPont Company. In a sense, this was spreading a risk among the thousands of stockholders of the company. Sometimes large corporations make investments in other smaller companies. But there are serious limitations on this —partly legal, partly because of the obligations of company officers to their stockholders, and partly in line with sound business judgment.

This problem of promoting the life and vitality of our economic system through new businesses cries out for the ingenuity of business leaders and organizations and also for a measure of co-operation by government.

In such approaches to the problem private business judgment should be retained in lending, and risks should be spread widely.

Some communities, eager to attract new businesses, have set up privately supplied pools of credit, administered by groups of local business and professional people.

Some states have done this officially. In Mississippi, the state government has helped cities and towns issue bonds to buy and build plants to be leased to private enterprises. This is known as the B.A.W.I. or "balance agriculture with industry" plan. The state government of Maine has chartered the Maine Development Corporation, designed to lend to small businesses. This corporation is operated and financed by private banks, each of which contributes a small percentage of its available capital. The adoption of this Maine plan is being seriously considered in several other states.

An adaptation of this plan on the Federal level has been proposed in bills introduced in the Senate by Senator Taft and by Senator O'Mahoney.

Such measures as these, however, only reach the fringes of the problem. Intelligently conceived tax reform could release the natural forces essential to business growth. The worst possible way to treat this problem is by direct government lending.

PRIVATE UTILITIES UNDER PUBLIC REGULATION

The principle that government's role in business should be that of a judge rather than that of an administrator applies especially to the production and sale of electricity. It should also apply to atomic energy. Such enterprises are essentially monopolistic, and for that reason are properly called public utilities. For that reason, too, the role of government is very important in their regulation. But despite the evils that have marked private ownership in the electric power industry in the past, and despite the growth of public ownership, the advantages of private ownership and operation remain.

The costly battles between government and this industry, the threat of public ownership, and the wide range of restrictive legislation have had a beneficial effect on private management. In recent years this industry in general has devoted itself sedulously to technological progress, to a reduction of rates, to better public relations, and to a calculated restraint on its old tendency to play politics.

Regulation by the states has reached a degree of competence that assures the protection of the public interest. Experience in framing regulatory laws and a vast accumulation of judicial decisions have clarified many points formerly contested by management and the public. In short, we have developed a relationship between producer and consumer that measurably assures justice and progress under free enterprise.

There is no legitimate reason why there should be further government intervention in this business except under very special circumstances. Moreover, where government, notably the Federal government, has developed electric power incidental to other projects, such as navigation, irrigation, flood control, and the like, it should equitably sell that power to private distributors. It might even safely, as in the case of the Bonneville Power Administration, enter into a co-operative arrangement with private companies. The government should operate in the wholesale rather than retail field. Private companies under state regulation should deal with the final consumer. Public monopoly in this field would, according to as ardent an advocate of local public ownership as Morris L. Cooke, be "a calamity."

The trend toward government monopoly should be stopped.

FAIR COMPETITION WITH CO-OPERATIVES

The development of co-operatives was originally the result of a constructive effort to provide a simple means for the exchange of goods at a minimum cost. The ideal of co-operatives is control and administration by the people who are directly concerned. The true co-operative is wholly in harmony with free political and economic institutions.

Co-operatives, however, have been the victims of over-solicitous politicians. As we have seen, they have been granted legal privileges and exemptions that tempt them to expand into a multitude of businesses, some of which are unrelated to the original reasons for their creation. Because of legal advantages, they are able to compete unfairly with private businesses. Often private businesses, attracted by these advantages, reorganize as co-operatives. They become co-operatives only under the law. They have none of the genuine incentives that inspired the earlier co-operatives.

The remedy is equality with private business under the law. Tax advantages should be removed.[4] Immunities and preferences under antitrust, securities and exchange, and other legislation should be repealed.

Under such equality, the genuine or "natural" advantages of certain types of co-operatives would remain. Wholesome competition would spur both co-operatives and private businesses that deal with the same products and services.

Roswell Magill, former Under Secretary of the Treasury, in collaboration with Allen H. Merrill says this of the principle that should be followed in fair and equitable taxation of co-operatives: [5]

Equity would not be established by taxing to the co-operatives merely that part of their income which is accumulated, or is reinvested in corporate stock or obligations, while exempting cash distributions from income tax, for their actual income consists as well of the net profits or net margins distributed in cash, as of amounts reinvested in the co-operative. Moreover, other competitive corporations are taxable on the entire incomes, whether

[4] A distinct trend toward the taxation of co-operatives became evident in the Eighty-second Congress. The tendency seemed to be to remove exemptions wholly from certain co-operatives engaged in specific businesses, such as savings and loan associations and mutual savings banks, and also from all co-operatives of large size; also to tax co-operatives the members of which are corporations rather than individuals; and to tighten the rules under which co-operatives may deduct their patronage dividends (refunds to members and customers) from their taxable earnings. Such changes were vigorously resisted by President Truman and his Secretary of Agriculture.

[5] "The Taxable Income of Co-operatives," *Michigan Law Review*, December 1950.

accumulated or distributed. . . . Tax gratuities, or subsidies, in favor of worthwhile social experiments, such as co-operatives, may have been sound and desirable under the low tax rates prevailing during the first two decades of the income tax. They cannot be justified, however, in the political, economic and tax climate of the 1950's.

Regulation without Regimentation

RESPONSIBILITY IN ADMINISTRATIVE COMMISSIONS

After a decade of agitation for Federal legislation to curb and regulate the procedure of Federal regulatory commissions, an act designed for that purpose finally became law in 1946.[6]

This act, under fair interpretation by the courts, should measurably curb the irresponsible practices of commissions and reduce the danger of "administrative absolutism." [7]

The important requirements of this act are:

1. Federal administrative agencies must make public their rules, opinions, and public records, and opportunity must be offered for hearings on the adoption of new rules.

2. Officers who assume quasi-judicial activities in hearing cases shall be separate from and independent of investigation and prosecution. This should end the bad practice of vesting prosecuting and judicial authority in the same person or persons.

3. People who are brought before commissions shall be given the right to counsel and the right to obtain copies of data and evidence against them.

[6] *An Act to Improve the Administration of Justice by Prescribing Fair Administrative Procedure.* 60 Stat 237 (1946). A very large measure of credit for the enactment of this law belongs to the American Bar Association. The chief architect of the act was Carl McFarland, former Assistant Attorney General and now President of the University of Montana.

[7] See above, pp. 139–41.

4. Hearing officers, who in the past have been imperious in their exercise of power, may be challenged for bias. Their powers are strictly regulated.

5. Persons adversely affected by decisions of administrative agencies are given reasonably free access to the courts. Courts may not only decide all questions of law, but may review factual evidence and may set aside arbitrary or capricious judgments not supported by the facts.

This act has not yet been given full interpretation by the courts, and until that happens, it is not possible to determine the extent to which old conditions have been remedied. Moreover, the Civil Service Commission has failed to improve the quality of hearing officers by the removal of the arbitrary and inefficient.

The dangerous practice by boards and commissions of substituting their business judgment for that of private management,[8] while open now to challenge and argument, is still possible. It should be fully corrected by court decisions and, if necessary, by further legislative action. All that is needed is to return to the principles under which these commissions, notably the I.C.C., originally operated under the laws establishing them and defining their powers.

JUSTICE IN INDUSTRIAL RELATIONS

Principles. 1. Since government intervention in the relations between employee and employer becomes necessary only when free bargaining and other direct relations fail, primary responsibility for industrial relations falls on management, the individual worker, and the union.

2. Management should seek a high level of wages. As economies in production are achieved by greater efficiency, some of the benefit should find its way into increased wages. But labor unions should recognize that the consumer is en-

[8] See above, p. 141.

titled to the major share of the proceeds of such economies. Labor itself is vitally concerned in relief for consumers. Its true interest is in capacity to buy, not in higher wages. Management should also seek stability of employment through continuous planning. The interests of all are prompted by measures that protect the health, safety, and happiness of all concerned.

3. Management, the individual employee, and the union should have open channels of intercommunication. Employees and unions should be free to express their views, suggestions, and complaints about the policies and methods of management. Management bears a responsibility to keep employees individually and collectively informed of its policies and of the problems and conditions facing the company. Management cannot, however, surrender its final responsibility for decisions on policy and methods of operation. There should be co-operation, not co-management. Since it is a wise policy to welcome labor into discussions of management, it should also be a policy on the part of union leadership to welcome the suggestions of, and joint discussion with, management on union policies.

4. With or without legal compulsions, management should recognize the principle of bargaining collectively and through freely selected representatives of employees. This should be a practice whether unions are involved or not.

5. While our essential liberty allows the formation of political groups aimed at any legal objective, there are principles that union leaders should observe in their political activities. It is unfair to union members as free citizens to use their money and organization, contributed and created to further economic ends, for political objectives determined largely by union leaders in alliance with a political party. Such practices are likely to result in the neglect of the true purposes of union organizations, in the alienation of members who want no political dictation, and in the irresponsi-

ble, not to say dishonest, use of money for which leaders are trustees. A political group intent on a single economic objective must of necessity distort the true purpose of political action, which should be the general public interest. However, legal measures can and should effectively prevent perversions of union activity. Such measures should require strict accountability for union funds, prohibit coercion in exacting contributions, and strictly protect the exercise of civil rights by union members.

6. Government, through legislation and executive action, should seek the ideal of a free market in industrial relations. Hence, its efforts should be directed toward lessening, as far as possible, all intervention by government.

7. Legal compulsion by government should be designed for the sole purpose of protecting the freedom of all parties in industrial relationships. This principle should extend to the protection of the right of an employee to join or not to join a union, to protection of all parties from violence and from all forms of intimidation. It should guarantee and protect free speech for all parties.

8. In all cases, whether under compulsory laws or by mutual accord, the bargaining representatives of employees organized industrially should be chosen not solely from the group that has a majority, but by some method of proportional representation. For example, if 30 per cent of the employees affected belong to one union, 30 per cent to another, and 40 per cent to no union, the representatives should be in the ratio of 3–3–4.

9. Industry-wide bargaining is a direct invitation to Federal government control and also to domination of labor by a monopolistic group of national union leaders. Bargaining should take place between the management of a specific company and representatives of the employees of that specific company, chosen as indicated in the foregoing paragraph.

10. The right to strike should be inviolate, except in cases

where the public safety, health, or national defense are involved. For such instances, government should provide means of fair and equitable adjudication of the issues, with free access to the courts for the interpretation and enforcement of law.

11. In the selection of members of administrative boards and of mediating agents, true impartiality should be scrupulously sought by the executive charged with the power of appointment.

12. The law should prohibit all strikes, boycotts, and picketing for reasons other than those directly affecting the company itself. Secondary and jurisdictional strikes should be outlawed.

13. No Federal or state law should compel an employer to bargain collectively with members of his own management. This applies particularly to foremen, who are specifically the agents of management.

14. Mass picketing or other forceful means of preventing free access to property that is under the responsible care of management should be prohibited by law.

15. Minimum-wage legislation was originally designed to prevent the employment of persons at pay insufficient for a minimum standard of living. The trend under statist policies has been toward forcing all employers to pay "average" or "prevailing" wages. This would lead to the regimentation of both management and labor. The original purpose should be adhered to.

16. Monopolies of union labor as well as of ownership and management should be subject to antimonopoly legislation.

17. All legislation should be based upon maintaining free and equitable conditions in the present and the future. The Wagner National Labor Relations Act was conceived, drafted, and justified on the ground that, since labor had been unjustly denied its rights in the past, it should be compensated by inequitable advantages in the future.

18. The accountability of union officials for funds, including political contributions, should be enforced by the same legal conditions that apply to corporations.

19. Strict accountability for the use of funds is a major measure for the protection of union members from exploitation by union officers. Further measures to that end are required to assure real democratic control and accountability in union affairs.

20. There should be equal legal responsibility by unions and management for the keeping of contracts.

FAIR PROTECTION OF FAIR COMPETITION

There is general agreement that the antitrust laws should be revised in the interest of clarity, fair trade practices, and fair administration by government. Everyone shares in needing this, except demagogues and socialistically inclined people who would use vagueness in the law to enlarge the police power of government.

The following principles would seem to be appropriate and fair means of guiding such revisions:

First, it should be clearly specified in law not susceptible to judicial distortion that mere size should not be conclusive evidence of monopolistic power. It should be recognized that in certain areas of industry large companies are desirable, indeed necessary.

Second, in a given field a monopoly of the market should carry with it certain responsibilities and amenability to regulation not imposed upon business generally. This applies to public services, where monopoly is necessary and desirable. But in other fields, and without further extension of the concept of public utilities, there should be specified the legal obligation to maintain fair prices, services to all who legitimately want such services, and access to raw materials. There are those who would specify a definite percentage of the market as the limit for any one concern. That is neither practical nor necessary.

Third, a way of getting court approval of specific trade practices which is more appropriate than the present "consent decree" method might be that of permitting businesses to go to court to get a declaratory judgment against the government. This would eliminate the long wait for Department of Justice action.

Fifth, there should be more specific laws regarding property rights in patents and proper means of exercising such rights.

The health of our economy and the preservation of liberty are generally conceded to be dependent upon the presence of competition and the absence of monopoly. All sides agree on this, statists and libertarians alike. But it should be noted and underlined that altogether too prevalent an opinion exists that competition in the United States over the past seventy-five years has been on the decline and is still declining. This belief is assiduously stimulated by statists who would accept the pessimistic alternative of statist policies to the further enlargement of the area of liberty. The facts do not justify this widespread belief in the decline of competition and the growth of monopoly. Here, as in other economic fields to which I have referred, honest debate has been closed by the development of scientific economics. In a very careful review of the available data on the subject, Professor George J. Stigler makes the following observations and conclusions:

> It seems conservative to estimate that the competitive industries were producing seven tenths of the national income in 1939, and utilizing four fifths of the labor force.[9]

Then, presenting the results of a study of the labor force by Daniel Carson, Stigler goes on to say:

[9] George J. Stigler: *Five Lectures on Economic Problems* (New York: The Macmillan Company; 1950), p. 50.

So far as broad industrial composition goes, the monopolized sector doubled in relative importance from 1870 to the nineteen-twenties, and thereafter declined moderately.

The chief cause of the relative growth of monopolized sectors to the 'twenties was of course the relative decline of agriculture in the economy. . . . The broad pattern is attributable to the relative (and in the thirties, absolute) decline in mining, transportation, and utilities, and the relative growth of trade and domestic and personal service. It is commonly believed that these trends favorable to competitive industries will continue in the future.[1]

Finally, Stigler adds:

. . . there is no obvious evidence for the more popular thesis that competition has been declining steadily (and in many versions, drastically) for a half century or more. This popular belief, I think, is partly fictional history, partly symptomatic of increasing sensitivity to given departures from perfectly competitive behavior. Unless it can be given a documentation which I do not believe exists, it should be abandoned as an obstacle to clear thinking on social policy.[2]

Big and small businesses are growing more interdependent.

The figures of the government itself prove that over the past half century there has been no increase in concentration in large companies. The bigs are not destroyers of the smalls. The ratio between large and small corporate businesses has not changed over the past twenty years.

Figures of the U.S. Department of Commerce on the relative growth of 200 big concerns and 800 small ones between 1939 and 1946 show an advantage for the small ones. Growth and health, as there defined, are based on assets, working capital, sales, and profits.

An extensive literature exists on competition and monop-

[1] Ibid., p. 52.
[2] Ibid., p. 54.

226

oly, but nowhere is there real evidence that, when lawful rules of fairness are enforced, bigness injures either the small companies or the consumers.

Bigness in some lines may be advantageous to all concerned, and in others smallness may be better. The determination of this must be left to the rule of the market.

After clarification of the laws on trade practices and monopoly, there should be no problem of bigness with which government has any concern.

GOVERNMENT BY BELIEVERS

In many discussions with advocates of statist policies, I have been struck by a similarity in the premises of their thinking. Most of them assert, and generally with sincerity, that they believe a free system of enterprise is ideally the best. They assert their faith in competition and even in profits as essential to individual and national well-being. But they say: "We do not have free enterprise; in fact, we have never had it. And what you call free enterprise is doomed to extinction. We are advocating more government intervention because we want to save what is left of freedom as long as we can. But ultimately free enterprise, or capitalism, will destroy itself." [3]

[3] In Professor Stigler's comment on competition, to which reference has already been made (p. 226), he makes this further observation concerning those who assume the decline of competition because they favor some type of new social policy: "Many people make assertions about the competitiveness of the economy, and of the rise, or more often, the decline, of competition through time, and usually their views on these questions seem to exercise a material influence on their views of desirable social policy. There is no necessary relationship between one's views on the extent of competition and on the type of economic policy that should be pursued. One can believe that the economy is 99 per cent monopolized, and still argue for policies designed to revive competition and private enterprise; or one can believe that the economy is 99 per cent competitive and still argue for syndicalism or socialism. Such positions, however, are not popular. People are prone to favor goals which they think are quickly attainable, perhaps because they wish to be present when the goals are reached, perhaps because they distrust the competence of other people's progeny." Ibid., p. 46.

This is a pessimistic dogma of statism. It differs little, except in degree, from the Marxian thesis. It is a denial of the reality and the future possibilities of a free economic society.

When people who share this point of view occupy posts in government, in which they exercise regulatory power over economic life, their pessimism makes impossible a healthy and constructive relationship with the people and institutions whom they must regulate.

The remedy rests in part with the authorities responsible for appointments to regulatory agencies. In the Federal government that means the President, his major department heads, the Civil Service system, and the Senate.

The final answer is political. A free people should, if they wish to remain free, elect to public office those who truly believe in a free economic system.

Sound Finance and Liberty

TAXATION FOR REVENUE, NOT REFORM

While the unlimited power of Congress to tax incomes is a continuing threat to liberty, it is impracticable in these times of international stress to expect any constitutional change until normal times return.[4] Since the income tax can be conditioned to any sort of social or economic system that Congress and the President prefer, the problem now is to labor for the election of a President and of members of Congress who will preserve liberty under a sound system of taxation. And so far as possible, the bureaucracy must be rid of people who would misuse the power of taxation.

[4] In 1949 the legislature of Michigan adopted a resolution proposing the calling of a constitutional convention to limit the taxing power of Congress. Under the Constitution of the United States, when 32 states adopt such a proposal Congress must call such a convention, which can then submit amendments to the states for ratification. The Michigan resolution proposed the form of such an amendment. A number of state legislatures have since adopted this proposal.

A number of principles should underly tax policy:

1. The objective and ideal of all taxation should be revenue, not reform.

2. For the normal civil functions of government, Congress should adopt a self-denying ordinance limiting expenditures and taxes. No such self-imposed restriction could be proof against a spending Congress and Administration. But Congress could by a solemnly adopted joint resolution specify such a policy.

3. In order to preserve personal incentive and business growth, there should be assurance that rates will be progressively reduced when normal times return. The surtax scale should be moderated; the double tax on corporate dividends should be eliminated; the administration of the depreciation allowance should be more liberal; and the entire Internal Revenue Act should be overhauled in the interest of clearly indicating to the Supreme Court the meaning and purpose of Congress.

4. There should be new legislation limiting the discretion of the Treasury in administering the famous Section 102, which has the effect of inducing companies to pay out reserves in dividends. A good rule would be to place the burden of proof on the government to show that the withholding of dividends is for the specific purpose of evading taxes.

5. A far-reaching reconstruction of the tax system should be started at once, for the purpose of giving sources of taxation back to the states.

6. Consciousness of taxes should be sharpened among all ranges of the population by taxes at some rate, however low, on all incomes. No group of any considerable size should be wholly exempt and thus be dependent on the rest of the population.

7. The principle should always be stressed, however it may displease the political mind, that direct rather than in-

229

direct taxation is to be preferred. Taxes should be seen and felt. The abiding concern of a political government is to levy taxes so that as many people as possible will not know that they are paying them. In the old days under the property tax the citizen had a more or less reliable gauge of what he was paying for government. Now, with the enormously complex system of indirect taxation, there is little opportunity for the citizen to place responsibility—to reward or punish his public servants. With the spreading of the income tax there should be an elimination of as many of the hidden and indirect taxes as possible. The sales tax also is a consciousness-awakening tax. Shall we have some time a political leader who advocates "share the consciousness of taxes"? Taxes are already being more and more widely shared because "share the wealth" has progressed so far. What is needed is to let people know more clearly what taxes they are paying and to whom.

8. Taxes should, so far as possible, be aimed at consumption rather than accumulation. A tax on consumption, in the form of a sales tax, for example, is easier to collect. It also allows a limited freedom of choice to the person who pays it to decide on the time he pays or whether he chooses to pay at all. It also reminds him that he is paying taxes.

9. The theory of "ability to pay" should be reconsidered. This cliche has been recklessly used, with little consideration of the fact that a person with "ability" to pay large taxes may also have the ability to use his money for productive and wealth-creating purposes. Drastic taxation of large incomes reduces capital formation and immediately gives an argument to the statist who would, following the Marxian principle of credit control, thrust government forward as a provider of the necessary capital. The theory of the politically minded economists of recent years that government spending adds to capital formation is largely an illusion. The

230

real and safe sources of capital are the savings of individuals and private businesses.

10. The ideal of a balanced budget needs hardly be mentioned. An unbalanced budget means an unbalanced future.

SAVING OUR SAVINGS

It is elementary that when the Federal government spends more than is raised by taxation, piling up of government debt results. That, in turn, produces inflation. Inflation progressively destroys the value of savings accumulated in the past. The debt also places a burden on the future.

The prevention of this reckless squandering of personal resources becomes a major concern of everyone and a first responsibility of government.

There is no alternative to spending except to keep spending within the limits of income. The economic jargon of government economists seeks to deny that, of course. Their formula is to borrow and spend first, and then from the increased "wealth" that results, to take enough in taxes to balance a future budget and to pay back the borrowed money. That is an illusion, because if more dollars are realized from the inflation caused by borrowing, they have less value. To a politician thinking about the results of the next election or so, a borrow-spend-to-repay policy is attractive. He cares little for the more distant future.

The way to check that delusive, dishonest, and perilous policy is political. Those who have savings and who stand to lose by inflation because their incomes are more or less rigid must resist the trend.

PUBLIC ECONOMY

The only way to check Federal borrowing is to balance spending with receipts. There are several approaches to this problem. All of them should be used.

1. A great many functions recently assumed by the Federal government should be restored to state and local governments. These are closer to the taxpayer and are more subject to his watchful eye and control. Hence, the restoration of functions and powers to the states, as well as the return to them of certain tax sources now pre-empted by the Federal government, is essential not only because it is necessary to the preservation of our constitutional system, but because it is a measure of economy.

2. Government expenditures abroad for the development of backward areas and for the recovery and expansion of the economic life of friendly allies can be measurably reduced by a sound encouragement of private investments. This would introduce better business judgment into such ventures.

3. The same principle can be applied to great Federal projects in this country, such as dams, reclamation, great bridges, tunnels, and public roads. If, as is claimed, these will be self-liquidating, the test would be the sale of bonds by the states or by interstate public corporations or "authorities." Thus, responsibility is laid upon the state or region benefited and the business judgment of private investors is brought into action. Under Presidents Roosevelt and Truman, this wise though less spectacular principle has been generally ignored.[5]

4. The rationalization of relief and welfare would relieve the future of a burden that may well be intolerable.[6]

5. The lending policies of the government are wasteful as well as wrong in principle. Relief from this drain would save considerable amounts.[7]

6. The elimination of useless jobs and other forms of waste in the vast Federal bureaucracy means much more than

[5] See above, pp. 204–8.
[6] See above, pp. 191–5.
[7] See above, pp. 213–14.

232

across-the-board slashing or aimless pecking away by committees of Congress. It involves the great task of bringing the Federal establishment under sound mechanisms of control. One example of this is the General Accounting Office, under the Comptroller General. This office was designed to provide not only a means for accounting of expenditures, but an instrument through which Congress could control expenditures and guide itself in making appropriations. In practice, accounting has almost completely overshadowed the controlling job of the Comptroller General. This was pointed out by the Hoover Commission. Likewise, the President has practically lost control of his huge administration because of a faulty budgetary system. This also was a point made by the Hoover Commission.

With the restoration of these controls, the immense task of weeding out the bureaucracy might be achieved, with a saving of great sums.

7. Ultimately, the voters of the nation should realize that only frequent changes in the Presidential office, even without change of party, can bring about large-scale economies. The vested interests that develop in a regime cannot effectively be eliminated by Congress alone. A new President who is genuinely economy-minded could save billions. Thus this problem, as well as others, is a political one.

PART FOUR

LIBERTY THROUGH POLITICAL ACTION

CHAPTER VIII

The Myth
of a Two-Party System

The Two-Party Ideal

The theory of a two-party system is one of the most intelligent political concepts since the birth of constitutional government. A constitution, however wisely constructed, is still a lifeless pattern. The political party activates the constitutional body. It is at once a mechanism between the people and their government and a cohesive element holding together people of similar or related ideas and interests. Burke's expression of this purpose is classic:

"A party is a body of men, united, for promoting by their joint endeavors, the national interest, upon some principle in which they are all agreed."

John C. Calhoun offered a somewhat more realistic appraisal:

". . . the community will be divided into two great parties—a major and a minor, between which there will be incessant struggles on the one side to retain on the other to obtain the majority—and thereby to control the government and the advantages it confers. . . ."

That is the ideal concept of a two-party system—one party

to govern; the other to oppose and criticize and, when majority sentiment changes, to take over.

In practice, the two-party system has demonstrated great superiority over the multi-party system in efficiency, in stability, and in the preservation of liberty.

This magnificent ideal of governing the republic through two alternative parties has been preserved through all the vicissitudes of our national life. In the past it has probably done more to preserve liberty than any other national tradition. No effort to achieve an immediate purpose, however worthy, should aim at replacing this ideal. On the other hand, the preservation of our free institutions demands that this ideal become a workable reality. The facts of our party system deride the principle.

For nearly a century, we have had no real national two-party system. Because of reasons for which responsibility need not and cannot be fixed, a very large section of the country has rejected the Republican Party. More recently, in an effort to express the essential schism in the nominal Democratic Party, a large proportion of Southern statesmen have rejected the leadership of that party. And all over the North and West the Republican and Democratic parties have revealed such internal differences on principle that neither party can be described in the terms of classic definitions. What is called a two-party system in the United States is a myth that still enjoys a hazy but durable respect.

Historical experience as well as common sense justify the two-party system. Two parties have been and should be the great harmonizing agencies in our republic. From the beginning, two parties made possible the operation of our meticulously disjointed Federal system. In the preservation of the essential continuity of government services, the parties have performed a function neither provided by the Constitution nor perhaps anticipated by its framers. They have made possible harmonious action among the units of government—

Federal, state, and local—without denying them independence.

There have been rough seas for party government. In the generation that reached maturity in the 1860's, the Federal system almost perished. In that struggle fissures were opened that have never been completely closed. But the Republican Party, despite its sins and stupidities after the Civil War, made it possible for the nation to survive the crisis and to escape chaos. For the Democratic Party was torn asunder and for a time ceased to function.

Our parties, despite their shortcomings, perform a notable service to national unity. They have harmonized, however imperfectly, the social, economic, religious, racial, and geographic interests of the nation. For both the parties have always proclaimed the principle of the unity of the nation.

Their protestations altogether too frequently have been gross hypocrisy. But hypocrisy, "the homage that vice pays to virtue," served a benign purpose. It prevented the public display of bitter differences and prejudices among groups and factions, notably religious and racial.

The proof of this is that when nonpartisanship becomes embedded in legally constituted local institutions, the void left by the evicted parties is occupied by loyalties with little relevance to political affairs. Prejudice and bigotry then raise their heads. The voter confronted in an election merely by a choice between personalities lacks the guidance and sense of group action that a party provides. Hence, he tends to identify his choice with some other sort of group. He may vote for a candidate because he is a Pole, an Irishman, a Catholic, a Protestant, or a Jew. Or he may vote as a member of an occupational group—a labor union, farm organization, chamber of commerce, or what not.

These substitutes for party cohesion are not only unsuitable for political action, but their appearance in politics creates dangerous class, racial, and religious antagonisms. Interests are inevitable in society, but the broader the base of unity, the less room they will have for the exercise of selfish aggrandizement.

These great national services are possible of real fulfillment through a two-party system. But they are growing more and more difficult, because our two national parties lack vitality. We have the names and the formal organization and the requisite legal formalities, but not the reality.

Parties are Born with a Purpose

Generally, parties in America originated in the interests of great economic groups. The Federalist Party was the first to appear after American independence had been won. It was a means of rescuing the republic from the chaos that prevailed under the Articles of Confederation. Hamilton and others realistically built their party firmly upon solid economic interests. These were, in the main, interests that crossed state lines. They were personified in the merchants engaged in foreign and interstate trade, bankers concerned with sound money, and owners of government securities, who were concerned with establishing a national government that could redeem its promises. There were also those who lived on the frontiers, who needed the backing of an authentic government as they faced foreign soil. And among Federalists there were many who regarded democracy as repugnant to their traditions.

To oppose the Federalists, Jefferson and others equally realistically created the Republican Party and based it upon smaller, intrastate interests—farmers, shopkeepers and, here and there, large landowners.

The Whigs later supplanted the Federalists, and the Jeffersonian Republicans were succeeded by the Democrats. Then, in the 1850's, the Whig Party died and was succeeded by the present Republican Party, which was dedicated to the

Union, free labor, and the new industrial and agricultural life of the East, the North, and the emerging West.

Our present alignment, therefore, arose out of the great conflict in the mid-years of the nineteenth century.

The Democratic Party barely survived the struggle, but managed to live through many years of Republican supremacy because it had the support of the Southern states and of some powerful urban machines in the North. It would undoubtedly have disintegrated and disappeared, but for those bastions that, it should be noted, were provided for it by groups of voters whose purposes were wholly unlike and who in many economic issues were bitterly opposed to each other. The incongruity of the members of this party was remarkable. It included Southern capitalists and farmers, masses of newly naturalized immigrants, free traders, inflationists of all sorts, and certain nationalistic strains. Some were attached to it by tradition; some, merely by the glory of the word "Democratic."

In its national gatherings it paid vague and usually irrational tribute to Jefferson as its founder and Jackson as its hero. Unity was found only in a desire to defeat Republicans and get office for itself. It won Presidential elections only when Republicans fought among themselves. Even in 1932, the Democratic Party needed an economic cataclysm to attain a majority. Its revival since 1933 has been possible only because the South has found no way to escape from it; because the rising power of minorities such as labor unions has supported it; because the memory of the great depression lingers on; and because Republicans have had no unity in foreign policy.

Parties Live to Govern and Enjoy

Great economic issues rise to national importance only once or twice in a generation. The elections of 1800, 1828, 1860,

241

and 1896 were probably the only times when fundamental decisions were debated and made. After 1932 it was proved that a great decision had been made in that election. But it was not clear in that campaign that a fundamental economic issue was at stake. In other elections issues were relatively minor, and only the power and perquisites of government were at stake.

This, however, is a reason neither to dispense with elections nor to minimize the importance of continuing parties, contending however selfishly for the right to govern. The routine processes of government are essential, and it is important that they be carried on with reasonable efficiency, intelligence, and honesty.

Hence, a party is not only an agency through which citizens express their convictions on great issues, but it is a means of providing people for public office. The party regulars acquire a special interest of their own, not necessarily antagonistic to but distinguished from the interests of citizens in general. The politician conceives of issues only as means of attracting votes. He is concerned with power and with the preservation of his official status, usually at any cost to his personal convictions.

Again and again, this has been revealed in Republican behavior. For years after the Civil War, Republican politicians thrived on the bitterness and hatreds born of armed conflict. Those who were in power after Lincoln were concerned only with perpetuating a Republican Administration. Their course proved profitable to themselves but catastrophic in its effect on the two-party system. The burdens and indignities they laid upon the South and its leaders were so unbearable that the South found the way to political protection by denying existence to the Republican Party within its borders. It found security in remaining solid.

When the South made this decision in the days of "reconstruction," it might well have said with prophetic vision to its Republican persecutors, as did Socrates to his enemies: "A fate far worse than you have inflicted upon me shall surely await you."

That curse has hung over the Republican Party for two decades. But like most kinds of retaliation, it visits a part of its force upon its creator. For the South is a prisoner in a party from which in every passing year it has less and less to gain. And it may be added that, with characteristic political ingratitude, the Democratic Party it helped now adopts what remains of Republican reconstruction policy in its civil rights program. Never have we seen a more ironical turn in political evolution.

The South Has No Party System

Not only is the two-party system in the South practically extinct, but by the strange process of social and economic evolution the South has lost the reality of any party system. This fact, so significant in appraising our present national problems, is convincingly set forth in a notable book, *Southern Politics,* by Professor V. O. Key, Jr., and associates. After making his case with a wealth of striking detail, Professor Key offers these conclusions:

The one-party system of the South is an institution with an odd dual personality. In state politics the Democratic party is no party at all but a multiplicity of factions struggling for office. In national politics, on the contrary, the party is the Solid South; it is, or at least has been, the instrument for the conduct of the "foreign relations" of the South with the rest of the nation.[1]

The resulting political maneuverings under this dual arrangement are indeed strange to see:

The Democratic party in most states of the South is merely a holding-company for a congeries of transient squabbling factions,

[1] (New York: Alfred A. Knopf; 1949), p. 315.

most of which fail by far to meet the standards of permanence, cohesiveness, and responsibility that characterize the political party. . . . In the conduct of campaigns for the control of legislatures, for the control of governorships, and for representatives in the national Congress, the South must depend for political leadership, not on political parties, but on lone-wolf operators, on fortuitous groupings of individuals, usually of a transient nature, on spectacular demagogues odd enough to command the attention of a considerable number of voters, on men who have become persons of political consequence in their own little bailiwicks, and on other types of leaders whose methods to attract electoral attention serve as substitutes for leadership of a party organization.[2]

This passage calls to mind the great diversity of the South. It suggests colorful names, titles, movements, sections, interests—the planters, "rednecks," "Pappy" O'Daniel, the "Texas Regulars," James Byrnes, Harry Byrd, the Delta and the Piedmont, city and parish, the "Kingfish" and all his men, the Black Belt, hillbilly bands, Mister Crump, "Big Jim" Folsom, "The Little Man's Big Friend," the Talmadges, the Populists, the "Big Mules," "Dixiecrats," and many more.

All together under the banner of the Democratic Party, this diversity has presented the rest of the nation with the Solid South. Yet, the incessant strife and shifting about among organized political groups in the South lead the observer to the inescapable conclusion that for most practical purposes true parties are lacking. The discipline that accrues from a party system does not exist, nor can it be expected to exist for some time to come.

Only in Virginia is there a single, disciplined hierarchical party. In some other states there are partially formed parties. But generally, high office goes to the leader who can sway the voters throughout a sufficient number of counties beyond his

[2] Ibid., p. 16.

home, and win a state election over other ambitious leaders in other groups of counties.

Southern Republicanism, a Hungry Dream

In the South the Republican Party is a minority so small that it serves none of the useful purposes of party government. It consists of a handful of Republican Party officials in each state, such as national committeemen, county and state party chairmen, and a scattering of voting party members. In eastern Tennessee there is a small area of Republicanism, largely a relic of Southern Unionism in the Civil War. There has been some increase in the Republican vote in sections where many Northerners, attracted by industrial opportunity or by the salubrious winter climate, have moved in, carrying with them their traditional political attachments. In some states these new arrivals are already becoming a vital force in primaries and, in a few cases, in elections. Since a considerable proportion of them are Republicans and conservative by interest and tradition, they often throw their weight with the more conservative Democrats. This was quite apparent in the 1950 primaries in Florida and North Carolina. The Republican vote in Florida has been gaining rapidly both absolutely and relatively, and there is some validity to the claim that before long the parties in that state may be fairly evenly balanced. In North Carolina in the vote for President in 1944 and 1948, the Republican ticket captured about one third of the vote, a great gain over previous years. The Dewey vote in Texas in 1948 was nearly fifty per cent higher than in 1944.

But a party must grow from the bottom, and on the county and local levels traditional Democracy is firmly embedded. Generations have grown to maturity with nothing but Democratic loyalties. The idea that decisions are made at primaries rather than at elections is part of the mores. In the counties, townships, and parishes, small political machines hold a firm grip.

The possibility of developing a vital Republican Party over most of the South is limited also by the character of the official Republican organizations in several of the states. Generally, those who hold the nominal party offices live only in the hungry expectation of a Republican in the White House elected by Northern votes. Then there will be Federal jobs again for those who have sustained the vigil over these long years. Some of these nominal leaders do not even have the confidence of authentic Republicans who have moved South during the great economic developments of the past few years. They have done little to build their party from the grass roots.

Even in Texas, where the former "Texas Regulars" are still a well-integrated group opposed to the Democratic national Administration, and despite the gain in the Republican Presidential vote, Republican ascendancy is very remote. Conservative Democrats themselves, even when opposed to the national Democratic machine, discount the idea.

Moreover, as long as the national Republican Party clings to the issue of civil rights enforced by Federal law, no candidate of that party can hope to make much progress in the South.

Northern Democrats, Homeless or in Captivity

Since about seven million Northerners voted for a Democrat as conservative as John W. Davis in 1924, while they had the choice of Robert M. LaFollette as another alternative to Calvin Coolidge, and these millions voted for Alfred E. Smith in 1928 and Franklin D. Roosevelt in 1932, both running on conservative platforms, it can be assumed that sev-

246

eral million traditional Democrats are by ideals and interests wholly antagonistic to the socialistic implications of the Fair Deal. It can be further assumed that the party that nominated President Truman in 1948 and approved the platform then adopted was dominated by other millions and their leaders, who are in fact a minority not only of the total body of eligible voters, but of those who voted at the polls and of those who voted for Truman.

Franklin D. Roosevelt, and the powerful leaders who supported him, calculated toward the end of his first term that there were about 15,000,000 Democrats who could be counted on to vote by habit and tradition for any Democratic candidate. There were also some 18,000,000 voters who were Republicans by habit and tradition. Since on any fairly conservative program the Democratic Party was doomed to minority status, it was essential to attract several more millions by a radical appeal. Hence, the later Roosevelt program and the present Truman program have been designed to attract the decisive votes of a minority of certainly not more than eight or ten million, and probably considerably fewer than that.

It also should be noted that a few million who were by conviction opposed to the Roosevelt-Truman domestic program voted Democratic in 1940, 1944, and 1948 on the issue of foreign affairs.

The conclusion must be reached, therefore, that under the wry, disjointed party system by which we live we are being rushed along toward an objective that a large majority of our people do not want. Without a clear way of making a decision in a national election, we are taxed, regimented, and generally governed according to policies that we would repudiate if we could.

The plight of the millions of Democrats who by habit and tradition do not favor the Truman program, but who find it hard to break away from their political moorings and vote

247

Republican, points forcibly to the necessity of new means by which they can once more make their power felt in determining the policies of their government.

The Infirmities of the Republican Party

In thirty-two states the Republicans are reasonably well established as a fairly responsible party. They elect frequently, and in perhaps half these states they usually elect Governors, Senators, and most of the Congressmen. They have in the past swept enough of these states to win Presidential elections, despite the handicap of the Solid South.

But the party also has handicaps within these thirty-two states. In several states, mostly Western, election laws created in the great surge of progressivism forty years ago make it very difficult to maintain a responsible party organization. Direct primaries, the filing of names of the various candidates under more than one party designation in primaries, and freedom for voters to cross party lines in primaries are all serious bars to party responsibility.

Thus, the Republican Party is not a true national party. It is something less than two thirds or something more than half of a national party. It cannot fairly be called a sectional party, although it is excluded from an important part of the nation.

It has vitally important, almost malignant internal weaknesses. In foreign affairs it has serious schisms that endanger its very existence. In domestic policies its extremists, radical and conservative, almost pull it apart at the seams. Torn by differences in ideology and by personal ambitions, it wallows in the high seas of policy like a ship in a mutiny. In 1948, with a victory in sight almost too easy to imagine, it chose a role of vagueness and generality, and the voters whose support it should have had remained at home and allowed it to lose. It has lost votes since 1940, while the nation's voting potential has increased by many millions.

Whenever it seeks to create a credo, its varied elements bury their divergent convictions in a mess of ambiguous phrases. It has strong members, but as a party it has no specific plan or program and little confidence in itself. And now, despite the wealth of many of its nominal members, it has very little money.

It has a successful past, but a part of that past prevents it from winning the marginal vote that might mean so much in its future. It clings to principles of the 1870's, when it sought by Federal force bills to establish civil rights in the South. This is a threefold mistake. It denies the party the opportunity to gain strength in the South and in the border states. It gains no votes among Northern Negroes, for they dance to the seductive music of Democratic statism. And in espousing the various civil rights proposals, it is attempting to pass patently unenforceable laws.

Under the delusion that it is the party of Federalism, it has failed to make a strong issue of the stolen powers and responsibilities of the states. It cannot regain the policies of Hamilton and Theodore Roosevelt. Those were appropriated by Franklin D. Roosevelt years ago.

In foreign affairs it has permitted three Democratic Presidents to steal its laurels. Despite a distinguished record in world politics, with the luster of such men of vision as Seward, Blaine, Hay, Root, and Hughes, it has permitted its enemies to convince millions that it is a party of a little and isolated America.

In four successive Presidential campaigns the Republican Party has not shown itself to be a responsible agency to which men may rally for the preservation of liberty and of conservative principles. To a greater and greater degree it has failed to win the support of young voters. Its candidates have hopelessly compromised with the opposition. Its voters have been divided on foreign affairs and on the issue of government intervention in the domestic economy.

Even in the Republican membership in the Senate and the House of Representatives, the party has failed to maintain the discipline necessary to a responsible party. The caucus, which should be the very heart of a responsible party, operates with very limited efficiency. There is either compromise with party radicals or there is open division within the party on vital votes.

The Federal Machine Takes Over

With party government thus broken, scattered, and disintegrated, the Federal machine has taken over under the direction of the Federal Executive. The wonder is that this has not happened before. For some years there has been an evolution from a party system to machine dictatorship. Instead of a system under which a responsible majority party controls those who hold the reins of government, as is still true in England, we have a system in which those in official power control their party. This is always a mark of political decadence. It happened to the party of Jackson in the politically dark years of the 1840's and 1850's. Federal office-holders now control conventions, write party declarations, shape party policy, and make dubious alliances with groups that are neither authentically Democratic nor of any party at all.

This perversion of the party began with Franklin D. Roosevelt. Rapidly, in the first years of his ascendancy, he gathered the party controls into his own hands. In his second term his White House favorites virtually took over party management, patronage, and policy-making. The momentous Supreme Court Plan was not developed in consultation with party leaders. It was a personal scheme. When it was ready, bewildered party leaders were told, not consulted. A bold effort to purge the Senate the next year was managed by intimates who had no standing in the party at all, despite the protests of the national chairman of the Democratic Party.

All this has been spelled out by James A. Farley and others. Farley believed in party government and finally retired. Since then, Presidents have employed and directed party chairmen like messenger boys. The Democratic Party became the private army of the President.

When Harry S. Truman humbly bowed before the awesome post to which Roosevelt's death had elevated him, he was regarded as a mediocre man. But it was not appreciated that the job he confronted was that of running a political machine, not the infinitely difficult task of leading a party. Fortunately for him, among his meager talents was the well-learned trade of a professional machine politician. Carlyle observed that a dwarf behind a steam engine can move mountains. A political machine, well organized and well financed, has a certain momentum. A new master can survive a long time if he is shrewd and if he understands simple political mechanics.

Harry S. Truman, who knew little of statesmanship but a lot about the prosaic knack of politics, shrewdly did what he was trained to do. He knew how to give orders, because he knew how to take them. He had breathed the atmosphere of politics from the beginning of his adult life. He had given his allegiance to the Pendergast machine in Jackson County and Kansas City. He had labored in its interest and accepted its discipline and rewards. Truman made no protest against its habitual, proved corruption. And when fate carried him to high places and his home machine was in trouble, he loyally defended it.

His unexpected election in 1948 was in part due to this sedulous development of machine loyalty throughout his official family. Since that election, his supreme confidence in machine methods has been openly proclaimed. He uses those methods to build and perpetuate his regime. His Fair Deal program is regarded by him not as a pattern for a nation's destiny but as a means of attracting votes.

Such a mind is essentially not concerned with the real merits or consequence of government policies. It is concerned with their usefulness in winning votes and building power. To a large degree it considers national interest to be identical with machine interest. Victory at the polls determines right; defeat, wrong. And when such a mentality is entrenched in the powerful Presidential office, it enforces its standards and purposes on every subordinate. Deviation from loyalty is regarded as a personal attack and is punished as such. Machine loyalty is rewarded at the expense of the national interest. Criticism of policies is regarded as political and personal enmity.

Truman has gathered into his Cabinet a larger number of professional politicians than has any President in recent times. The entourage around the White House has the complexion of practical politics, as have the heads of great so-called "independent" agencies such as the Social Security agency. Even the more recent Truman appointments to the Supreme Court have the color of agreeable political cronyism.

In five short years, this man has managed and directed the most potent Federal political machine in our history. And he has made it clear that whoever works for the government works for the Democratic Party.

Keeping in mind this political mentality at the top, consider the available resources of power. In many states the number of Federal employees is as great or greater than a normal electoral majority margin. If the dependents of these employees are considered, some state elections could be measurably influenced from Washington.[3]

[3] But the influence of Federal employees has been overemphasized. It must always be remembered that employees may feel resentment against, as well as

Other factors in machine power are those who receive the favor of the government through loans, contracts, special privileges, and benefits of all kinds.

This dispensation resembles the traditional Democratic Party only in name. It is no longer a party. It is a machine—hard, disciplined, ambitious, and puissant.

Party government has ceased to function.

Proposals for Coalition

The foregoing analysis of the disintegration of our two-party system would draw no serious criticism from most Northern Republicans or conservative Southern Democrats. Five successive defeats have heavily underlined the weakness of the Republican Party—a weakness apparent to even the most loyal of its members. The party might speak through its chosen Presidential candidates with the tongue of an angel—which it has not—but it must enter every campaign with a handicap of more than one hundred electoral votes. Even if it should win, it would still represent only a majority of the conservative strength of the nation. Under the prevailing conditions it cannot become a securely established governing party.

Recognizing this clearly, many intelligent Republicans have been seeking some form of party reconstruction, either to alter the party to make it acceptable in the South, or to create a workable coalition with the conservative elements in the South.

A favorite idea is to change the name of the party. Some

loyalty to, their employers. In Washington, where the conscience of government employees is in a great many cases stricken by what they see of waste, favoritism, and lax moral standards under the protection of civil service, there is a great deal of virile opposition to the party in power. The Republican vote in Maryland and Virginia counties, where many government employees live, is proof of this. There can be no sound reason for assuming that Federal employees can be counted upon as a certain political asset to the party in power.

suggestions have been made to rechristen it the Union Party, or the Union-Republican Party, or the Freedom Party.

There are also those, mostly of dubious Republican identity, who would adopt a rival statist program and thus steal from the Democrats the allegiance of some voting elements in the North. These "me-too" people have made no important headway. Desperate as traditional Republicans may be, they cannot now accept such a course.

The creation of a coalition between conservative Democrats in the South and conservative Republicans in the North has been proposed by as authentic a Republican as Senator John W. Bricker. His Republican colleague, Senator Karl E. Mundt, in 1951 suggested several steps to carry out the proposal. Mundt has described his plan as "a formula whereby people of both political parties on both sides of the Mason and Dixon Line can join their forces and their votes in a great national effort to elect a President and a Congress dedicated to restoring the Federal government to its proper sphere of activity and thus putting a permanent end to today's drift toward the shoals of national socialism."

Such a plan as Mundt's, or any similar plan, would depend for its success on vigorous citizen action in the states, Congressional districts, and local communities of the nation.

Northern Republicans, however, must realize that as long as they cling to their purely nuisance-value adherence to the Truman civil-rights program, they are not only pursuing a phantom of their dead past, but are denying voters an opportunity to preserve the traditional rights of all of us. They are also probably denying themselves a chance of winning the Presidency.

Northern Republicans must also understand the attitude of leading citizens of the South, including most Southern politicians. Southern leaders have a punctilious sense of who-joins-whom. They are certainly not going to "join" the Republican Party. Any alliance must be on even terms and under neutral auspices. The South, moreover, has serious legal problems to solve before any coalition could be successful. In some states there can be only one party labeled "Democratic" on a ticket. It would be difficult in some states to elect a slate of electors unpledged to the choice of the Democratic National Convention.

Another problem has to do with a Presidential candidate chosen by the Republican convention. That candidate might well be under obligations to certain Republican leaders in the South who, though discredited at home, carry delegate strength to the convention. If these delegates were, as some of them are, pledged to Negro organizations intent on a Federal civil-rights program, they might exact some sort of pledge from their chosen candidate. That would make it very difficult to win Democratic support for that candidate in the South.

Any possible coalition is always confronted with the confidence of many northern Republicans that they can win without Southern support. This was undoubtedly true in 1948. It may be true again. Such a victory is always possible, and it was the rule in many elections before 1932. But it requires an overwhelming landslide of public opinion, which no party that hopes to win consistently can expect. Or it requires a badly split opposition, which cannot be anticipated except on extraordinary occasions. Or it must anticipate the decline of the Democratic Party to the condition of weakness that prevailed from 1896 to 1912 and from 1920 to 1932.

The latter condition is not likely to reappear in the foreseeable future, for a number of reasons. One is the relative growth of the cities. The drift toward urban areas continues, and since fewer farm workers are required in a mechanized agriculture, traditional Republican areas are declining in voting importance. The long hold that Democratic Administrations have had upon states that receive large government grants has built up vested Democratic interests there. There

255

is also the immense growth of the unions, which, while it does not guarantee a solid labor vote for any Democratic candidate, nevertheless provides many Democratic state and local machines with strong auxiliary support. There are also the many, many thousands of beneficiaries of government support who find the statist policies of the Democratic Party in line with their supposed interest.

For these and other reasons, Republicans cannot hope for a return of the conditions that existed during the many years when they were the majority party. Nor can conservative principles prevail when conservatives in the North are separated from people of like mind in the South by the present party division. The restoration of true party government calls for some sort of coalition that will grow into a genuine national conservative party. There are more and more evidences that seriously concerned people are turning to that solution. But it would be a risky prophecy to suggest when such a consummation may appear.

It would be very shortsighted to overlook the possibilities of the Dixiecrat movement as a possible factor in some future coalition. That revolt, which came into the open after the Democratic convention in 1948, was hampered more in its first campaign by its lack of leaders than by any lack of principle or of popular sentiment behind it. It was not merely a revolt against the civil-rights program of the President. It was a genuine drive for states' rights and the curbing of Federal statism. In New Orleans, for example, the principles behind the movement were generally approved, but its leadership was distrusted. We shall hear much more of that revolt in years to come.

The Meaning of the Coalition in Congress

An informal coalition of Republicans and conservative Southern Democrats in Congress has wielded great power for

256

a number of years. It has been an effective check on the most extreme proposals of two Presidents. At this moment, it is stronger than ever. Its influence is in the main negative, but that is inevitable while the Northern Democratic machine centers in the Presidency. In the present Congress a safe majority, perhaps two thirds of the members of both houses, are essentially conservative.

In the House of Representatives, both the Democratic and the Republican leadership lose party votes on an important roll call. The Republicans are likely in the present Eighty-second Congress to lose from twenty to fifty of their leftist members, but the Democratic leaders expect to lose from thirty to a hundred conservative members of their group. This, on all matters of fundamental importance in the domestic field, means a comfortable conservative majority.

The meaning of this Congressional coalition is very clear. In the only way that the voters of the nation can now express themselves, they are insisting on a preservation of economic liberty, economical government, and other traditional principles and institutions. So far as representative government has meaning, the coalition in Congress embodies the collective will of the people of the nation.

Since this is so, the immediate task of conservatism becomes clear. It is to strengthen this coalition by strong support of its members at the polls by citizen action, to increase the proportion of conservatives in Congress, and thus for a time to hold the line against statism. Beyond that is the task of reconstructing the two-party system in a manner that will assure the majority of voters control of the Presidency as well as control of Congress.

CHAPTER IX

Leadership,
Actual and Potential

A Personal Note

Since this chapter and the one that follows are designed to suggest practical, specific, and immediate means by which citizens may preserve their inherited liberty through political action, it may be useful to explain how I have arrived at some of my conclusions. In general, the conclusions set forth in this book are based on a lifetime devoted to the observation and study of politics. But in the two years during which this book has been in the process of gestation and composition, a number of my earlier conclusions have been modified in the light of what I have learned from many people who are also seeking an answer to the problem with which I am concerned. I have also had the benefit of observing many efforts throughout the country to organize citizens for political action, especially in the 1950 primaries and elections.

One conclusion is that there has never been a moment, at least within the orbit of my own experience, when the thinking of the vast numbers of citizens whom I have described as those who share the middle interests has been so out of line with and critical of the prevailing philosophy and competence of the two major parties. A great number of these people want to do something about what they know is happening to their savings, their hard-earned tax money, and their economic and political liberty.

Some of these people are already starting to do something at the local and state level, but they need more advice, guidance, and leadership.

A second conclusion is that the results of the 1950 election clearly showed a disposition of voters to take matters in their own hands. The Korean War, diplomatic blundering, and military miscalculations were powerful factors. But the drift toward statism was also an important issue. The candidates who individually and forcefully presented these issues did very well, with or without effective party organization. That was notable in the Senatorial contests in California, Utah, Illinois, and Ohio. In those states, there was, outside the Republican Party, aggressive citizen action for the successful candidates, and that help unquestionably turned the tide. Many, perhaps most, voters made their choices on the basis of personalities and issues rather than party loyalty.

A third conclusion is based on what I learned from people, not active party members, who took part in primary and election campaigns in a dozen or more states in 1950. They were unanimous in asserting that they should make no effort to set up a national nonpartisan organization before the election in 1952. They were firmly convinced that they could work more effectively in 1952 gathering people together on local levels in support of party candidates for the Senate and the House, North and South, Democratic and Republican, with additional effort in support of a conservative candidate for President. It was their opinion that convinced me that the creation in the near future of a conservative A.D.A. or P.A.C. at the national level would be a mistake. The A.D.A. and the P.A.C. in 1950 actually did their cause more harm than good, because they gave their statist principles and policies "a habitation and a name," thus "something to shoot at."

259

From this, I drew another conclusion: that there should be very energetic efforts to create citizen groups on the state, district, and local levels. These groups might work without specific names or adopt some innocuous name merely to hold their members together.

There is already plenty of specific experience to provide blueprints for such local efforts. I might, if it seemed necessary, heavily burden this chapter and the next with lists of examples of such activities in past primaries and elections. But because there are so many patterns of action and such varying degrees of success, the effect of such a catalogue would be to confuse and frustrate.

I am therefore limiting myself to generalized comment based on the practical experience of many groups, with only a few specific examples. These hints may be useful to supplement the effort of leaders to improvise methods for meeting specific conditions in specific communities, districts, and states.

The Essential, Decisive, Elective Offices

It will be clear to those who have followed my discussion to this point that American liberty can be preserved and socialism can be avoided by electing to public office leaders who are capable of shaping policy. In the determination of policy some elective offices are essentially decisive. Others are not. Members of the Congress of the United States hold offices of the first importance in determining policy. The coordinate office of President is vital. And experience has taught us the potential importance of the Vice President. Next in order are the governors of the states, not only because so many go to the Senate or the Presidency, but because they play a vital part in shaping state policies. Finally, there are the state legislatures. Many other public elective offices are important to a political party. But the foregoing are paramount. And for the immediate purpose of stemming the statist tide, the Congress and the Presidency should come first in any conservative plans. The election of the right people to these offices and the defeat of the wrong people are what I have in mind in this and the next chapter—in fact, throughout this book.

I am not concerned here with "good" citizenship generally, with municipal or county government, or with the details of government housekeeping. These are important but not of first importance. The preservation of free institutions comes first.

The Indispensable Citizen

The durable fame of Machiavelli rests upon much more than his cynical description of how a prince gained and kept his power in sixteenth-century Italy. Many of his comments on statecraft and military affairs in addition to those in *The Prince* were for his time revolutionary, but sound and of enduring value. He argued in his *Discourses on Livy* that the people were wiser and more constant than rulers, that republics were more to be trusted than principalities, and that the faults of the people were generally derived from the faults of their rulers.

There are two other pieces of wise advice from the famous Florentine which apply to my argument here. The first is that while people as isolated individuals, haunted by fear and distrustful of each other, freely sell their liberty to a ruler who promises security, the same people bound together in a common cause reveal invincible courage and audacity.

Another lesson can be learned from Machiavelli's classical military maxim that the safety of states must depend upon citizen armies. He reviewed with a mind sharpened by experience the dangers and weakness in mercenary and professional military forces and drew a conclusion that has since become a fundamental policy of modern nations. An army recruited from the ranks of citizens is best.

From this, a sound rule of political action can be derived. Free people cannot safely entrust the operation of their political machinery to professional politicians. The businessman who acquits himself of personal responsibility by merely giving money to a political organization and the poor man who gives his vote to a boss for gratitude, protection, or the hope of security are virtually employing mercenaries to fight their political battles and to run their government. There is thus created a class of politicians who acquire a vested interest all their own. They reveal a selfish urge for profits, for power, and for their own official perpetuation. Their concern is not the public interest; it is their political organization's interest. Despite pious protestations, this interest is usually quite independent of and in conflict with that of the nation, the state, or the community.

In a group of machine politicians there is a body of loyalty to the machine, with priority over that owed to the city, state, or nation. Based upon that loyalty, there operates a code of ethics that is apart from, and often antagonistic to, the standards that govern the general relations of individuals. In 1949, a candidate for mayor of the city of New York was offered to the people as vote-bait, although it was clear to those who saw beneath the surface that he had no intention of serving his term. As it happened, he did not. Also, in 1944, Democratic leaders urged Roosevelt to run, although, according to James A. Farley and many others who knew the facts, they were sure that the President was a dying man. He was their choice because he could save the ticket. The safety of the nation was a matter of lesser or of no importance.

The lesson of this is the need for the citizen's participation in politics. Citizens should not "hire" someone to care for their political interests.

In the Field of Public Opinion

THE PRESS AND RELATED ORGANS OF OPINION

The only members of that immense and diversified interest known as the press which enjoy independence are those who receive their support from the public generally, in the form of the sale of their product and of advertising. A newspaper, magazine, radio or television station that is dependent on a subsidy is not free, no matter how worthy its purpose may be. It is dedicated to a specific point of view. Its opinion is a labeled product. If it is supported by a special interest, it furthers that interest. If it is supported by an "angel," its opinions must conform measurably to those of its angelic master.

Thus, the preservation of a free press is utterly dependent on a free economy. When its major financial support comes from advertising, the press must sell its space impartially in a system of competitive business enterprise. The greater the competition, the more ample will be the field of sales. A newspaper or magazine must submit itself to a public vote of confidence every time it rolls off the press. And the advertiser, if he expects to stay in business, is concerned not so much with his personal preference for this or that newspaper or magazine as he is with the number and character of the people who buy and read it.

The faults of the press are open and palpable, and they have been freely exploited. But when the critics propose remedies, they usually suggest a form of public or private subsidy or more government control. They have not yet found a practicable substitute for what they call a "commercial" press.

The vital relationship between free enterprise generally and a free press is recognized by the press itself. For an overwhelming proportion of the American press has ceaselessly opposed the growth of statism and of Federal power over the past two decades. The fulminations against the press by President Truman and by his predecessor have not injured it or denied it public support.

True, Presidents and hundreds of lesser political officeholders have shown time and again that they can win elections despite the opposition of a large part of the press. But the press has survived and will outlive its present-day critics. For the fact that an electoral majority refuses to follow the editorial advice of the press is no proof that the press performs no useful purpose in expressing its opinions. A political party may lose a series of elections and still, by its opposition, preserve the very essence of free government. The value of an opinion is not lost through a defeat at the polls. The essential purpose of the press is not to organize voters and win elections. It is to inform, to criticize, and to provide news, and thus to serve people in and out of government.

The tendency, so generally deplored by critics, toward consolidation and therefore a decline in the number of daily newspapers, especially in the larger cities, has served the interests of liberty. Consolidation has resulted in more stable and solvent newspapers. Such newspapers are more able to resist pressures from minorities, from special business interests and from government. Nothing invites corruption more than weak and impoverished newspapers. A big paper that enjoys a "monopoly" in the morning or evening field must appeal to the generality of interests of the people, and nothing is more generally to be sought than liberty. Moreover, there is in large and profitable newspapers a capacity to provide more information, better reporting, and more diversified opinion. This is a net educational gain.

The value of the press as an agency of education in domestic politics has been limited since the outbreak of the war in Europe in 1939 by the heavy emphasis on news of war and foreign affairs. This has made it more and more difficult to provide a forum for debate on serious national issues. This shift in emphasis has also been notable on the radio.

Political news in newspapers and magazines as well as on the radio has been to a considerable degree colored by the left-wing and radical opinions of many members of the working press and of radio commentators.

Opinion thus subtly presented is very effective. When presented on the editorial page or signed by responsible commentators, opinion can be read and evaluated as such. But opinion inserted in biased news accounts is difficult to detect. The reader, moreover, is unable to identify and judge the value of its source.

To a degree, the responsibility for this has been due to the growth of the Newspaper Guild, which, according to its public pronouncements, has been and is not only an organization dedicated to the improvement of the working conditions of its members, but a vital political agency dedicated to statist policies.

Despite its faults, the press still fulfills its mission in the history of liberty. Without it, any effort to mobilize citizen action nationally against the entrenched power of a machine in office would be hopeless.

CONSERVATIVE AGENCIES FOR RESEARCH, EDUCATION, AND PROPAGANDA

There are dozens of privately supported agencies actively engaged in promoting free economic enterprise and in distributing general information favorable to free institutions. Some sponsor various sorts of programs on the radio and elsewhere. Some distribute books.

It is obviously impossible here to list these agencies, for their number is very large, their methods diversified, and they vary immensely in size and financial support. Nor is it possible to evaluate the results they attain, for their bread is scattered on many waters.

There are, in addition, innumerable business organizations and trade associations operating at national, state, and local levels which influence public opinion. Their material is also available for citizens' movements.

The case against statism has been effectively made many times in the printed and spoken argument put out by these agencies. It is quite probable that a majority of Americans are already convinced. The need remains, however, to bring arguments down to the immediate concerns of the individual voter, to repeat and repeat the arguments in different ways and with many homely examples, and finally, through personal contacts, to get the voter to act.

The persuasion of voters is a matter of trial and error. No one, however scientifically equipped he may be, can fully anticipate the specific arguments that will prove effective. They must be tested in the give and take of a campaign and modified in the light of experience.

The major service of the agencies described above is to provide leaders in local movements with material that they can adapt for their own campaigns.[1]

Potential Personal Leadership

SOURCES OF LEADERSHIP

Since our liberty is endangered by the political apathy of immense numbers of American citizens, it is important to

[1] An excellent example of how this can be done is provided in the activities of The American Economic Foundation, of which Fred G. Clark is the founder and the moving spirit. Its literature brings the fundamental principles and practices of economics down to the immediate day-to-day concerns of the worker and the consumer. Economics is presented within the framework of the individual's own "job security." Its aim is to get economics discussed "on buses, on street corners, in the lunch rooms and taverns."

know where this apathy is greatest. It is also important to know where political activity is now most likely to be found. An exceedingly interesting contribution to answers to these questions is a study by Julian L. Woodward and Elmo Roper, entitled "Political Activity of American Citizens." [2]

In this study, political activity was defined in five categories:

(1) voting at the polls, (2) supporting possible pressure groups by being a member of one or more of them, (3) personally communicating directly with legislators, (4) participating in political party activity and thus acquiring a claim on legislators and (5) engaging in habitual dissemination of political opinions through word-of-mouth communications to other citizens.

Questions covering these points were submitted to a national cross-section of 8,000 persons.

The general result showed the following percentages:

	Percentage of Total Sample Qualifying
Voting:	
Once or more in last four years	75
Three times or more	47
Five times or more	21
Discussing Public Issues with Others:	
Discusses frequently and takes an equal share in the conversation	21
Discusses frequently and usually tries to convince others he is right	6
Belonging to Organizations That Take Stands on Public Issues:	
Belongs to one or more such organizations	31
Belongs to two or more	7

[2] *The American Political Science Review*, Vol. 44, No. 4, December 1950, pp. 872–85.

*Percentage of
Total Sample
Qualifying*

*Written or Talked to Congressman or Other
Public Official to Give Own Opinion on a
Public Issue:*
> One or more times in past year   13
> Two or more times in the past year   7

*Worked for Election of a Political Candidate
in Last Four Years:*   11

*Contributed Money to a Party or Candidate in
Last Four Years:*   7

Assuming the correctness of the sample cross-section, one point is very clear: only a small percentage of our people take part in operating our political machinery.[3] Therefore we do not have "popular" government. The next question is: "What kinds of people are more active than others?" The Woodward-Roper study gives this answer:

AMOUNT OF POLITICAL ACTIVITY EXHIBITED BY
VARIOUS SUB-GROUPS IN THE POPULATION

*Percentage Within Each
Sub-Group Who Are
Politically Very Active*

Sub-Groups	
"A" economic level	36
Executives	34
Professional people	31
Stockholders	28
College-educated	24
"B" economic level	24
Republicans	15
Men	13
People 50 years of age and over	12
People 35–49 years	11

[3] This suggests why a citizen who chooses to be active in politics can exercise influence far beyond his own vote.

268

AMOUNT OF POLITICAL ACTIVITY EXHIBITED BY VARIOUS
SUB-GROUPS IN THE POPULATION (*Continued*)

	Percentage Within Each Sub-Group Who Are Politically Very Active
"C" economic level	11
White people	11
Farmers	11
Independents in politics	10
Total adult population	10
People with only high school education	9
Democrats	9
Non-stockholders	8
Women	8
People 21–34 years of age	8
Laboring people	6
Housewives	6
People with only grade school education	5
Negroes	5
"D" economic level	3

The authors do not tell us the basis of the "A," "B," "C," or "D" classifications. Presumably, they are based on incomes or on equivalent economic factors.

The authors caution us to note that while a much smaller percentage of "D's" than "A's" are politically active, there are many more "D's." The very active group is made up of 13 per cent "A's," 23 per cent "B's," 54 per cent "C's," and 10 per cent "D's."

The study analyzes the activity of four types of political affiliation in the sample.

Thus, the degree of activity among Republicans is greater, despite their inferiority in numbers in the sample. But the crux of the situation is in the "independent" and the "know nothing" groups. The "independents" should be the objectives of those who would win elections. They are, as we see,

	Percentage of Total Sample	*Percentage of Very Active*
Republicans	29	43
Democrats	44	38
Independent	16	16
Others, Don't Know and No Answer	11	3

fairly active, but unwilling to be listed as orthodox party members. They are also afflicted with apathy, and public apathy is the greatest asset, the very life blood, of those who are already in office.[4]

To avoid any misconception of the foregoing study, it should be clearly understood that, while the degree of political activity is higher in the "A" and "B" groups, they are numerically so small that their efforts are overwhelmed by the great numbers in the "C" and "D" groups. Thus, the efforts of those in the "A" and "B" groups must be greatly increased to overcome their inferiority in numbers. They must also direct their attention to the education and activation of as many as possible of those in the "C" and "D" groups. Individually, they are doing more, but nevertheless the percentage of the politically active among them is alarmingly small.

MILLIONS OF POLITICALLY IMPOTENT SALESMEN

One of the most remarkable aspects of the current American political situation is the political impotence of those who

[4] An important conclusion from the foregoing study is that new voters, hitherto politically detached and indifferent voters, and, what is also very important, people who live in new neighborhoods need the appeal of new types of leadership. The prospective recruit must first be won over to some effort to achieve nonparty objectives in his own neighborhood, such as an "improvement association" or a "Main Street merchants' association." He must contend with the reluctance of the old leaders to move aside and make room for new and younger leaders. Any organization should provide an avenue for the promotion of new leaders, "coming men." In a political organization failure is commonly due to this lack of opportunity for new leaders. The potential leaders of each new generation must see room at the top.

have the greatest capacity to sell goods and services. In normal times increase in demand is maintained by salesmanship. This makes possible more mass production, lower prices, abundant employment, and a high standard of living. From the clerk in a country store to the heads of the great advertising agencies of the nation, millions of Americans are selling their goods because they can make people believe in them. They take billions of dollars from the public in exchange for their products. Salesmen know the home life, the likes and dislikes, the preferences and prejudices of their customers, with whom they have invaluable personal contacts. But all over the land demagogues and self-seeking politicians are selling bad ideas to the very people to whom these salesmen are selling a variety of goods, from life insurance to shoelaces.

The salesman operates in the center of a free capitalist economy. His success depends on his customers' freedom of choice, free competition, and stimulated demand. Socialism is his deadly enemy. Under a planned society, people would get exactly what government decided they should get—no more, no less. Salesmen should help check statism before it reaches the point of no return or they, like Othello, will find their occupation gone.

This sales power should be applied to effective political action. These people should learn the art of selling sound political principles as well as goods.

Salesmen learn by trial and error and gradually develop their art in conformity with their personal capacities and traits. One will approach his prospect armed with reason and facts. Another will win through a spirit of good will and a shrewd use of flattery. One will force the issue directly and quickly, while another will use indirection and infinite patience. One insurance agent will sell a life policy by portraying the tragedy of unanticipated death; another will portray the mental peace of preparedness.

Hence, few specific rules can be laid down for the salesman

271

in politics. He must use his judgment as intelligently as he does in selling goods. He must understand the effect of his personality on those whom he would influence. And most of all, he must realize that in politics a face-to-face contact with a prospective voter is the most potent means yet known of exercising influence. As a beginner in politics he will enjoy learning how to meet the new and diverse human situations that will confront him.

As in selling goods, the important thing in politics is to win confidence and to be believed. One politician said to another, after a disastrous defeat in New York City: "We had a wonderful case. By all odds the better case and the better candidate. But they didn't believe us."

Automobile dealers and salesmen who sell millions of units a year and service other millions are important in the life of their communities and of outlying regions. They know many people and, what is more, they know those vital things about those people which enable them to appraise them as potential buyers. They operate in a keenly competitive atmosphere, but when they are trying to elect sound and intelligent public officials, they can work together despite their competition in business. In several states in 1950 the influence of automobile dealers was very important. In Utah, many of them organized among themselves in support of the Republican Senatorial candidate, Wallace Bennett, who incidentally was himself an automobile dealer.

Potentially important also are the farm-implement dealers who represent nationally known companies. There are also dealers in the oil products of many companies.

Consider also the immense potential influence of insurance agents. Their business brings them into every household, and the interests of their companies and of themselves are clearly in line with sound, economic, and free government.

A large number of these salesmen operate as free agents, businessmen in their own right, although they represent and

272

sell the products of nationwide companies. Surely those companies should place no restrictions upon the political activities of these agents. For the companies' vital interests as well as those of the country are involved. Some, in fact, would view such activity with genuine approval.

The salesman need not fear the loss of sales by a judicious use of political persuasion. For there are ways of persuading people that are more effective than argument. The salesman can serve his customer well if in a friendly manner he conveys sound advice far beyond that which concerns the excellence of his goods. The salesman and his manager have a common interest with the customer in a sound economy.

ADVERTISING MEN AND WOMEN

The advertising business exists because people demand freedom of choice in buying what they need and want. It does more than offer varieties of products to desirous customers. It also creates the desires that lie behind demand. Because it is the means of creating as well as of meeting demand, it has performed a major role in building America's miracle of mass production.

Not only is the business of advertising essential to our American economic system, but advertising men and women have a vital reason for maintaining it. There is no lack of appreciation of this among the members of the business. Immense amounts of talent and money have been devoted to the interpretation of, and arguments for, a free economy. Many advertising men have taken active parts in political campaigns.

The specialized talents of the advertising profession have great political potentialities. These have already shown themselves in the promotion of the basic ideal of economic liberty. The great need is to channel advertising talents directly into political activity. Creating public opinion is important. But to deliver the votes is essential. This large group is a most promising source of help in creating, aiding, and directing citizen action.

THE BUSINESSMAN'S CHOICE

Business management is a widely inclusive term. It refers not only to those responsible for general direction and control, but to those engaged in hundreds of specialized activities, including production, selling, and research.[5]

There is a theory, altogether too prevalent, that "business and politics don't mix." The concept behind this is that since business ministers to all, regardless of political distinctions, it is inappropriate for people in business to engage in active politics. There might have been some validity in this theory long ago, when government had only limited functions, when it was managed largely by lawyers and professional politicians, and when business was largely unaffected by party changes. In those days it was believed that when a businessman participated in politics he lost customers and neglected his business. It was taken for granted that the businessman must be outwardly neutral in politics.

But government now touches business on all sides. Political decisions profoundly affect economic life and condition almost all business decisions. The businessman must understand political as well as economic processes. Moreover, in the present choice of ideologies, which must be resolved in the political arena, the businessman is faced by the plain issue of self-preservation. He must, through political action, protect the system under which his business operates or he will ultimately lose the control of his business altogether. This is true for every type and size of business.

[5] In the next chapter there are set forth some specific suggestions for businessmen, based on the experience of some of them in political activity. It suffices in this chapter to consider some of the factors that have limited the usefulness of businessmen in politics.

Another deterrent to the activity of business managers in politics is a widely held belief that political activity should be delegated to specialists. A company, for example, employs a public relations man and vests in him certain responsibilities, which usually include political and governmental relations. There is, of course, room for specialized public relations. But the top managers of a business can no more delegate all political relations than they can delegate all functions of thinking, eating, or sleeping.

Nor can they delegate their political responsibilities to a political party by occasional cash contributions. This is as naïve as the idea that to contribute to a missionary society is to buy the way to Heaven, or that a gift to the Community Chest relieves a company of the responsibility for the welfare of its employees. Politics sorely needs the fine judgment and intelligence, as well as the money, of business managers.

Still another factor that deters businessmen from political activity is the widespread belief that the businessman is inept and incompetent in politics. His mental processes, it is held, do not fit the subtleties of political action. The prevalence of this view overcomes the businessman with a sense of futility. He yields to his fears and stays aloof.

There are solid reasons for his reluctance. Politics largely deals with what seems to be true rather than what is true, with what people can be induced to believe rather than what is the truth. In business calculations two and two must be four. Two and two in politics are what people can be made to believe they are.

Professional politicians have discouraged businessmen from developing an interest in politics. The professionals want to keep things in their own hands.

Finally, there is the bitter fact that demagogic attacks upon "business" during the past two decades have taken their toll. They have prejudiced people against business in government. And they have driven the demoralizing belief into many businessmen that, since they have been depicted as pariahs, they will actually impair public confidence in whatever they join.

This reluctance will pass as more businessmen brave the rigors of politics and win public confidence by their activity in politics or in office. The example of Wallace Bennett of Utah, a past president of the National Association of Manufacturers, in winning a Senatorship in that state against an entrenched politician should go far to dissipate the concept of the businessman as a political pariah.

With some practice the businessman can acquire the important political art of public speaking. In the British Parliamentary campaign in 1950, Lord Woolton was, I thought, next to Churchill the best Conservative speaker.

Lord Woolton demonstrated another important service that a businessman can bring to organized political action. He understands organization, for he has great executive ability. Lord Woolton directed the building up of the machinery of the Conservative Party in preparation for the 1950 and 1951 campaigns, and he did a magnificent job. The Conservatives excelled the Labour Party in the direction of hundreds of constituency campaigns, and in the quality of their propaganda and their speeches.

Of all human activities, political campaigns probably represent the low mark in efficiency and economy. In large part this is due to the fact that politicians generally have little executive ability. Their mental processes lack the precision essential to comprehensive planning. No one talks so much of planning as do politicians. Few do so little planning. Here is where businessmen have a genuine contribution to make.

The gap between business objectives and political objectives is not so great as it may seem. Business, too, is concerned with making people believe things, with presenting facts attractively and persuasively.

276

The businessman should realize that in politics the best protection is usually attack. In politics, strangely enough, the man in front who is throwing punches is least likely to get hurt. His opponents will usually resort to attack at the flank or the rear. They will put pressure on his more timid followers, on the bank that lends money to his business, on the union to which his employees belong. It is the fearsome, the reluctant, the timid warriors who can be "handled."

A final word might be helpful to rekindle the courage of those businessmen who have seen politicians make a whipping-boy of "business" for many years and who are obsessed with the belief that businessmen are unpopular. Politicians have invested a mythical creature called "business" with all the sins of a small minority of businessman. It is a hackneyed expression but a true one that the sins of the few are not the responsibility of the many, especially in such a vast and diverse area as business.

This is recognized by the common sense of most people. They may listen to denunciations of "business," but they like and trust individual businessmen. Despite the confidence of demagogues that prejudice can always be effectively created by attacking the prosperous and successful businessman, there lies in most people a fundamental respect for the man who can be so described. His economic position offers assurance that he does not have to steal the public's money and that he has little or nothing to gain in politics. It lies within the capacity and province of businessmen to increase this respect and confidence.[6]

[6] A businessman in a successful citizens' movement suggest the following functions that businessmen should perform in a similar organization: "First they should provide most of the finances. Next, they should be heavily concerned in the creation of the organizational machinery in campaigns. They should fully participate in the delicate relations with the political party with which co-operation is desired. They should have a hand in selecting candidates. And they are essential in selecting paid workers for publicity, advertising and the training of other paid workers and volunteers. They should participate, perhaps in a less important way, in formulating campaign literature, slogans and research."

THE LAWYER'S ROLE

In the first half of our national life, the legal profession held almost a monopoly of leadership in politics and government. Since then, the political influence of lawyers has declined. It is still potent, however, and in a citizens' movement it is indispensable. Lawyers' training in the principles of politics and jurisprudence, their understanding of law, their training in dialectic and public speaking are their major contributions. The jury lawyer, moreover, knows how to pitch his appeal to all sorts and conditions of people—to explain, move, and persuade.

The slant of mind of lawyers, despite many contemporary exceptions, is conservative. *Stare decisis* still prevails in their training. Moreover, in private practice many of them serve businesses and individuals whose interests are opposed to statism. In private practice, as distinguished from government service, their personal interest is in freedom from government control. In socialist England there was persistent pressure to "socialize" the profession. That danger is definitely latent here. Lawyers thus have not only a moral responsibility, but this special concern in protecting their profession.

AWAKENED DOCTORS

These hitherto nonpolitical people have been hurled into public controversy by the threat of government medicine. They are alerted recruits.

The organized efforts of their professional associations have already trained them in the arts of political action. In recent elections their influence in many places has been effective, and in some places decisive. They must learn, however, that freedom is indivisible. Private medicine cannot be saved alone. The doctor must generalize his struggle. His use-

278

fulness in citizen action is very great, for his concerns reach every type of citizen. He must learn to prescribe sound political ideas as well as medicine.

While over the past few years there has been a great increase in the political activities of doctors and dentists, there are already ominous signs that this interest is subsiding. It is essential that their leaders keep them awake to the danger to their professional interests and to their concerns as citizens in statist policies. There will be no abandonment by statist politicians and others of the intent to take the medical profession into the custody of government. It is a primary objective of socialism here, as it was in Britain.

UNDERRATED WOMEN

In political activities the usefulness of women is distinctive on two grounds: greater opportunity for leisure has enabled many of them to read more about public issues than their husbands and brothers; and the average married woman of thirty-five and over in the middle or higher income groups has more time to spare for political work. And, what is also important, they are often able to contribute not only time but money.

The proportion of women who complete high school and college has greatly increased in the past generation. Ultimately, their formal education will exceed that of men. And I can testify, after many years' experience in teaching government and politics to college men and women, that the capacity of women to comprehend the realities of politics is fully equal to that of men.

It should be added that the amount of property possessed by women grows relatively larger. Since so much of this is in the form of savings and inheritances, their stake in the preservation of the kind of government that will protect their property is tremendous.

279

In political activities, women are likely to put more emotional drive into their efforts than are men. The testimony of political managers indicates that women in the field and in the office work harder and produce more results than do men in the same jobs. Moreover, women are more likely to do with speed and enthusiasm the prosaic jobs, such as addressing and stuffing envelopes and making house-to-house calls. Such jobs are the very life blood of successful campaigning. If women feel that the cause is good, they will conquer boredom and fatigue to get the mechanical work done.

In several instances of citizen action on local and district levels in the past few years, women's capacity to participate seems to have been overlooked by the businessmen in charge. This is a great mistake. Responsible and able women and their many club connections should be fully utilized.[7]

TEACHERS AND EDUCATORS

Since education to a large degree is a recognized function of government, the enlisting of teachers and others concerned with education in politics presents a special and delicate problem. Political activity is largely proscribed in tax-supported schools. This, of course, does not apply to educators employed in privately supported schools.

In the public schools at the elementary and secondary levels, teachers are, like most white-collar workers, confined to salary ranges that make them the first victims of inflation. But since their salaries are paid from tax collections, teachers

[7] Scott Wilson, veteran of many campaigns in the South and manager of two successful campaigns of reform Mayor Morrison in New Orleans, says this of the value of women in political campaigns: "Women's vote—their activity in Independent Voters' League, etc.—is frequently the balance of power. As former Mayor Maestri of New Orleans said: 'Dem skirts beat me.' I've seen society women precinct workers stand down and rout tough political bosses. Their endless love of argument is something near impossible to cope with at the polls—where coming and going voters only get flash impressions. Logic gets lost in wordiness in political debate—by women. God love 'em."

are likely to look to government rather than to private sources for relief. School board members, trustees, and directors of higher educational institutions should understand that a low-salary policy that thrusts a heavier and heavier burden on teachers will drive its victims into movements antagonistic to free enterprise. The most effective way to enlist the members of the teaching profession on the side of the middle interests is to provide them with salaries and working conditions commensurate with those prevailing in private business. For these teachers shape the attitudes of the growing generation for or against traditional liberties. The influence of teachers, directly and indirectly, upon parent voters must not be overlooked.[8]

WAGE EARNERS

I have already pointed out [9] the great shift in political outlook of wage earners since their incomes have moved upward among the middle groups. This suggests the increasing possibility of enlisting wage earners and their wives in citizens' political movements. Above all, such political activity, even when originated by business leaders, should seek a cross-section of all interests. Even such political action organizations as the C.I.O.-P.A.C., sponsored by union leaders, have energetically proselyted many groups other than wage earners. There is nothing exclusive about their membership. No exclusiveness should be permitted in a citizens' movement. It should be as broad in its base as a national political party professes to be.

Great numbers of wage earners still fail to realize how rapidly they have moved up in the economic scale relative to other groups. They can be apprised of this without offense to them. Moreover, the few who do appreciate their

[8] A Southern politician makes this wise comment: "Country school bus drivers bring to the home more than kids in lots of rural areas."
[9] See Ch. III.

great stake in conservative government policies can become useful exponents of these vital economic facts among their fellow workers.

FARM LEADERS

Farmers, once the embodiment of individualism, have shown surprising capacity to organize in recent years. The great national farmer groups such as the Farm Bureau Federation and the National Grange are composed of thousands of local groups. The officers and members of these groups have great influence in their communities. There is no inconsistency in their enlistment in citizens' movements. For, of all people, the farmer has probably the most to lose through dependence upon the government.

OTHER SOURCES OF LEADERSHIP

Many more groups of leaders will suggest themselves and, without attempting to exhaust the list, a few should be mentioned.

There are the executives of clubs and associations of all sorts, whose activities bring them into close contact with public life. Among the organizations they serve are the various service clubs, chambers of commerce, farm organizations, church and women's clubs, and others.

Such clubs and groups must realize that the success of their principles and policies must depend on their influence, which extends beyond their membership. Their members have multitudinous outside contacts. Weekly meetings at which current national policies are denounced and deplored serve only the limited purpose of exciting the converted. Indignation that never bears fruit in action withers away in sterile pessimism.

There are also many officials of labor unions who have no

obligation or duty to conform to the political objectives of the top leaders or political arms of the great federations. These local union leaders are a part of the communities in which they live. Their fundamental political interests lie for the most part with those of other members of their communities.

A great source of political leadership can be found among retired farmers and retired business and professional men and women in every community. They have leisure, which is indispensable for political activity. Since statism is a threat to savings and personally attained security, and since conservatism is an attribute of age, these elder citizens are obvious recruits.

CHAPTER X

Organizing for Freedom

The Arduous Ways of Politics

George Santayana, whose spiritual and intellectual roots are in his Spanish ancestry and the aristocratic atmosphere of New England society, has taken a doubtful view of the excellence of popular government. In his opinion pure democracy, if it were to produce a high culture, would require more of the common citizen than his past behavior might promise. "If a noble and civilized democracy is to subsist," he wrote, "the common citizen must be something of a saint and something of a hero. We see, therefore, how justly flattering and profound, and at the same time how ominous, was Montesquieu's saying that the principle of democracy is virtue." [1]

Santayana also pointed out that it is not in the spirit of democracy to offer prizes. Even public office, he continued, confers no great distinction, and no great profit if honestly administered.

The effective exercise of influence in a free society requires a sedulous and unremitting devotion to very prosaic activity. Its meager rewards are offset by personal sacrifice, bitter reverses, and periodic frustration. Perhaps because the rewards are so doubtful and unsatisfying to the fastidious, sensitive

[1] George Santayana: *Reason in Society* (New York: Charles Scribner's Sons; 1905), p. 136.

mind, political activity has been left in large part to those whose satisfactions are material and self-serving.

But since in our time government, through doing very ordinary things, has attained an enormous power over our life, the direction of political life should become the task of extraordinary people.[2] What Henry Wallace calls the age of the common man can be attained only by uncommonly good and brave men and women.

Superficial people can find excitement in politics because they regard it as a game. But it is much more than a game. It is a serious struggle for existence and for the values that make existence worth while.

With this in mind, devoted people in increasing numbers have fortunately been willing to scorn delights and give themselves to the hard task of lifting the levels of political life.

Despite the pessimism of such observers of free government as Santayana, political activity does offer exciting rewards. Woodrow Wilson once said: "Nothing that is human is alien to the science of politics." As a person works beyond the preliminaries into the vitals of politics, the boundless concerns of human life unfold before him. A voter's motives are a mosaic of personal interest, altruism, prejudice, habit, and factual knowledge. While a political appeal, addressed to wider and wider audiences, seeks common denominators of interest, personal appeals to prospective voters to go to the polls or to vote for specific persons and policies must be designed for each individual. This requires resourcefulness, hu-

---

[2] I made this point in my 27 *Masters of Politics* (New York: Funk & Wagnalls; 1949): "To a philosopher, a scientist or a great lawyer, the preoccupations of a politician seem to be the interests of a person too lazy to apply himself to serious things. This is a gross underestimation of the politician's job. For beneath the surface he is applying his mental faculties to exceedingly complex subject matter, and if he is to be successful he must labor with incessant energy and meticulous care. For political genius is the capacity to give continuous, undivided and sedulous attention to matters that to most serious people seem too trivial to bother with."

man sympathy, sensitiveness, and skill. The details of political action that seem so dull at first become more important and attractive. But the ultimate values that political action should seek are beyond reckoning.

The Moral Responsibility of Free Men

As Santayana so clearly points out, the person who dedicates himself to the tasks required of a citizen in a democracy must indeed be exceptional. It is a sad commentary on human nature in this age, perhaps in every past age, that so few people are stirred by a sense of duty to participate in public affairs and that whoever dedicates himself to political action, with a full appreciation of its dangers, trials, and dearth of personal gain, must be stirred by unusual moral convictions and courage.[3]

It is a pity, too, that an effort to stir people to participate in politics must be largely based upon appeals either to the material interests of those who stand to lose by present trends or to the possibility of personal advancement in public life. Those who have been more favored by their position in the moderate or more fortunate ranges of our society should primarily be moved by a moral sense toward the interests of their country. They owe a great deal to the free institutions under which they and their forebears have lived. They have a deep obligation to those who will come after them. They should not in conscience permit the nation's liberty to be wasted away by rapacious and misguided leaders. Their sense

[3] A perceptive student of politics, after reading this chapter in manuscript, made the following comment: "I wonder whether there is enough of the old Presbyterian sense of duty to make the appeal even stronger by the introduction of the idea that it is a stern duty and obligation of the upper orders to perform a leadership of trusteeship. This struck me quite forcibly the other day in reading the biography of Henry L. Stimson. I had never thought of him as out plugging a precinct, but he started in that way."

of what the country deserves should move them to save it from error, waste, and ultimate disaster.

Citizen Action Must Be Militant

Business and professional men are altogether too prone to limit their political action to applauding the speeches and writings of others, to heated private denunciations of the op-position, and to occasional small contributions to their favored organizations and parties. They hate to declare them-selves publicly in an election campaign. They are like mem-bers of a religion who will kneel down for their faith but will not stand up for it. A passion for political anonymity per-vades a large majority of our people. Often it is shrouded in protestations of independence, neutrality, or open-minded-ness. Essentially, it is based on the fear of losing friends or business, of endangering a job, or of hard work.

The fight against statism cannot be won by the timid and noncommittal. People must forego convenience, and security from criticism. They must get into politics personally, di-rectly, and actively. They must be for someone and against someone, despite the consequences. Citizen action must be militant.

The Vote Is the Payoff

All the effort, money, and ingenuity devoted to selecting good candidates, arguing for a cause, writing, printing, and distributing literature, making speeches, and organizing ral-lies are in vain, if on Election Day voters do not vote. For the vote is the payoff, the power and the promise of the future.

That, of course, means getting out the right kind of voters.

We can count on the opposition and its allies to get out their supporters.

But what assurance have we that citizen action for more votes will get out the right vote and not the wrong vote? There is no real assurance. But there are many evidences that the "right" people have been more laggard in voting than the "wrong" people.

Between 1940 and 1948 the total number of Americans eligible to vote rose from approximately 80,000,000 to 91,000,-000. That is an increase of 11,000,000. The figure is probably over 95,000,000 now.

In 1940, approximately 50,000,000 people voted for President. In 1944, 48,000,000. In 1948, 48,833,680.

This is an indication that something is radically wrong. Part of the trouble was with the candidate in 1944 and 1948. But we cannot blame it all on Governor Dewey. Mr. Middle-Interest American deserves the heavier censure because, if he is going to wait until just exactly the right candidate comes along, he may lose his liberty in the interim.

Willkie received, in round numbers, 22,300,000 votes in 1940. Dewey received 22,000,000 in 1944 and almost exactly the same number in 1948. The Republican failure in 1948 becomes glaringly apparent when it is considered that in 1948 there were nearly 5,000,000 more potential voters than there were four years earlier and also that in 1944 there were some millions of men and women in military service.

But the Roosevelt and Truman votes fell off even more, relatively and absolutely. Roosevelt had 27,200,000 in 1940 and 25,600,000 in 1944. Truman had 24,100,000 in 1948. And even if we add to the Truman 1948 vote the votes for Thurmond and Wallace, the total fell below the Roosevelt 1940 vote by a million.

Those who believe that a more "colorful" candidate can answer their need should note the relatively small difference between the vote for the most "colorful" Roosevelt in 1944

288

and the least "colorful" Truman in 1948. That difference was 1,500,000. Such a difference would not at this rate bridge the gap between the parties. It is organized action that is needed, not a more glamorous candidate.

Citizen action can shop in a colossal market of more than 42,000,000 possible stay-at-homes. To be sure, no one knows how these will vote if they come out. A little faith and a bit of knowledge must suffice. If those who want a change believe in their cause and feel that intelligent people believe in it, they ought to get out as many people as possible. They ought, of course, to beat the bushes with more vigor in sections where people live whose interests are most endangered by socialistic trends.

In the British Parliamentary elections of 1950 and 1951 about 84 per cent of the eligibles voted. In that large turnout socialism was effectively checked. In 1948 in the United States 54 per cent voted! That points to the heart of the problem.

Personal Contact Is Indispensable

The business or professional man or woman who decides to engage in political activity, in fact any beginner in politics, must learn one lesson above all others. There is absolutely no substitute for personal, face-to-face contact with the voter. In our complex life outside the realm of politics we have the habit of delegation, of contacts by telephone, telegraph, and letters, of dependence upon advertising, publicity releases, and other forms of printed persuasion, or speeches. But in politics, where the final and indispensable act is the voter at the polling place casting the vote, there is nothing that can be substituted for personal contact. Political machines operate on this principle as a matter of course. Their methods are based upon experience, tradition, and habit.[4]

[4] For an interesting confirmation of this, see Paul Lazarsfeld's *The People's Choice* (New York: Duell, Sloan & Pearce, Inc.; 1944). In this book the author

This stresses the necessity for people who engage in political action of any kind to get out of their homes and offices and go into the highways and byways, no matter how difficult it may be for them to find the time, and no matter how unaccustomed to such activity they may be. This also stresses that workers whose job it is to make direct contacts with voters are a first consideration in any political plans and budgets.

Citizen Action for, Not of, a Party

The attitude of organized citizens toward parties should not be hostile. A citizen who participates with other citizens in nonpartisan action against statism can also be a party member.

But we face an immediate, emergent need. The decisive millions are in neither party. And the machinery of one party has been captured on the national level by the statists.

The real function of parties as legally organized groups is to serve the purposes of citizens. In many districts the parties provide the bus, the driver, and the maintenance men. Nonpartisan citizen action can and should furnish the passengers.

The late President Lowell of Harvard said that parties are brokers. If public opinion favors this or that, the party will adopt this or that as its objective. The party should act as the means through which public opinion accomplishes its purposes in government. It operates in the field of ideas as a broker operates in commodities. It acts as an agent without too much regard for the value or the nature of the product. Its compensations are the perquisites and honors of office.

A party should not be regarded as a creator of policy. It se-

---

presents the results of a study of how people made up their minds to vote in 1940. The point made is that those who changed their minds were influenced not by newspapers, magazines, or radio, but mostly by personal contacts, often more or less chance contacts.

lects policies and ideas as its means of attracting votes. If enough voters want a policy supported, and if under capable leadership a considerable number of them are organized to work inside and outside a party, that party will adopt their policy.

Understanding the Politician

Since the citizen who engages militantly in political action must deal with professional politicians of all sorts and conditions, he should grasp clearly the motives, the personal characteristics, and the manner of thinking of these complex but indispensable people. It would take volumes to explain the politician, and even after such an effort the conclusion would have to be registered that this species is almost as diversified as man himself. A few general hints, however, may be helpful to the novice in politics. In a most realistic study [5] of the master politician Sir Robert Walpole, F. S. Oliver offers this general statement:

"To gain power, to keep it, and to govern—these are the special business of the politician, just as it is a working bee's business to make honeycomb and honey . . . if a politician, having gained power, should neglect to govern, and should dissipate his energies in an endeavor to do good in other ways, he will certainly fail both in his endeavor and in his duty."

There is an unwritten code that imposes itself upon a professional politician, in part separated from the code that governs his nonpolitical relations and to a degree detached from that which governs his conduct as a patriotic member of his nation. His job—his duty—is to win elections and to hold power as long as he can. He pursues this objective with devo-

[5] *The Endless Adventure* (London: Macmillan and Company, Ltd.; 1931), p. 31.

tion and often at great sacrifice of personal comfort, of material gain, and of the personal relations that others regard as their prime concerns. Politicians can put the interests of party above that of country. Or to put it more charitably, if you will, they can conceive the interests of party and country to be identical. Considerations of complete frankness can be waived for political advantage. When there are erring party brethren, there may be in the politician's mind more than one interpretation of the meaning of being a brother's keeper. In dealing with facts, the politician is moved not by a desire to portray things as they are, but by the urge to present them in a manner to move people to do this or that.

The citizen who enters politics may be constrained to reform the politician's code. If he should succeed, he will be doing what has never been done before. He is most likely to fail, and, for his pains, he will make resentful enemies. In any event, we can leave these realities for consideration at some other time and seize upon another fact, also pointed out cogently by Oliver:

If a politician would keep his followers loyal to him, he must be careful not to outrage their feelings of right and wrong. His course of action is therefore determined from the beginning by the morals of other people. . . . An artist, starving in a garret because he has ventured to outrage the public taste, may yet paint masterpieces; but political masterpieces can be made by a politician working in energetic partnership with a prevalent opinion.[6]

This shrewd observation points squarely at the objective that citizen action should attain. For citizens so engaged may, without any danger of acquiring the occupational morality of politics, bend the professionals' energy and interest to their side by winning a public following of their own and by shaping a public opinion consistent with their ideals. They will then find ready acceptance and invaluable co-operation

[6] Ibid., p. 31.

among the politicians whose side they decide to support. This will suffice to satisfy the moral requirements of the moment. The recasting of traditional codes of the politician can wait for a more leisurely time.

What Level for Citizen Action? [7]

There can be no generalized, specific answer to this question. The answer in each specific case must depend upon the practical circumstances that confront those who initiate and lead citizens' movements. Limitations of acquaintance and resources may make it advisable to begin with a city block or a township. The county may be a practicable area. The Congressional district not only offers a wide scope for action, but results there are directly measurable in terms of national influence. A citizens' movement in a Congressional district or a state should be subdivided into smaller geographical units.

Leaders should plan the geographical scope of their activities in line with the number and the area of residence of the voters they want to reach. In whatever area they select, they should have the resources and a potential supply of leaders and workers to reach every voter directly—to push every doorbell—and to learn something about every family. An attempt to organize in too large an area leads to spotty, imperfect work, the results of which are impossible precisely to

[7] In what follows, I have incorporated ideas and methods gathered in a large number of states, districts, and localities. The general idea of citizen action is far from new. But in recent years, notably since the advent of the Truman Fair Deal, there has been increasing evidence of a national trend toward citizen activity outside the parties. Some citizen's movements, as I have already noted, have been notably successful and have continued and expanded their efforts. Others have been more or less impractical, impermanent, and visionary. Some have limited their efforts to a get-out-the-vote campaign. Others have covered a wider range of political activity, from active participation in selecting candidates to more or less formal alliances with one or the other party. And some have worked within the party framework with the definite purpose of capturing party control.

measure. And when such a movement fails to have the stimulus of some success, it is most likely to ebb away in discouragement.

Perhaps the best rule is to divide and subdivide activities in line with the common interests of groups of voters. The geographical areas selected may not always be identical with such political subdivisions as counties, towns, wards, and precincts. In cities they may center in racial or religious groups, where there are homogeneous areas of that sort. They may be based on common economic ties, such as employment in specific plants or industries. In rural areas, it may be more convenient to work in such political areas as towns, townships, or counties.

On the other hand, operations may be confined to special groups of leaders. In recent campaigns, groups of leaders from specific businesses or professions have operated over a large area—groups comprising lawyers, doctors, advertising people, automobile dealers, insurance salesmen, and others. In these cases the leader-workers have a specific clientele that they can conveniently reach.

In the Taft campaign in Ohio in 1950, where the opposition comprised various labor units, dozens of small organizations were formed to get out Taft voters in many areas, from single streets to counties and districts.

What Objective?

We are concerned here with militant political action, which means positive support of specific candidates and policies and opposition to other specific candidates and policies. I am not concerned here with vague and generalized efforts to teach "good government," to clean up affairs in specific cities, counties, and communities, or to create and distribute educational and propaganda material. Such objectives are generally good and sound. But their consideration lies beyond the scope of this book.

The first decision that must be made by any group intent upon organizing militant political action is its objective.

1. Does it intend to keep itself independent of any legally constituted party organization but support the candidate or candidates of one or the other party? In short, will it co-operate with a party without being identified with it?

2. Does it intend to work within the legal framework of a party for the purpose of gaining party control?

3. Does it intend to limit itself to a specific function, such as to get out the vote?

It is very important to make this decision. For to confuse the first and second of these possible objectives will result in misunderstanding, waste, and duplication of effort, and the ultimate weakening of both citizen activity and party responsibility. The ideal of all effective citizen action should be the creation of responsible party government of such a character as to win the active and devoted support of many citizens.

Some Blueprints

INDEPENDENT ORGANIZED POLITICAL ACTION

Preliminary Organization. In an area of some size, such as a county, Congressional district, city, or even a state, small groups of twenty to thirty carefully selected men and women should first be called together. Then the initiators can explain the need, purposes, and methods of action. Since members of such groups have many contacts and connections through their businesses, clubs, clients, and the like, further meetings can be held by the initial members. Such groups should later be called together in every strategic place in the area to be covered.[8]

Since the members of such groups are generally quite inexperienced in political activity, a process of education should begin with them. It is best to move slowly at first, until complete understanding has been reached on objectives, policies, and methods, and until adequate financing has been assured.

It is significant that some of the most successful citizens' organizations in this country have operated from the beginning without a specified name, without a letterhead, without any formal officers. Perhaps nothing more than some such unpretentious name as "Citizens' Committee" is needed. The purpose of anonymity has been to frustrate opposition attack.

In the preliminary movements of such a group it should be remembered that its strength will at first be overestimated by the opposition. Professional politicians are panicky people. They rush into hostile counteraction. This must be anticipated and effectively met with firm and rapid action by the citizens' group. A citizens' group must not start until it is ready, and then it must move fast.

Expert Management. Those who initiate and control citizens' organizations should themselves serve without compensation, but they will find it essential to employ expert management. A businessman who started a highly successful movement says: "A political campaign is like a sales campaign. The candidate and his principles must be 'sold' by

[8] Scott Wilson, the successful manager of a citizens' movement in New Orleans, has this to say of the preliminary steps in setting up a citizens' group: "It is best to start with a small group first—say four business and professional men. Then have another meeting with the group enlarged to eight. Then twelve. But if for the next meeting twice that number is invited, maybe only fifteen will come. That may be because somebody is scaring off the early converts. It is best then to put the whole matter square on the line publicly and have a big meeting and get under way."

word of mouth and by advertising. 'Sales' managers and division managers direct routine 'salesmen' and hundreds of volunteers."

Top management and training talent should be selected for genuine competence, tact, and proven capacity in the work required. When it seems advisable, such people should be adequately paid. It is better to pay a good worker than to accept an incompetent volunteer. To pay or not to pay depends on circumstances that must be decided by those who initiate and support the movement. Successful movements have found it advisable generally to pay most of their full-time workers who must be employed over a period of months or years.

Top staff workers should be neither public office-holders nor seekers for public office. When such personal interests are present, there is a temptation to build relationships or organizations to be used later for personal purposes. Moreover, relations with a party are impaired by any suspicion of self-seeking.

Since a political movement is a militant effort to win an objective against entrenched opposition, its operations should be disciplined and under unified command. An expert manager should be in command. The initiating committee should not cross lines. It should work solely through the manager, just as a corporation's board works through its president.

Finances. A citizens' organization should operate on sound budgetary principles. A yardstick should be established for contributions. The C.I.O.-P.A.C. has tried to get one dollar a member; the A.F.L. two dollars, although both have fallen far short of their goals. Businessmen and professional men and women should contribute according to their means and importance. Paid solicitors are not suitable for collecting contributions and pledges. This should be done by businessmen and others in the original group who can talk plainly to their friends and business associates.

Too much money is just as dangerous as too little. The appearance of opulence may be deadly. In a citizens' group it antagonizes the political party that is the object of its help. The public, however, is quick to penetrate any phony demonstration of poverty. Tammany leaders have never lost the support of their followers by living well, dressing well, and assuming a reasonably dignified and forthright appearance of well-being. Perhaps the golden mean is an efficient, well-equipped organization that is neither wasteful nor parsimonious.

The finances of a citizen's group must be competently and responsibly handled. Payment for party work should be forthright and strictly equitable. If a precinct needs five workers on election day, each of these workers should receive precisely the same pay and each one should know that the others are getting the same. Payments to workers should be made by the supervisory official in charge, and he should give headquarters a receipt for the money.

These details are vital. Money must not stick to the hands of intermediaries. It must not be surreptitiously given to anyone. For there are no secrets in the inner councils of politics. Money should be paid at fair rates, and only for actual work performed. Payment for anything else is sowing dragon's teeth.

Political organizations are notably erratic in matters of finance. Part of the time too much is spent, and the rest of the time there isn't enough to spend. Sound financial management is essential, particularly in a group whose main purpose is to work for better financial management in government.

A citizens' group should scrupulously observe the law in collecting and spending money in political activities. Competent legal advice and direction are essential to the staff of the group. It hardly needs to be stressed that the Federal as well as state corrupt-practices laws should be studied and carefully complied with.[9]

Contributions to the Party. A citizens' group must make it clear that it is not getting money that otherwise would go to the political party whose candidate is getting support. That sort of thing helped to wreck the Willkie campaign in 1940.

A clear understanding should be had with the official leaders of the party with which a citizens' group is co-operating. Since the political party must employ precinct or township leaders who work to get out the party vote, who provide poll watchers, canvassers, and the like, some means must be found to help pay them whatever is allowed under the law.

In all these matters of contact with the formal political party, liaison should be constantly maintained by the citizens' group through a political manager or agent. He can see that contributions really get to the people to whom they are due, and he can maintain friendly relations with the party officers, the candidates, his manager, and others.

Getting Good Candidates. A primary task of a citizens' group is to use every legitimate means to get good candidates to run. That is not easy. To run for Congress and to remain there is a formidable matter for anyone who has a successful business or profession that needs attention. And most people suitable for an important office have such obligations.

Even if elected, a person in political life has financial and other obligations that are heavy. He must ordinarily depend on and get along with a political organization at home that may be sluggish, incompetent, indifferent, or worse. He gets

[9] A memorandum on the Federal laws governing citizens' political groups appears as an Appendix, p. 337. The statements of law therein I believe to be accurate as of 1951, but they should be checked by any group using them for possible changes by amendment or judicial interpretation.

little financial help in campaigns, poor publicity, tepid encouragement, and plenty of criticism. Moreover, there are always enemies and rivals at home working against him while he is struggling with his job in Washington.

Citizens' organizations can help greatly in inducing better people to run and in helping good men who are running for, or are already in, office. And leaders of an organization can do a great deal to induce the official party to select or accept better candidates. The whole tone and character of public life, notably of Congress, can be immensely improved by the presence in districts and states of strong citizens' organizations, dedicated not to this or that special interest, but to sound, economical government and the traditional interests of the nation.

A citizens' movement that collaborates with an existing party organization can show the organization that it has real political strength, and thus can greatly influence the selection of candidates for Congress and other offices.

Enlisting and Training Political Workers. When groups of leaders have been strategically placed in the area from which activity should fan out, when some money is in hand and more is pledged, and when expert professional workers are employed, the preliminaries are completed.

The second step is to get volunteer workers to make direct contact with voters. This can be done first by carefully going over the ward, precinct, town, and township election returns to see where work should be concentrated. It is important to recognize that the greatest need and opportunity for citizen action are in the spots where there has been the highest proportion of stay-at-homes in recent elections.

Then the poll lists should be examined, by someone familiar with the community, to find promising workers who appear to have views that harmonize with the purposes of the movement. Then the expert workers (part-time, paid or unpaid, according to the circumstances), should call on these people and enlist them for volunteer work. Then the volunteers should be trained. This training should be quite thorough. It should emphasize the importance of good government and good candidates. The relationship of the movement with the party that is to be supported should be explained. Also, supplementary printed material should supply the facts about election districts and divisions, registration, primaries, and elections. The laws governing elections, particularly with respect to legitimate and forbidden practices, should be taught. These volunteers should, above all, receive printed material to use among voters describing taxation, proposed legislation, the trend to socialism and its dangers, and the nature and dangers of socialism elsewhere, notably in England.

If, after training, it appears that some of the trainees by lack of sympathy or by personality are unfitted to act as suitable workers, they should be dropped or employed in unimportant activities.

As soon as a larger division such as a city, ward, or county has been equipped with groups of trained volunteers, there should be larger meetings of those volunteers in groups of two or three hundred each. These meetings should be addressed by some informed and inspiring speaker, not necessarily a member of the citizens' group. The meetings should be social as well as educational. It would help to have each volunteer contribute some small sum, perhaps not over a dollar, to defray the expenses of the meetings. So far as possible, workers should be encouraged to make the movement truly their own, not a drive by some hidden supplier of money and direction.

Later, meetings of this sort, at which the candidate can be introduced to the volunteers, should be held in each ward or county. Every volunteer should know the candidate personally.

Above all, the candidate should be induced to write letters to volunteers from time to time, thanking them and telling them of the progress of the campaign.

These volunteers should be the very heart of the movement. They are the people who deliver the indispensable means of success—the voter who casts the right vote. And from their ranks will rise major leaders of the movement and eligibles for future public office.

The people who initiate, support, and direct a citizens' movement can adopt, without impairing the integrity of their efforts, the very practical political principle of remembering and in some manner rewarding those who have helped. Permanent records of the names and addresses and services of all workers, paid and volunteer, should be kept. There is always the need to acknowledge and reward past service and to be prepared for the next campaign.

Publicity and Advertising. Candidates usually know little about means of getting publicity or about the nature of good publicity. Expert service is needed.

Here the citizens' group can find and pay the right person, perhaps on the advice of advertising agency men or editors. It is almost always possible to get a skilled newspaperman or a public relations man.

A political campaign has many of the characteristics of a commercial sales effort. The candidate and his attributes and views need advertising. His name, his face, and his right hand should be everywhere. The impression of success must be put over. Campaign "literature," various forms of paid advertising, outdoor advertising, press, radio, and television should be expertly prepared. This function might, with the consent of the party, be taken over by the citizens' group.

It should be stressed that with the development of radio and television important new resources for campaigning are available. "Visual aids" are already in use that enable a candidate or worker to present his case by records and projected slides. There are sound trucks equipped with phonograph records and loudspeakers to carry messages through the streets. Since routine party workers are usually most backward in their adoption of new methods, a citizens' group can well vitalize campaigning with new ideas.

Expert advertising and publicity people, in citizens' movements as well as in party campaigns, have often wasted much effort and money in political advertising and "literature" by pitching their tone on too lofty a scale. There is such a thing as too much "slickness." The mass of voters still think of politics in terms of torchlight parades, slogans, and other simple appeals.

There is also a great distinction between the sort of printed material that goes well in cities and the sort that has an appeal in rural areas. The city dweller gets more reading material than he can use. For country readers "literature" can be printed in smaller type, it can be more voluminous, and it should be written with less smoothness and not so much effort toward stylized prose. The farmer has more time to read such material. He has relatively fewer newspapers and magazines. He will take a piece of campaign literature home, read part of it, put it aside and return to it for further and more careful reading.

Between Elections. After the primary, as well as after the election, whether the outcome be successful or not, citizen leaders might well give a dinner meeting for the candidate and party heads. Such a meeting need not be given publicity. It would, however, be an investment in good will and permanent friendly relations within the group and the party.

There should also be post-election dinners, barbecues, picnics, or other forms of appreciation for party workers, especially for volunteers.

Various means should be devised between elections to

maintain a spirit of permanence in the organization. A good political leader never rests between elections. Success requires round-the-year care and attention to organization. Leaders should always remember that the next election is just around the corner.

After a successful election, it is of great importance to keep contact with and to help the winning candidates. Perhaps the creation of a permanent citizens' advisory committee is the best way to do this. A newly elected official will be subject to the devoted attention of the professional politicians whose interests will lie in what they get rather than in the success of the official. The citizens' group is concerned primarily with his success and with his adherence to its ideals. The citizens' group can assist a Congressman or a member of a state legislature in many important ways. It can provide him with expert help in his job of contending with a mass of issues and legislation. It can keep his political fences at home in good repair. It can explain his actions and votes to the people at home and also keep him informed of conditions and the state of opinion at home.

The preparation for the next campaign should begin immediately after election. It can be taken for granted that the forces of opposition will be at work alienating voters and attacking the record as it unfolds.

It should never be forgotten that the professional politician conceives it to be his duty to win elections and to govern. It is the citizen's duty to see that the right politicians govern and that they govern well.

ACTION WITHIN THE PARTY FRAMEWORK

A second type of citizen action operates in part within the party framework, with the objective of either taking over control of the party or vitalizing the party and influencing party policy and the choice of candidates. Such a movement exists in Texas. In various forms it is also found in a number of other places.

The Texas movement, while it is a very positive force, has no formal name or precise organization. It originated in 1944 and was known then as the Texas Regulars. After the events of that year, when it almost gained complete party control, it assumed its present form and adopted its present strategy. It consists of a very large group of active and influential Texans, resident in all parts of the state. Its leaders are well known to each other and to many other people who are not members and participants.

Its objective is the maintenance of our constitutional principles and the curbing of socialistic trends in government. Needless to add, it is opposed to President Truman's Fair Deal. Many of its members hold official positions on party committees.

The major concern of these Texans is the election and maintenance in office of members of Congress and the state legislature who are, on domestic issues, consistently conservative. A majority of the Texas delegation in the U.S. House of Representatives answers to that description. The Texas legislature is definitely conservative. It may be added that the voting records of the two Texas senators are conservative on domestic issues.

The activity of the Texas citizens' movement has not, of course, been wholly responsible for this, but it has been very influential in stiffening the resistance of people in official life against radical policies. The movement is a practical and ever present force in state elections and party councils.

Its presence gives assurance to members of both Congress and the state legislature that when they refuse to do the bidding of powerful minority groups or the Federal machine they will have strong backing at home in the next election.

This Texas group has voluntary leaders in every large town and city in the state. It seeks to stimulate active partici-

305

pation in party politics, from the precinct level up. To that end, its workers and leaders try to instruct, in the legal and procedural facts of party life, people who are in sympathy with its conservative policies.

One of the original leaders of this Texas group has this to say of the methods employed to mobilize citizens in political activity:

It is presumed that our staff and field leadership will be competent to do and instruct others how to do such basic jobs as explaining: (1) *modus operandi* of party politics and why it is necessary for believers in constitutional government to control their own precincts; (2) why it is necessary *always* to attend their precinct conventions and to know personally the voting habits and leadership qualities of their neighbors in the precinct; (3) how to go about getting a list of qualified voters; (4) how to organize a pre-convention caucus among their friends, in their own homes for the purpose of planning business at their precinct convention and getting out the vote of neighbors who will support their candidates and resolutions; (5) how to go about drawing up the resolutions which should be presented at the precinct convention; (6) the importance of electing their own secretary and the giving of proper instructions to this secretary to make sure that the records of the convention are properly kept and safely transmitted, with adequate provision for duplicate attested set of records to remain with the secretary until their group knows for sure that a probably unfriendly county political administration cannot possibly throw out their vote or disqualify the candidates their group has elected; (7) the power of a postal card sent to the right people in the precinct (under some conditions when there is danger in sending a postal card there should be sent a confidential letter); (8) the long-range importance of the precinct convention in selecting better candidates for county, state, and Federal offices.

It should be explained by the field workers that our perilous political situation today is simply the result of the "middle-interest group" letting the professional politicians run the precinct political convention. It should be pointed out, as one authority has estimated, that one vote in a precinct convention carries more real power than 2,000 votes in a general election. It is the professional politician who wants to tax and tax, to spend and spend and to elect and elect. Our "middle-interest group" has failed to carry the political responsibilities of our forefathers who spent days and weeks riding on horseback and traveling in covered wagons to discharge their political responsibilities. We have abdicated to the professional ward politician because it was too much trouble for us, we were too busy doing something else—more important than freedom—usually trying to make money, or because politics is often considered "dirty."

We have proved in this state that what the professional politician could do for his selfish, personal interest, we have been able completely to offset and supplant with a sound, good-government philosophy through out efforts.

In 1951 the Texas legislature passed a comprehensive revision of the primary, convention, and election law, which will greatly increase the influence of this group. The legislation was very effectively supported by the group and also by many other groups and individuals anxious to break the hold of the Federal machine.

GET-OUT-THE-VOTE CAMPAIGNS

All over the nation during the past few years citizen groups of various sizes and capacities have been formed in political campaigns for the single purpose of getting out the vote. Most of these resolved, of course, to see that most of the votes that came out should be favorable to their political and economic points of view. They decided to do something besides talk about conditions. As Freeman Guerin of Columbus, who helped to form such a group, has put it: "Instead of wringing our hands, we decided that ringing door bells would be a more effective way in combatting this growing intrusion into our liberties."

Mr. Guerin says further that the people who started the Columbus movement—named the Active Citizenship League—asked themselves at the outset three questions: Whose doorbell should be rung? Who should ring it? What would take place when the bell is answered?

This is his answer to these questions:

(1) Election Board statistics showed that roughly 50 per cent of those eligible to vote were not registered to do so. Closer study revealed that the majority of those not registered lived in political subdivisions where our opposition would find little sympathy for their political ambitions. Obviously, then, these areas should be concentrated on and an effort made directly to the individual to get him to register and vote. Consequently, certain considered political subdivisions within the county were singled out as the proper places in which the doorbell ringing should take place.

(2) Who should ring the doorbell? There was no question in our minds but that the doorbell ringer should be a resident of the area or precinct in which the work of registration should be done.

(3) How should we go about recruiting these volunteer workers? This is the key to the success of our program and where, we believe, the Active Citizenship League is unique. In the first place, we solicited members in the League by interesting men of influence in our program and then had them interest five other men who, in turn, would enlist five or more and so on. Each member thus acquired agreed to work in his own immediate neighborhood and interest his neighbor to the extent that he would be willing to help when called upon. Certain amplifications and refinements arose from this method as the membership spread and finally resulted in a nucleus of enthusiastic ward and precinct workers and organizers in the political subdivisions in which it was considered advisable to work.

There was then prepared an organization chart which described the line of responsibility of workers down to the city block supervisor, with a detailed definition of the job assigned to each member of the working staff.

Mr. Guerin says further:

308

The organizational work was carried on to the point where there was a worker in almost every block in the precinct. Each worker was furnished with a list of the names of the unregistered persons in the area to which he was assigned. These names were gotten from the records of the Board of Election. In so far as possible, the worker lived in the block to which he was assigned. Under no circumstance was he asked to go beyond the confines of his own precinct. Meetings were held where they were properly schooled as to the most effective approach to be made at the time of the call. A sheet was used by the block worker for recording the results of his interview after which he returned it to headquarters for checking at the Board of Election to determine whether or not a follow-up was needed.

The time between the close of registration and election day was used to good advantage in seeing to it that absentee ballots, sick ballots, etc. were attended to. These situations appeared in the course of the workers' calls and accounted for a great many votes that would have otherwise been lost.

On election day the organization was used to get out the whole vote, complete with baby-sitter, transportation for those who were in need of it, etc. This was considered an easy task by the workers who had gone through the rigors of registration. And this getting out the vote was really what paid off. When the program was at its peak, we had about 800 doorbell ringers and leaders on the job.

The results attained by the Active Citizenship League in the 1950 election were impressive. This organization was operating in the face of stiff competition with the C.I.O.-P.A.C. In the 222 voting precincts in which it operated, it was estimated that it added 6,500 to the registration rolls. In its follow-up work, it succeeded in getting 85 per cent of those who were registered to vote. Their candidate, Taft, received 80 per cent of those votes. This, according to their claim, greatly exceeded the results attained by the C.I.O.-P.A.C. in the districts exclusively worked by that organization.

If such an effort were multiplied many times in such a

state as Ohio, and thousands of times in the United States, the political history of this country could be fundamentally altered. It is an excellent example of public spirit, energy, persistence, and capacity to organize.

The Lessons

There is no magic way to avoid the danger that we face. Fine theorizing about it, adorned with all there is of piety and wit, will not avail. The way to preserve liberty is to induce American citizens to do their duty at the polls.

The first lesson taught by every successful effort I have seen is that people in the mass simply will not perform this duty without leadership and organization.

In plain terms, this means that somebody must take the initiative. This somebody must get the co-operation of other somebodies who are of like mind and spirit. These leaders must be moved by a genuine spirit of duty, pride, patriotism, impending danger, or what you will. They must not expect acclaim or glory. Rather, they must face many sacrifices of time, comfort, and peace of mind; for the way is arduous and wearisome, and the job is prosaic, generally uninspiring, and mostly thankless and barren of direct reward.

When they have found that there are enough of them to begin, they must find the means and develop the skill to organize. It will be a long, long time before their first efforts reap a harvest at the polls.

They must reach and move the sovereign American voter who, however glorified by politicians and poets, is in the majority of cases a politically lazy and careless fellow. In most places he must be induced to register, and after he does that he must be watched, and then induced to vote. And he must have pounded into him the facts that will make his vote productive of results.

310

The leaders in citizens' movements must keep everlastingly at it, for one victory does not make a millennium. The fight for liberty is unending. In the calendar of politics there are no holidays.

It would be pleasant indeed to bring to the major point of this book the luminous tone of inspirational verbiage. But that would not be keeping faith with the facts. There is, however, the satisfaction of knowing that the job I am proposing to men and women of spirit can be done and has been done, and the way to keep our liberty is to get many others to join in doing it.

The Ultimate Need

It is probable that out of one or more successful local citizens' movements organized effective action will be extended throughout the nation. Left-wing organizations such as the C.I.O.-P.A.C. and the A.D.A. are at least nominally nationwide. It is idle to speculate on what exact form a similar organization with more conservative objectives may take. Perhaps there will be a process of amalgamation among local groups.

Successful citizen efforts are already widely known and studied. In the main, these movements are concerned with national problems, and their trend is toward national influence. After successful work in electing Congressmen and Senators, it is inevitable that in Presidential campaigns these groups will labor for the final election of a national administration favorable to their aims.[1]

[1] In the large cities voters generally know very little about any candidates, up to and including those who are running for Congress. Workers, therefore, cannot attempt to "sell" too many candidates to the voters on whom they call. If they concentrate on candidates for the legislature and Congress, they will be reaching the main concern of the prospective voter, which is the making of laws, the voting of money, and the levying of taxes. Experience has

There are a number of groups working on a national level whose objective is to stimulate civic interest, participation in politics, and more use of the right to vote. There are also many agencies concerned with the distribution of literature of various sorts expounding conservative national ideals. Other organizations are dedicated to the dissemination of conservative views by the spoken word at dinners, over the radio, and on various forums.

It seems probable that ultimately there will be some sort of clearing organization through which these and many local groups might become better acquainted with each other. Such a clearing organization should provide blueprints for new local groups in the initial stage or organization.

Since it is evident that the ultimate need is some sort of party realignment, all leaders of citizens' group with a conservative bent might well keep that objective in mind. Their influence in both parties can be very considerable.

Party leaders are enormously responsive to any group or leader with an assured supply of potential votes. And since the political and economic objective of these conservative citizen groups should be a national conservative party, they can help break down the obstacles, especially in the Republican Party, to such a consummation.

Unless this happens our parties will further disintegrate and for a time party chaos is likely to result. That may well be the moment when citizen leaders may bring about the creation of a new, national conservative party.

Local Action Is Needed Now

The major need now, however, is to hold the line against Federal statism. Citizen action is essential here and now in

---

shown that if a voter can be persuaded to vote for these legislative candidates, they will vote for other people on the same ticket, down to candidates for the lowest range and up to candidates for Governor, U.S. Senator, and President.

supporting conservative members of Congress from the North and South. It cannot wait for the slow evolution of party policy or for the creation of a new party or of nonparty machinery at the national level. It can and should develop in villages, cities, counties, and Congressional districts. It should drive for the winning of minor victories, for supplying the margin of votes needed by candidates who meet its ideological specifications for members of state legislatures, for governor, for Congress, and for the Presidency.

Above all, citizen action should waste no time speculating about or hoping for a Presidential Moses to lead us out of the wilderness. Every citizen with capacity for leadership must be a Moses. For the wilderness is growing more dense and neglected with every passing day.

Regardless of the outcome of the Presidential election in 1952, the activity of citizen groups should continue in the years ahead. If there is to be a continuation of the present regime, the need to hold the line in Congress will be greater than ever. If, on the other hand, a conservative wins the election, he will need vital and active support in every corner of the nation. The fight for the preservation of liberty should be eternal, because the forces that threaten it are not created by this or that party or Administration. They are inherent in the complexities of human nature and in the relations of men with one another.

PART FIVE

THE BLESSINGS OF LIBERTY

CHAPTER XI

The Promise of the Future

The Incomparable Achievement

The incomparable economic achievement of the United States is revealed in the most obvious facts of our daily life. It is all around us in the present, and it is in the pages of our history. Countless volumes have been written about it; it is the theme of much of our oratorical discourse. It is necessary here only to note briefly the fact of this achievement, for our main concern is with its causes and the relation of those causes to future progress.

Among the many American achievements during the past thirty years has been a capacity to measure our own economic system. The science of economics, when it was largely devoted to theory, provided plenty of room for disagreement. In certain respects that is still true. But it has, through improved capacity for factual measurement, established a number of reliable calculations that are well known.

For example, we now have fairly good estimates of the volume of national production year by year. We know that in the decade from 1899 to 1909 the physical output of factories increased 55 per cent. From 1919 to 1929 we increased it by 65 per cent. In the ten years following 1929 we established the worst record in half a century, for the increase was only 3 per cent. But from 1939 to 1949 the rise was more than 100 per cent.

In addition, the record during that half century has shown a great increase in efficiency. The per capita output has been rising at a tremendous rate. From 1899 to 1939 our production per man hour increased at an average rate of two per cent a year, and our working population increased by the same yearly percentage. A few simple comparisons will illustrate this gain. In 1914, an average worker devoted nine hours of labor to earn enough to buy a pair of work shoes. In 1949, the figure was three and a half hours. In 1914, he worked 41 hours to earn enough to buy a baby carriage; 102 minutes to buy a lamp bulb; 49 hours to earn the price of an electric fan. In 1948, the figures were 15½ hours for the baby carriage; 7 minutes for a lamp bulb; and 4 hours for an electric fan.

We have a volume of production almost equal to that of the continents of Europe, Africa, and South America combined—an area inhabited by ten times our population.

Eighty-two per cent of our national income goes to individuals for personal work. Eighteen per cent goes to property in the form of rents, interests, and profits.

Americans, with only 6 per cent of the world's land area and 7 per cent of the world's population, own and use one third of the world's railway mileage; half of the improved highways, telephones, and electric power; 60 per cent of the life insurance policies; 85 per cent of the automobiles. They consume three quarters of the world's silk; 60 per cent of the rubber; half of the coffee; and 40 per cent of the salt. Salt consumption, according to economists, is an important indication of a nation's standard of living.

These figures have been reliably interpreted to mean that Americans are nine times better off than the average of the rest of the world's population. The distribution of these and other indices of living standards are on an incomparably wider basis than elsewhere.[1]

Since it became the habit of some left-wing economists to speak of a "mature" economy, a number of wholly new industries have appeared, are employing hundreds of thousands of workers, and are producing billions in wealth. Notable among them are plastics, viscose, and television, all of which have been developed since one of those economists induced Franklin D. Roosevelt to say "our industrial plant is built."

Many inventions originated abroad, but the United States immediately adopted them, mastered them, and leaped ahead in their practical application.

The technique developed in the United States for mass production is recognized as a marvel and model for the world. It has been an indispensable factor in building our high standard of living. It will raise the standard of living everywhere, once its principles are mastered throughout the world.

One of the factors in mass production, although not the fundamental basis of the process, is the principle of duplicate or interchangeable parts.

Charles F. Kettering of General Motors once said that the printers were the first to start mass production.

"The invention of movable type," he continued, "was the greatest thing that ever happened in the development of education and civilization, because with movable type all sorts of things could be set up and duplicated readily. Every word that was printed was reproduced over and over again, exactly the same."

Centuries passed, however, before the revolutionary character of this principle was fully realized here in the United States. Eli Whitney, who had invented the cotton gin, sug-

[1] See Ch. III.

gested the idea of interchangeable parts to the army as a method of making rifles. But many years passed before manufacturers grasped the idea that behind the principle of interchangeable parts is the careful preparation known as "make ready."

B. E. Hutchinson of the Chrysler Corporation once asked me if I knew the meaning of mass production. Out of my imperfect knowledge I said: "The principle of interchangeable parts."

"The interchangeability of parts," he answered, "and the benefits that derive from it were only the by-products of mass production. The fundamental idea behind mass production is the substitution of tooling for individual skill, with a consequent highly functionalized individual operation. This means a highly specialized design for the machine, created by very skillful engineering. Then, when the machine is operated to produce the parts, there is required of the operator only a very narrow, specialized skill. The operator—and this applies to the great mass of employees—needs to acquire only one skill, which can be acquired quickly. The product which emerges in great number from this combination of long, expensive 'make ready,' plus the fine machine itself, plus the operator with a narrow, specialized skill, will be superior to anything produced as an engineering sample."

Kettering provides a forceful example of this process:

"The machine gun is a very good illustration of the point I am trying to make. I remember when one of them was brought to the Frigidaire Plant in Dayton. Our men said, 'We don't know anything about the machine-gun business.'

"I happened to be there and I said to the colonel who had brought the machine gun in, 'Will this gun shoot the way you want it to?'

"He said, 'Yes, that particular gun has been through all the firing tests and is O.K.'

"I said, 'That's all we need to know. If you have drawings

of the parts of that gun all we need to do is make parts exactly like those in that gun, and what can it do but shoot when we put it together?' "

Thus, the combination of ever and ever more accurate design and tools for standard duplication lies at the basis of an infinitely rich material life. This is an American achievement.

We have created capital at a tremendous rate. During the Second World War we added, in 1939 prices, $25,000,000,-000 in value to our industrial plant, which was a greater investment than that represented by the industries of England, France, and Germany, which were built up over 150 years.

We have reached a point at which, unless taxation and other government policies impose a bar, the problem of progressive production is solved. The greater problem is increased consumption. A philosophical specialist in retailing has deplored the saving instincts inherited from Puritan ancestry and has called for an anti-Puritan economic philosophy. He calls his methods the "selling of discontent." That, essentially, is what modern salesmanship strives to do—to stimulate human wants and thus to create a market for mass production. This aggressive force multiplies both production and consumption and raises the standard of living. While other nations ration their scarcity, we have had to organize our abundance.

We have beaten back the poverty line that has enclosed the mass of the world's people for ages and that still encloses 85 per cent of them. Right before us, not in the flickering dreams of hope but in the probability of achievement, is the goal of enough for the reasonably healthful and happy maintenance of all.

Marxism professed that a bed-rock security for all could come only by planning for all, by eliminating the "wastes" of competition and luxury—in short, by destroying capitalism. We have arrived very close to that goal of security, not by destroying but by preserving capitalism. We have proved that the "wastes" of competition are the fires that turn the wheels of production. Like the gardener who prunes a tree, competition, by continuous cutting away, produces more and richer fruit.

The system that created our achievement we are asked to abandon for another that was planned a century ago by Marx, a man who knew only the infancy of free industrial enterprise, and who considered only its infantile gropings for the means of life.

Incontestable Causes

In assigning causes for the American achievement, we should avoid the twin fallacies of coincidence and *post hoc, ergo propter hoc.* A vast amount of special pleading and careless thinking has attended efforts to interpret our past in terms of cause and effect. Some socialists claim that the people who settled America merely stumbled on a section of the earth with incomparably rich resources and that greatness would have emerged under any system and with any kind of people. Some nonsocialists fall into a like error in singling out one factor, to which they ascribe the qualities of magic. The old Bancroft school of historians credited our good fortune to the hovering wings of Providence.

When we direct our attentions to the many specific reasons for our national eminence we find that nearly all of these causes, including the use of God's gift of natural resources, have something to do with liberty.

Our unassailable location has protected these resources from barbaric invasion and spoliation. It preserved this continent until a congeries of nationalities came with the authentic seeds of modern civilization. The Indian races were relatively few in number, indisposed to develop resources

322

and only remotely related to the springs of great ancient civilizations. The people who came after Columbus energetically set about to retain the advantages inherent in location by pressing forward to all the areas looking out to the sea. The people of the United States over a century, by hook or by crook, by conquest, purchase, or pure bluff, pushed their sovereignty over a continent perfectly suited to the development of nationality. They made a few gestures at Canada, but either failed in these or gave up because of a recognition of political and racial kinship in which neighborly living was profitable to all.

This location, protected by the oceans, made it possible for our people to develop institutions of their choice, with no threat of interference from alien attack or from any sort of foreign influence that they were not willing to welcome. The British Isles had a similar advantage, and historical judgments assert that their protected location was a major factor in the development of free institutions. Our physical detachment has been incomparably greater.

It is hardly necessary here to enumerate the great natural resources that have been and still are available to our people. These resources, in terms of minerals, land, water, and climate, are common knowledge to our schoolchildren. Our enormous coastline, affording access to all the world, is not only an agency of commerce but it opens to us resources, real though almost wholly untouched, in and under the sea.

It is a valid law of nature and of history that the pressure of need and cupidity moves people of all sorts to greener fields and richer hills and valleys. The lure of America moved the more venturesome, resourceful, and liberty-loving individuals of the Old World more quickly and persistently. Thus, there is a connection between these personal qualities and our natural resources which cannot be denied.

William A. Dunning, a great historian, used to say that we were settled by a hardy breed of "kickers." They were people who hated the restraints of entrenched authority. They wanted to be free, they asked no odds, no dearly purchased protection, no subsidies but a piece of virgin land or a post for profitable trade. This was a manifestation of the love of liberty.

The peopling of the United States and Canada was a selective process. And this selection was, except in small instances, no act of a government, but a matter of free choice. Generally, it took imagination, courage, and a deep sense of independence to tear loose from tradition, home ties, and political allegiance, and come to the New World. It is too general and too complacent to say that we are descendants of the best people of Europe. But it is accurate to say that we are descendants of the kind of people best suited to build a new nation; in whom faith, imagination, inventiveness, hardihood, and the love of individual freedom were foremost qualities.

Collectively, they had an infinite assortment of skills. Their superficial habits and traditions were of all origins. The least common denominator, however, was a matter of spirit and purpose, and that spirit and purpose were embodied in opposition to the growth of authority, especially state authority.

The anthropologists, notably Franz Boas, have proved that superficial characteristics, even physical lineaments such as color and head shapes, change in a generation or so. But the mental characteristics of a people create new political and economic institutions and traditions. These have been the patterns within which our great achievement has been created.

These people also brought their inherited political institutions. There were Anglo-Saxon institutions and French ideas. There were German and Scandinavian concepts of industrial and community life. These, too, were favorable to great material and cultural development.

324

As the nation began to grow, there was an energetic tide of migration toward the frontier. Here again, a selective process operated. Those who pulled up stakes and moved were of many kinds. There were the imaginative, the young, the ambitious, the cantankerous, and the visionary. There were also chronic failures like Tom Lincoln. But failure is not too seldom a mark of nonconformity. The indolent failure is too lazy to move. New sections filled up with those newly arrived, and they grew to importance in the national scene.[2]

Another characteristic that has greatly contributed to material growth and a very high standard of living throughout America has been the uniformity of American life. James Bryce in his *American Commonwealth* devotes a penetrating chapter to this. He noted uniformity of landscape over vast stretches of his journeys and almost indistinguishable towns and cities. "The same fields and crops, the same rough wooden fences, the same thickets of the same bushes along the stream edges . . . the same solitary farm houses and straggled wood-built villages." There is even less variety in the great mountain ranges than in the short ranges of Europe, he added.

Bryce wrote that a generation ago. He would now be confronted by vastly greater evidences of uniformity. The same makes of automobiles line the streets of thousands of towns and cities. The same products are sold by similar stores, agencies, and stations, and the same motion pictures are shown in the theaters. The same national magazines are on the newsstands. The same features appear in hundreds of newspapers. The same programs are on radio stations.

Bryce complained about our uniformity. It was "the one serious drawback" to the pleasantness of American life.

[2] An old friend of mine, Lewis A. McArthur of Portland, in his years of retirement made a study of the geographical names in the Northwest that signalized the boundless optimism of the pioneers who settled there. Among them were Eureka, Utopia, Joy, Enterprise, Lovely, Paradise, Promise, Eden, and Arcadia.

True, but a civilization does not grow for the purpose of providing satisfactions for a traveler. It grows to supply the needs of those who live in it. There are great values in our uniformity. It makes possible a stupendous market for goods produced in mass. It was an important precondition to the mechanization of labor, because demand became too great for the labor supply, and machines had to be created to multiply the products of men's hands.

Freedom from national frontiers and trade barriers created such trade as has never before been seen over such a great area. The American system permitted the mobility essential to rapid and substantial industrial growth. If the elder Rockefeller and other pioneers in the oil business had been compelled, when they built refineries and pipelines, to consult such boards and other authorities as the socialists in Britain created, they would have grown old before their product began to serve its purpose.

It has been a source of strength that all or most of those matters which required relatively great government expenditures were absent here: the fear of and defense against predatory neighbors, feudal and national hatreds, the maintenance of an unproductive and extravagant nobility, and a submerged class of the impoverished. Moreover, until recently there has been freedom from the burden that the support of a great bureaucracy places on an economic system.

The interdependence that prevails in our economy is a result of a free market. We have achieved on a massive scale, without government intervention, what has been recognized in socialist or semisocialist governments in Europe as exclusively the task of government or of government-sponsored co-operatives. The American chain store is one example.

A better example is the infinitely complex process by which food produced on the farm is finally delivered to the consumer's dinner table. That process involves, first, the production of the raw food on the farm at a reasonable profit to the farmer; second, the processing or preparation of the food for use by the consumer; third, the distribution of the food at an economical cost; and, finally, the delivery of the product to the consumer at a price within his means.

While there are millions of people engaged in this process —and many of them operate as individuals or small companies—a number of large companies that deal with a wide variety of products have also developed in this field.

Such a company buys directly the products of thousands of farms. The farmers, because of the size and stability of the company, are assured of a certain and profitable market from year to year.

The company, seeking the best means of producing a large output at constantly more economical prices, underwrites extensive research and experimentation to improve the processing of the products and to devise new, attractive, and nourishing types of finished foods out of the old staple products of the land.

Since the development of a market for new products depends upon a growing demand, consumers are educated by advertising. This advertising, far from being an economic waste, as many enemies of the free system assert, is a means of providing a market sufficiently large to bring down prices by economies in mass production and distribution. It is in effect the big show window for the company. The more that people can be made to want, the greater the means that can be provided to meet those wants.

Finally, the consumer is benefited by a wider and more interesting array of foods brought within his means.

In this entire process benefits are bestowed upon every participant—the farmer, the carrier, the various dealers, and the consumers. Finally, the large, stable company provides investors, large and small, with a sound place to put money at work to benefit the nation and provide security for savings.

In this field of economic activity, as in many others, small and large businesses live side by side with mutual benefits. The research and know-how of the companies that can afford them are quickly known by those that cannot. That gives the smaller companies ideas from which they profit. Individuals all along the line think of improvements that ultimately are helpful to all.

It might be added that the so-called Brannan plan is merely a bad method of doing what food manufacturers have been doing for many years at no cost to the taxpayer and with no restrictions on the freedom of anyone concerned.

Charles F. Kettering has described the part that freedom plays in our economic system by comparing it with our political system of voting:

"We refer to our nation as a 'democracy,' which is just a long way of spelling 'votes.' That's all a democracy is; a country where people vote for things. We think of elections as coming in the spring or in the fall; but these aren't the elections that count so much. These are only the political elections. We have continuous elections in this democracy. Every store, on both sides of the street, in every village, town and city, is a voting booth at which our citizens vote every day. A little boy says, 'I want that candy bar. I don't want the other one.' A man says, 'I don't want that color on my automobile. I want this color.' We are voting from morning until night, and out of that voting comes the decision that gives everybody more for his money because it leads to competition, and competition is what makes the nation run. . . .

"That's what stores are; that's what advertisements are: Voting and electioneering places for their articles, whether it be a drill press, a necktie or a hat. The man who can keep on making something and giving his customer a profit is the one who is getting the most votes, and that man is sure to succeed."

The process of linking production with consumption is the responsibility of business management. Modern management is a product of the past century, and its inventiveness and skill to a considerable degree account for the American economic miracle. Company management is the connecting link among factors in the modern economic system. It serves at once the consumer, the worker, and the investing owners. Management is the great moderator among many interests, as well as the innovator and director in the process of production and distribution. This role of management needs to be well understood by the public for, without it, America could never have attained its present standard of living.

The Promise of the Future

In a free society national goals are not fixed and attained by coercion, as they are in Soviet Russia. Liberty permeates the nation with a million forces; the achievement is unpredictable, and therein lies the zest of anticipation. As long as we are sure of the direction in which we are going and are sure of the motives and principles that guide us, we can anticipate a better life. That should be enough assurance for free men.

We cannot take a narrow view when we survey the facts of change in the half century just past. The transformation of travel and communication, the growth of new industries, and the revival and growth of various regions and communities should be enough to reassure us about frontiers.

We have the physical spaces for people and enterprise. Compared with more compact civilized countries, we are still quite primitive and empty.

Our resources, despite our past excesses and wastefulness, are bountiful though not boundless. We are nearing the bottom of the Mesabi Range, but beyond that supply are vast deposits of iron ore available for use when we devise better methods of refining and provide new capital for development. And there are unlimited amounts of pure ore in near-by Canada and Labrador and in the undeveloped countries to the south. Our coal supplies are good for centuries. Estimates of our oil resources have been revised and re-revised—always upward. There is an immense bed of oil shale in western Colorado, eastern Utah, and southern Wyoming that, according to the U.S. Bureau of Mines, could yield three hundred billion barrels of oil. The best of this is probably in Colorado, where a government demonstration plant is operating and beginning to show that the cost of extracting this oil will in all probability come down to a basis competitive with the present sources of petroleum. The Bureau of Mines estimates that the shale deposits contain more oil than has ever been produced in this country, and much more than is in proved petroleum reserves still in the ground. Supplies of nitrates in their natural forms may decline, but now we know they can literally be taken from the boundless air. Atomic power is already in sight. These are essentials, and they are to be ours.

We have the sea, too, open for the ingenuity of science. Charles Kettering tells the story of how science solved the problem of bromine. A short time ago, he says, only 800,000 pounds were produced a year. Then "out came the slide rules," and ways were devised to produce 150,000,000 pounds a year from sea water at a bearable cost. That water, says Kettering, has "potassium, magnesium, and all sorts of mineral and biological things." And we have the sun for heat and energy.

We have technological skill, which has not reached anything like its maximum development. The achievements in the late war clearly show a momentum that should project itself far into the future.

We have, above all, our national character, in which restless venture, imagination, energy, and impatience of restraint and routine predominate. That they cannot be taken for granted, however, is shown by the quest of so many of us for the illusory haven of bureaucratic security. Already, there are disturbing signs of change in our youth. Two years ago, a survey by *Fortune* indicated that an alarming number of our college graduates were enamored of a future security tucked into a job with a pension at the end. They manifested no special inclination to venture in business for themselves. But this survey also showed a minority of young men in rapidly growing states like Texas and Oklahoma who preferred a more risky course.

Our population is still moving. First it settled the coastal areas and river valleys. Scarcely had a civilization grown there than the drift toward the interior began. Later, there came the railways and highways, and people settled along these new lines of commerce and communication. Now, with the liberation of industry from the necessity of being located near coal, iron, and other heavy raw materials, another trek is under way. One line of migration is toward more kindly places to live. The increase in California's population in the past ten years has been equal to the entire population of New Jersey. More significant than this, because it has not been caused by any urge toward ease and government benefits, has been the movement of people into the South—into Texas, Louisiana, Mississippi—and the Southeast.

The per capita income in the eleven Southeastern states from 1940 through 1950 rose 200 per cent. The per capita income rise over the same period in all the states was 150 per cent. Inventions created by free enterprise have provided mechanized means for agriculture on small farms for Negroes and whites. Cattle-raising is moving in, and in large sections the reign of King Cotton is ended. Industry, also inspired by the promise of greater opportunities, has moved southward. Sixteen thousand new factories were built in the South in eight years after 1939. All this was in only a slight degree because of government planning or government help. It was owing to the energy of free men seeking economic opportunity.

331

It is likely that, even if the threat of Communist aggression should not be wholly removed, there will be a trend of capital, know-how, and venturesome people into undeveloped areas throughout a world revealed to us in the lurid light of war. The world has more than two billion people, and only a small fraction of them have ever had enough to eat or any of the amenities of life, despite the fact that everywhere rich resources lie undeveloped in the sight of dire need. We have, says Kettering, the arsenal to win the battle of plenty. But the slowly awakening people of backward areas must furnish the manpower and do the fighting. We can design the tools, but they must do the job.

The horizon of knowledge is still in the misty distance. To cite Kettering again, there is relatively little that we know. This great inventor and master of research, who did so much to revolutionize the automobile, still seeks the answer to such questions as these: What is friction? How do fuels burn in an engine cylinder? What is fatigue of metals? How do plants fix energy from the sun? What is a lubricant and how does it work? What is immunity to disease? What is energy?

"Every time you tear a leaf off a calendar," says Kettering, "you present a new place for ideas and progress. All along the future years is spaced new information. It comes by inventions, by discoveries and by research. We can't stop this development because we know practically nothing about anything. We have it all in front of us. We have the perpetual necessity of finding out new information based on the facts that we found yesterday, some proved and some disproved." [3]

But progress will not come through research, science, and invention alone. These are merely the loose strands of progress. They must be joined by cross-strands. The genius of leadership and management in economic, political, and moral life must give meaning and use to scientific discovery. Unless this is done, all our science may end in frustration

[3] "Get Off Route 25," *Colliers*, December 3, 1949.

and disaster. There must be freedom in many fields other than mere science. For science alone can be the tool of tyranny.

Liberty and Progress, One and Indivisible

The forms of authority paramount over the individual have been infinitely varied. In this book, however, we have been concerned only with the authority of the state as one of two alternative ideals. For that is the choice presented to us in the United States.

The reality of socialism is not a true merger of the will of many individuals. It is the claim of British socialists, in many cases sincerely uttered, that their ideal is a people's regime in which all individual wills are still existent and operative through free political institutions. It is the claim of Communism also that it is a people's government, existing without free political institutions but devoted to the good of all.

Despite much theorizing to the contrary, individual liberties thus fused result in the loss not only of material but of spiritual values to the individual. For when many wills are thus subdued, liberty of action and authority pass to one person or to a group of individuals, who become the master government. There is no such thing as collective planning or collective action, except when all are free. Somebody plans for all, and somebody directs all.[4]

When that happens, as I have pointed out, these some-

[4] "Government in this way becomes the rational art of minimizing the inevitable conflicts of primal irrational wills against one another and against the forces of nature at large. If government attempts to go further and to approve one set of irrational wills and forbid another, it becomes itself the agent of a particular irrational will; and instead of speaking for all wills that move in its domain, and showing each the best terms it can make with circumstances, it becomes itself a particular set of circumstances hostile to all other wills, instead of wise friend to them all." George Santayana: *Dominations and Powers* (New York: Copyright, 1950, 1951, by Charles Scribner's Sons), p. 434.

bodies are confronted with tasks beyond human capacity. The complexity of life forbids mastery of details. Also, the susceptibility of human nature to the virus of power is too pronounced to be trusted. For the intoxication of power progressively undermines rational judgment.

True, the poetry of history describes golden moments under concentrated authority. We all know the rhapsody of Gibbon over the Rome of Nerva, Trajan, Hadrian, and the Antonines. But the melancholy end is also known to us. We know, further, of the failure of socialist planning in many modern instances. And we have seen the slave states made according to the blueprints of Marx.

We have the alternative and we know its fruits. We have seen the progress of nations that over a century and a half have measurably kept vital the ideal of a free market. That progress has come from the fusion of millions of individual choices in the market without the imposition of any single authority. Free choice has delivered the goods. So far as human welfare or, if you will, the general welfare, is concerned, we have that in as rich a form as the world has known. We have also seen that where we have impaired the free market in the interest of this or that group, the result has been progressively and finally successful efforts to force surrenders of other interests. The Brannan plan is the lineal descendent of Alexander Hamilton's *Report on Manufactures*. "The other fellow got it" has been the theme of our political life. When everybody finally gets it, nobody will have it.

True Liberty Is Positive and Constructive

I have, except in a few specific instances, used "liberty" and "freedom" as synonymous terms. There is, however, a difference in what they connote, and it is essential by way of conclusion to underline that difference. Freedom implies the removal of or exemption from some sort of restraint. The condition that accompanies freedom may be empty, vacuous, aimless. Standing by itself, it implies no vital action, nothing that makes it a material or spiritual value in itself. The prisoner released from Chillon had only freedom—no capacity to participate in the processes of liberty. And in the sense in which freedom has come to be used in contemporary history, it often carries with it the necessity that some coercive power is essential to preserve it.[5]

On the other hand, the word "liberty," which is Latin, not Teutonic in origin, implies the capacity within itself for its own protection and the constructive power to create an environment favorable to those who possess it. This is the sense in which it was used by the framers of our institutions. I have used it in this sense in my suggestions for national policies which offer an alternative to the compulsions and spurious gratuities of government. The "free" market became an ideal in political economy when in fact the market was bound by a thousand restraints. But economic liberty has created a system of self-government and vital, creative forces. Today in the United States that system is struggling not to free itself but to retain its capacity to grow and serve as it has in the past. Liberty, despite attack and serious losses, is still the established order. It has served us well and can serve us better.

But material services have not been and cannot be the primary mission of liberty. If life is to have value, liberty must meet the need for a progressive growth in the mind and spirit of the individual. The lesson of all religion is that we are here because we need to be fitted for a destiny beyond the material world. Our inward impulses and instincts con-

[5] "But freedom from want and fear is only a condition for the steady exercise of true liberty. On the other hand, it is more than a demand for liberty; for it demands insurance and protection by provident institutions, which imply the dominance of a paternal government, with artificial privileges secured by law. This would be freedom from the dangers of a free life. It shows us liberty contracting its field and bargaining for safety first." Santayana: Ibid., p. 58.

335

stantly remind us of this lesson. Perhaps that is why in the long history of an individual's consciousness the central figure in his universe is himself, and his own well-being his incessant concern. The efforts of that individual to survive and grow create the energy that moves and sustains civilization. Personal dignity and goodness and cultural and spiritual values rise from that inner ego. Liberty, essential for personal effort, is therefore a value *per se,* a value indispensable for the attainment of spiritual fitness for an unseen but priceless destiny. The fruits of liberty are all around us, but its essential value is within us. Its preservation should be our business in life.

APPENDIX

Federal Laws Governing Political Action Committees

1. According to the Federal Corrupt Practices Act, a political committee is defined as an organization that accepts contributions or makes expenditures for the purpose of influencing elections for President, United States Senate, or the House of Representatives, providing the organization operates in two or more states. From this definition it can be seen that independent committees organized for the purpose of influencing elections for Federal offices, including electors for President and Vice President in only one state, would not in any way be subject to the provisions of the Federal Corrupt Practices Act. However, the Corrupt Practices Act does state that branches or subsidiaries of national organizations are included in the definition even if they operate in only one state. As a general rule, it has been accepted that so long as officers of local committees are independent of a national organization the local organization is a bona fide independent committee. Various states have their own corrupt-practices act that govern these local committees.

2. Every political committee, as defined above, shall have a chairman and a treasurer before any contribution can be accepted or expenditure made. No specific report of the organization of a new political committee is required. However, the treasurer of every political committee must file a report with the Clerk of the House of Representatives showing the name and address of each contributor of one hundred dollars or more in any one calendar year. The report must also show the name and address of each person to whom an expenditure of more than ten dollars was made in any one calendar year. In actual practice it is generally accepted that all expenditures are listed in order

of their payment even though they are under the ten-dollar limitation, because recurring monthly charges could easily run the total payments over the ten-dollar limit. Likewise, it can be seen that it would be more practical to list all contributions, particularly those paid on monthly basis, rather than wait until the aggregate contribution of an individual reaches the one-hundred-dollar limitation. The report must be filed between the first and tenth days of March, June, and September in each year covering the period through the last day of the preceding month. A report is also required to be filed on the first day of January, complete as of the last day of the preceding year. Reports are also required in a general election year between the tenth and fifteenth days preceding a general election, and another on the fifth day preceding the general election.

3. The Hatch Political Activities Act provides that no political committee may receive or expend more than three million dollars in any calendar year. However, here again this limitation applies only to political committees. Inasmuch as the Hatch Act states that definitions shall have the same meaning as assigned to them by the Federal Corrupt Practices Act, it is obvious that the three-million-dollar limitation does not apply to independent state committees. So in effect a local committee could spend an unlimited amount of money in a single state for Federal offices as far as the Federal Corrupt Practices Act and the Hatch Act are concerned. Of course they would be subject to the state laws.

4. The Hatch Act contains a provision that limits any one person's individual contributions to a political committee to five thousand dollars during any calendar year or in connection with any campaign for nomination or election for an elective Federal office. Contributions made to or by state or local committees are not subject to this provision. Here again it can be seen that this limitation applies to independently organized local committees, and an individual could contribute any sum he pleased to such a local committee. At the same time the local committee can make contributions to a national organization in any amount. However, a "national" political committee is governed by the same limitations on contributions as an individual. In other

338

words, a national committee is not allowed to make a direct contribution in excess of five thousand dollars in direct aid of any single candidate. However, contributions of greater than five thousand dollars may be made to independent state or local committees.

Index

i

iv

A NOTE ON THE TYPE

The text of this book was set on the Linotype in a type face called Baskerville. The face is a facsimile reproduction of types cast from molds made for John Baskerville (1706–75) from his designs. The punches for the revived Linotype Baskerville were cut under the supervision of the English printer George W. Jones.

John Baskerville's original face was one of the forerunners of the type style known as "modern face" to printers—a "modern" of the period A.D. 1800.

The book was composed, printed, and bound by Kingsport Press, Inc., Kingsport, Tennessee.